NO MORE TOMORROWS

NO
MORE
TOMORROWS

DOMINIC CARUSO

WESTBANK

PUBLISHING

FIRST EDITION 2008 PUBLISHED BY WESTBANK PUBLISHING

FOR INFORMATION ADDRESS
4408 BAYOU DES FAMILLES
MARRERO, LA 70072

COVER DESIGN BY DOMINIC CARUSO

ISBN (10) 0-9789840-3-X
ISBN (13) 978-0-9789840-3-8

LIBRARY OF CONGRESS CONTROL NUMBER 2008938240

1. CLINTON PUBLIC LIBRARY, CLINTON, MD - 2. ST. MARY CNTY. PUBLIC LIBRARY, ST.
MARY, MD - 3. NEWSPAPERARCHIVES.COM - 4. NYTIMES.COM

PRINTED IN THE UNITED STATES OF AMERICA

PREFACE

Convicted of murder and sentenced to death in the late nineteen twenties, Francesco Caruso known as Cheech to family and acquaintances changed the venue of medical practice in urban areas after that time.

Cheech was the head of my family; he was my father. I tell his story to honor my father's wish to do so, all aspects of it, the light . . . and the dark. Even more, I tell it to honor my mother, who worked publicly to free Cheech from prison when to do so went against her very reserved nature. In a strange country and language, she made speeches, gave interviews, and pleaded with public officials for her husband's life. Her strength and courage sustained our family through difficult times, none more trying than the period when Cheech waited upon death at Sing Sing Prison's Death Row. I choose to tell about my parents as a narrator of selected scenes that bring together family memories and news accounts. This allows me to combine family stories with news stories of the time in a cohesive, readable way. Dialogue among people in this account follows reports from different members of my family. Where possible, I used the very words related to me by Mom, Dad, my sister Lena and by my other relatives. This included my father's younger sister, his last surviving relative. Her memories of the time were most vivid. In all dialogue, I was careful not to change the gist of conversations as they happened or alter the nature of events by what they said. Despite the famous personalities on these pages, this is my parents' story, told by a son who wishes he had one more tomorrow to tell them he loves them.

Introduction

It was the decade of the twenties, a time of expensive watered-down liquor, speakeasies, the Charleston and flappers. It was two years before Black Friday, April 14, the stock market crash and the Great Depression. The year 1927 found Americans finally accepting the telephone as an important part of life. The Victrola, 78-rpm records and roller-playing pianos were becoming popular and more affordable. The first sound-equipped movie was made with the great entertainer Al Jolson starring as a black-faced songster in *The Jazz Singer*. A young Charles Lindbergh buzzed New York City trying to raise the money for a solo flight across the Atlantic . . . unheard of!

The greatest baseball team of all time, the 1927 World Champion New York Yankees, dominated the baseball world and the World Series with the help of the great Babe Ruth and his sixty home runs.

With great anticipation and amazement the longest underwater passageway, the Lincoln Tunnel, opened to the public. The Broadway musical *Showboat* entertained New York audiences for the first time.

Though 1927 was memorable for all those events, a single immigrant family's tragedy spread its effect like a cold fog off the docks of New York that year. In Brooklyn's Little Italy, the death of a small boy named Joseph Caruso drew public attention for far more years than he lived.

The influx of immigrants through places like Ellis Island became a deluge of humanity in the 1920's. Irish immigrants were the largest group of people to migrate to America, followed by the next largest group, the Italians. Almost half of the Italian immigrants returned to their homeland.

As immigrants settled into this unfamiliar land, they formed little homelands away from home, small communities within the city's and towns. These ethnic communities were sometimes no larger than a block or two. Each nationality grouped together to recreate a semblance of home, where language and culture was familiar and where they found time to enjoy each other's company in an unfamiliar environment. Dealing with this new environment was difficult. The immigrants needed the comfort of speaking fluently among themselves, tasting the usual foods, knowing what to expect in encounters with others. Villages of immigrants popped up all over New York City, New Jersey and Connecticut known as the

Irish neighborhood, Little Italy, China Town, the German neighborhood, etc.

The Statue of Liberty carried the inscription, "Give me your poor, your huddled masses. . . ." They came and kept coming, poor of everything but pride, tradition, spirit and hope. For the most part, they were hard-working people of limited means. Advantages and services were not generally available to them in this land of plenty, this country with mythical golden-paved streets. Many arrived here only to die of starvation or disease. Most immigrants lived in cold-water flats, apartments that did not have hot water or heat. Slum neighborhoods became over-populated, infested with pests. Roaches, rats, mice, and lice infested the better ethnic neighborhoods as well.

As conditions worsened, epidemics spread everywhere. Chicken pox, measles, malaria, whooping cough, and diphtheria were among the many illnesses immigrants had to survive. The medical community made a conscious effort to serve the needs of the public, including the poor. In the larger cities like New York of 1927, the population was mostly comprised of poor immigrants in concentrated areas. Realizing that the poor could not afford to go to hospitals or doctor's offices for their medical needs, the doctors and nurses went into poor immigrant neighborhoods to treat them. They treated these impoverished patients at their apartments and recruited midwives and nurses to do follow-up visits. By 1927, medical staffs treated millions of people on house calls from headaches to minor surgery and childbirth.

Epidemics knew no bounds. Stemmed at their sources, the medical community acted wisely to contain them and was none the poorer for it. By reaching out to the impoverished in their flats, they helped control contagious diseases while making money they would normally not have received. They arranged payment plans according to the family's ability to pay. Sometimes the amount was as little as 25 cents a week.

Common procedure in a contagious disease situation was for an authority to post quarantine signs on entry doors, notifying visitors of the risk from the condition. Only authorities could remove a posted sign, under threat of fine or imprisonment to all others. Penalties were strictly enforced.

Doctors, midwives and nurses who made house calls were easy targets for those who earned their livelihood by crime. Often healthcare givers were beaten and robbed of anything they had from money, medicine and vehicles to the very clothes they wore.

Though no one knew it, Medical care providers had protection in Italian neighborhoods. The organization, known today as the Crime Family or Mafia, that kept them safe was not widely known to the immigrants.

On February 13, 192, at one o'clock on a Saturday afternoon in Brooklyn, an event occurred that from that time forward changed the way the medical community viewed house calls nationwide. The event set the powerful organization of the New York Chapter of The American Medical Association against another organization not as well known, but just as dedicated, the Mafia. This event pitted one Italian against the other and posted a message that no doctor, mid-wife or nurse was truly safe anywhere . . . not even in Italian neighborhoods, which had been the exception.

In reporting the story, the newspapers, magazines and radio distorted the truth and warped details into sensational headlines. Because headlines sold, they wrung this chronicle for the lurid attention that sells newspapers.

The elements of high drama were easy to overplay the unfortunate death of a young boy, his grief-crazed parents that included a pretty, young mother and the brutal murder of a medical doctor in Little Italy.

Media personnel of all kinds must have assumed the immigrants involved had no power to prevent news accounts or to protect themselves and their surviving children from unwelcome public attention. Stories about the brutal murder of Dr. Casper S. Pendola separated readers into groups. Foremost were those for the death penalty and those against it. Not reported were the behind-the-scenes maneuvers of the New York Chapter of the American Medical Association and the Mafia. Battling each other for a man's life was the might of a powerful establishment organization and the little-known force of one just carving its niche in this country.

Francesco "Cheech" Caruso fled the scene after Dr. Casper S. Pendola's death and went directly to family, in the Sicilian manner. His older brother Rosario Caruso lived on Staten Island. About 4:30 p. m. on a cold Saturday February 13, 1927, Cheech sat in a welter of emotion at his brother's kitchen table.

Chapter 1

Down the common dark, damp hallway with flats on either side, Rosario speaks into the public phone mounted on the wall. He cups a hand around the mouthpiece, keeping his voice low. "Operator, please give me the Brooklyn *policia d*epartment." The operator does not hear or cannot understand his heavy accent. Clearing his throat, he speaks a little louder pronouncing the harsh English syllables with care. "Please give me the Hamilton Avenue Brooklyn *policia* department." His message understood this time, he adds, "Thank you." He curves his body around the wall mounted telephone box, closing out curious neighbors. He thought, Sicily not like this, people stacked atop each other in cold boxes so they no can break wind without neighbors knowing. Waiting in silence to be connected, he turns just enough to look toward the end of the hall through the open door into his apartment.

Inside, his younger brother sits at a small kitchen table. With his elbows on the tabletop and his head buried in his hands, Cheech waits, quiet and motionless.

Hearing a voice at the other end of the telephone, Rosario says, "Hello, Mr. *Policia*, this is Rosario Caruso. My brother Francesco is here with me. He wants you should come and get him. He wants to give up. He wants to go back to Brooklyn."

After a brief pause, the officer responds, "Who the hell is this?"

Straightening up in surprise at the officer's rudeness, Rosario speaks the difficult English language with all the precision he can muster. "My brother said he killed a man today in Brooklyn. He said the man; he was a doctor, Doctor Pendola. Do you know what I am talking about?"

After a pause full of muffled voices, the officer says, "Where are you calling from? Give me your address, and I will see that someone comes to get him."

"I cannot tell you that yet, Sir." He knows how some Americans think people are stupid if they speak English with an accent, especially an Italian accent. Rosario speaks as clearly as he can, pronouncing every syllable as carefully as he can. "Please! First, you must listen to me. I have something to tell you from my brother. He said that he will only give up to you if *policia*-man Sergeant O'Mally comes into my house to arrest him."

There is another pause. Then the police officer speaks again. "He's not working today; he's off duty. I can't get him now."

Rosario shifts, gazes at Cheech's hunched figure and says with urgency, "You must find him Mr. *Policia*-man. I will call you back in one hour. After my brother speaks to O'Mally, I will tell you where I am, one hour, goodbye!" Hanging up the telephone, Rosario wipes the cold sweat off his face onto his shirtsleeve and walks slowly back to his apartment. He thinks it is only right that his younger brother came to him for help, but he wonders if he can deal with this disaster, or maybe be deported for his part in it. Inside the apartment, he collects a bottle of Italian wine and two glasses and walks to the table. Easing onto a chair across from Cheech, he places the wine and glasses on the table and fills both glasses. He gestures for his brother to drink. In Sicilian, he makes an effort at rough humor. "Cheech, come on, drink up. Once they get here, you won't be drinking wine for a long time."

Cheech grimaces but takes up his glass. Both men taste of the wine in the silence of the little room.

Rosario watches, still shaken, as his brother sets down the glass, lips wet like his swollen eyes, and buries his face in his hands again. Cheech has always been the best looking of them, the seven Caruso sons, drawing women and men alike to him with ease and charm when he chooses. When he pounded on the door earlier and stumbled inside, Rosario felt shock at his ill, wild appearance. The shock deepened as he learned why Cheech came.

Shaking his head, Rosario says, "What have you done? what have you done? In this country, you will get the electric chair. Do you know that?"

Cheech takes his huge hands from his face and wipes his eyes. "My life is over anyway, Rosario, over. When Joey died in my arms, inside, I died with him. It's best I die. It doesn't make any difference if I live anymore." Cheech strikes his deep chest and flings up his arms. "All I do is cause misery and death everywhere I go. I killed Valenta, and then Papa, and now I killed Doctor Pendola. Now I lost Joey." His voice throbs with grief as he clutches his shirtfront. "I lost everything. I have nothing. My life is over. My heart is dead!"

Leaning across the scrubbed table, Rosario grasps his wrist and whispers, "Cheech, my poor brother, you still have a family, and you shouldn't give up. We love you."

Cheech pulls free and shakes his head looking at Rosario with angry eyes. "This isn't the first family I left. I left close relatives in Sicilia. Now I leave this family in America."

Removing the cork from the wine bottle, Cheech lifts it and gulps down a healthy portion of the bottle. Then he refills both their glasses and places the bottle on the table. The two brothers stare at each other and lift their glasses in a mute toast. Rosario stands up, walks to the icebox, find's another bottle of wine and returns to the table, placing the *vino* in front of his brother.

Cheech leans on his forearms, tragedy sagging his face and massive shoulders. He looks down at the tabletop. "I'm always running. I'm good at running."

"You don't run when you have me call *policia* for you." Rosario wonders how Cheech would know an Irish police officer. "This O'Mally, he is a good friend to you?"

Head down, Cheech nods. "He is like a brother, a real brother. He is my only friend."

"How long have you known each other? Are you sure you can trust him?" Rosario pours another glass of wine, wishing he had more to give Cheech in his devastation. "How did you meet this unlikely friend?"

"I did him a favor a long time ago. He never forgot it. It was my pleasure to help him." For the first time since his arrival, Cheech straightens up as he continues. "It was something he could not do for himself because he is a policeman. So I took care of it for him."

Rising from the table, Rosario sets his glass down with a thump. "The hour is up, time to call the *policia* again. Come on Cheech, you talk to O'Mally."

The brothers walk out of the apartment, broad shoulders nearly touching as they pace down the narrow hallway to the public phone at the other end. Rosario dials and is quickly connected with the Brooklyn police station. A male voice crackles down the line. "This is the Hamilton Avenue Police Station, Officer Ryan speaking!"

Clearing his throat, Rosario says, "This is Rosario Caruso. My brother is ready to speak to O'Mally. He would like to speak with Officer O'Mally."

"Hold on," Ryan instructs. Rosario hears distant voices and scuffling sounds.

Then a wary voice says, "Hello, this is O'Mally."
Rosario hands the receiver to Cheech.

Cheech leans forward, closer to the mouthpiece mounted on the box. This is his only chance. He is glad to hear his friend's voice. "Hello, O'Mally? Is that you, *Piason*?"

"It's me." O'Mally lowers his voice. "Are you okay, Cheech?"

Shutting his eyes, Cheech knows he will never be okay again. "I am as okay as I can be. Sorry I ruined your Saturday, *Piason*. Who else can I turn to?"

"Don't worry about it," O'Mally says, "Sure you call me anytime."

Leaning against the wall in relief, Cheech hears reassurance in O'Mally's tone. Still, he is a cop, and right now a roomful of his cohorts can hear every word he's saying. He tells O'Mally, "I know you're surrounded by policemen so listen to me and say yes or no. Will you come with the detectives to get me, and stay with us until I'm locked up? It is important."

O'Mally agrees at once. "I understand. I know what you mean. Of course I will come for you with the arresting officers."

The Irishman is a friend indeed. His presence will keep Cheech alive long enough to ask a special favor of his friend in the privacy of his brothers home. "Thanks, O'Mally; now I give the telephone to my brother so he can give you the address here." He hands the receiver back to Rosario who is leaning against the phone box. Listening to his brother, Cheech can tell that O'Mally has to search for paper to write on.

Finally, Rosario concludes repeating, "About an hour. We expect you. Thank you."

As they trudge back to the apartment in silence, Cheech feels the high ceiling and confining walls close in on him like a prison, like the prison that certainly lays ahead for him, if not worse. Once the door closes, Rosario reverts to their native tongue. "Tell me again what happened at the house with Joey, please, while we have the time. I want to know."

Cheech wipes his eyes and puts his hands together. He manages to say, "My Joey," before the tears start again and the saliva in his throat chokes him. Deep sobs shake his shoulders and wrench his chest until it hurts to breathe, but he needs to talk about it. He came here to spill the torrents of poisonous rage and grief to a brother who would recognize their headwaters. Finally, he gasps, "Joey was sick for about three weeks. He was getting worse all the time." His words struggle out as he weeps. "First he had a cold, and then a sore throat and a fever. Then he started to have trouble breathing. He had trouble sleeping. My precious son, my little boy, he was so sick." Tears slide down his cheeks and splash on the tabletop as the pain in his throat makes it difficult to speak. His son suffered far worse torment, and he could do nothing for his beloved boy. "One morning, I opened the door to our apartment to go to work and saw a quarantine sign on the door. I didn't know where it came from, but I knew what it meant. We couldn't leave our rooms, not for work, food or anything. Some neighbors, who were standing outside their doors, told me they would take care of the food for us. I thanked them and went back inside. I told Maria about the quarantine and explained that we had to stay behind the door until a nurse say's we can leave. Somebody will come to help us, I tell her. They will come." Anguish and a surging sense of betrayal set his blood pounding. He talks faster and louder. "But nobody ever comes, not anyone, not the doctor, not the nurse . . . nobody. Days go by. Joey, he gets worse and worse. Maria and I stay up with him for three or four days and nights with little or no sleep.

"The other children begin to get sick. We don't know what to do for Joey anymore. Maria and I take turns swabbing his throat. It is so swollen, so red, like it's burning with fire."

Cheech shrugs and grimaces, hands spread wide. He saw it hurt little Joey when he doctored his throat. He would rather cut out his own heart with a spoon than see Joey hurt. "Still, nobody comes. We don't know why. How can a man protect his son when an official sign imprisons him? What kind of government lets children sicken onto death behind a barred door? I didn't know what to do. Nobody came to help us. Other tenants had doctors and nurses visit them, but nobody came to help us.

Finally, I couldn't bear it anymore, to watch my Joey suffer. I told Maria to keep Joey warm, that I would be back with a doctor as soon as I could. So I went out to look for a doctor."

Rosario leans forward, frowning. "The quarantine, you broke the quarantine!"

Shaking his fists, Cheech roars, "By then I didn't care about the dammed quarantine or if they arrested me forty times over!" Clenching his teeth, he swallows the taste of bile. He needs to explain to Rosario before the police come for him. "Joey was bad, worse by the minute. I had to go. I looked everywhere for a doctor, but their offices were all closed. On the way back to the house, I stopped at Pendola's Drug Store. I went there for medication when Joey first got sick. I knew the man and his wife. I went inside and told the drug man that Joey was worse and I needed a doctor. I told him the doctor offices closed and I needed one right away. I pleaded with him to help me with his medicines, for my boy's sake. He tells me, 'my brother is a doctor. He lives at Queens. If he is home, he will come. Give me your address.' He told me to wait, and then he went to the back of the store."

Rosario nods "He's a good man, the druggist."

"When he came out, he said his brother was home and would leave right away. I was to go home and wait there for him. I thanked Pendola and hurried home." Bitterly, Cheech recalls Maria's expression of relief and her admiration for him when he told her he had arranged for a doctor to come for their boy. About an hour later, the doctor knocked, and I let him in. He looked at Joey, shaking his head and saying he was very sick. Joey was having trouble breathing. He said Joey should be in a hospital. We pleaded with him not to take him away. The doctor said he would try to treat Joey at home. He got fresh with me, saying to me 'Why did you people wait so long before going for help? When it comes to contagious diseases like this, home remedies don't work.' I was tired and his voice bothered me. He was blaming us for Joey being so sick. I got hot all over, grabbed his wrist and told him to not speak to me that way anymore, to stop being fresh with me. I told him someone put that the sign on our door over a week ago, and we sat in the house waiting and waiting for someone to come from the hospital . . . nobody came. Nobody came! If there was no sign, I would have gone to the hospital for help last week and my boy would be better by now, so be nice and don't be fresh no more. Then I asked who put the sign there. The doctor said he would look into it and find out. Then he said he would do his best for the little boy. I let go of his wrist and told him to fix Joey. How thankful Maria was, not to have our boy carried off to that monstrous place where people were cut on and died. The doctor turned Joey on his side and rolled up his little shirt. Out of his black bag, he took a needle and filled it with medicine. Then he stuck Joey in the back. Joey cried, but the doctor said he was going to be okay."

"He told you Joey would get better?" Rosario shifts on the hard wooden chair and frowns. "Then I don't understand what happened."

"I do!" Cheech pounds his thigh with a fist. He tells Rosario something he must know. "The doctor gave me a piece of paper with the name of another medicine on it. He said for me to go to the drug store and get it filled right away. I ran back to Pendola's drug store and gave the drug man the paper. He looked at the paper and told me that this medicine was too strong for a six-year-old child! He said, "My brother should not do things like this."

Rosario raises his dark brows. "He said that, about his brother?"

Nodding, Cheech gets up to pace the floor. He cannot sit still and relive the nightmare of the last few days. "Then the drug man shook his head and went in the back of the store. When I got back home with the medicine, the doctor was still there. I told him what his brother said, and he said his brother should mind his own goddamn business, that he didn't know what he was talking about." Cheech stops, flinging out his hands in supplication. "I didn't know what to do. The drug man, he was so sure it was wrong, but the doctor, he is a doctor! His job is to know the medicines for healing."

Rosario nods in agreement, thrusts thick fingers through his hair as Cheech resumes pacing in the small space. "Then the doctor says he will be back at ten o'clock the next day and he left. Maria and I are up all night long, never leaving Joey's cot. We keep him near the oven to keep him warm. Joey is restless all night, until after twelve o'clock when he has tremors and brings up foam. His voice starts to change. He does not talk like a little boy anymore. His little voice is like a low, rough whisper, heavy like a man. It is hard to understand him. Maria understands him better than me."

Cheech stops to swallow, but the knot in his throat seems permanent. "Then Joey, he can't talk anymore. He just stares into space." Cheech covers his face with his hands, shoulders heaving. "We could hear each breath going in-and-out, in-and-out. He worked so hard to suck air into his little chest. It hurt him; I ached with him for every breath." Cheech's heart feels like it is about to explode. "I sit down on the floor beside his cot near the stove and watch him breathe. I keep on telling him he was going to be okay, but he doesn't answer. He just looks away. Maria and I keep asking him if he can hear us, but he says nothing."

At this point, Rosario notices that Cheech resumes his tragic tale in the past tense rather than the present tense he was using earlier. He thinks that early on Cheech was not just remembering what happened . . . he was reliving it.

"Then Joey's little body stiffened and his breathing became softer. I moved one of his arms gently to see if he would respond . . . and he did. Then he said the last words of his life." Crying louder and out of control, Cheech sags and falls to his knees where he stands, holding his head as if it could fall off.

Rosario finds him a towel and leads him to a chair at the table. He embraces Cheech for a long moment, and then pours him another glass of wine. "You gonna be okay?"

Burrowing his face in the towel, Cheech tells him, "He told me, 'Papa . . . the doctor is killing me with that shot he gave me. I feel like I'm on fire. I'm dying, Papa, please help me; help me, Papa, don't let me die.'"

After another storm of weeping, Cheech groans and mops his ravaged face
with the towel. "I tell him, you are going to be okay, you will not die and
leave me. I will not let you die! He put his little shaking hand on my arm.
It was so thin by then; it is like a feather's touch. He looked at me one last
time. Then his eyes turned away from me. He said, 'I go now Papa.'
Cheech tries once, twice, before his voice grates out, "And he stopped
breathing." Cheech's head sinks forward. Tears rain on the wood tabletop.
"I watched him real close and looked for a breath, but there was none. I
whispered, "Joey breathe for Papa, please, no do this to me." I looked at
Maria on the other side of the cot. She was crying with no noise, both
hands on her mouth. I looked at Joey. All I could think about was Papa. I
killed him and named my son after him, and now I killed my son too."

Rosario shakes his head. "No, Cheech."

"Yes! I killed him, I killed both of them!"

"But the doctor . . . when did the doctor come back?"

"Let me think, let me think. My head hurts. It's difficult to think.
Cheech rubs his aching head. Since Joey died, his thoughts attack and
scatter like wild pigs, and the pain of his loss hasn't stopped for an instant.
"I started crying and acting like a crazy man. It's hard to remember what
was happening." His voice rises until he is almost yelling. Seizing
handfuls of his dark hair, Cheech pulls.

Rosario, taken aback by the change in his brother's mood, reaches
across the little table and grabs Cheech's wrists. His brother's fingers are
too intertwined with his hair to remove them. Hoping to prevent him from
hurting himself, Rosario says, "Stop! Cheech, Cheech, stop. Don't,
Cheech, please, no." With no response, Rosario begs, "Cheech you're
scaring me; stop!"

Cheech grabs his brother's hands in a painful grip and flings them
away, lips curling inward over his teeth.

Frightened, Rosario massages his wrists. Never has he seen his
younger brother act this violently before, not in the natural fights among
all the brothers back home in Sicily and not against outsiders. This
younger brother known to his family as being calm and calculating shows
a side Rosario has not seen before. Becoming aware of wetness, he looks
at his hands, red, covered with blood. In horror, Rosario shouts, "Cheech!
My hands are bloody. What is it, where did the blood come from?"

Cheech crosses his arms in front of him on the table and rests his
forehead on them. "Don't touch me, Rosario. Don't touch me again, not
anymore!" When Rosario rises causing the chair legs to scrape the floor,

Cheech says sharply, "Sit down!"

Falling onto the seat of the chair, Rosario holds on to both of his brother's hands. "The back of your head is covered with blood. What happened to you?"

"I don't know," Cheech says in puzzlement. He touches the back of his scalp, winces, and looks at his hand. "I can't remember. I can't remember." With increasing agitation, he cries out, "I wish I was dead! Rosario, give me your gun, I want your gun. I'll settle this now."

"No, no!" Rosario protests. "No more trouble. Enough is enough. Let me wash my hands, and then I'll take care of your head." At the shallow sink, he scrubs his hands, keeping watch over Cheech. Wetting a dishcloth, he returns to his brother and attempts to clean away the blood.

Suddenly, Cheech wrenches away, overturning his chair as he leaps up scaring Rosario. A snarl distorts his features as his eyes look at nothing. "You're the reason I killed Papa, you and your no good brothers. You're the reason Papa is dead. I will never forget that, never. You and your brothers should never have done that to me. I will never forgive you." Words fall over each other like ants escaping a kicked hill as he tries to express himself. "You all left me out there miles from nowhere with no clothes, no food and no way to get home. Because I made them pay for what all of you did to me, I am cursed. You got away; I couldn't find you, you son-of-a-bitch. You got away and hid like the rat you are!"

Rosario shakes his head no, but does not dare interrupt Cheech in this wild frenzy.

Cheech sways on his feet, looking into the distance. "First Valenta died, then Papa died and now Joey is dead. Will he be the last? No, I don't think so. I don't care with Joey gone." Hoping to calm his brother, Rosario takes a step toward him. His head snapping up, Cheech puts up both hands. "Don't touch me, Rosario! You touched me enough." Cheech raises clenched fists and yells, "You touch me one more time and I kill you too, *gabish*?"

Rosario returns to the table and sits down slowly on the far side, as far away from Cheech as the small table allows. He remains quiet knowing Cheech is crazy with grief. He doesn't know what he is saying, he tells himself. Maybe he doesn't know what he is doing, either. He tries to remain calm.

Chapter 2

Cheech looks and acts so strange as he raves on that Rosario thinks twice before he risks speaking. Softly he tells him, "Cheech, what happened to Papa was an accident. No one knew that would happen. We didn't mean it to happen like that. It wasn't your fault that Papa died; we didn't mean for it to happen like that."

Eyes red and glaring in an unfamiliar face, Cheech takes a step toward him. "After O'Mally comes and takes me away, I don't ever want to see you again, you Bastard. You are no goddamn good! You and your fucken brothers are just as bad!" He stumbles back, clutching handfuls of hair again. "I don't even know what I'm doing here; how did I get here? Why did I come to your house?"

Rosario says the only thing he knows to say, the truth.

"Because I'm your brother, still family . . . no matter what you think of me."

"You're no goddamn brother of mine, you son-of-a- bitch no good bastard." His eyes empty, Cheech does not look or talk like himself. "You stopped being my brother when Papa died, you and the rest of your goddamn brothers." Leaning over to look out the window, Cheech seems to see Sicily instead of Staten Island through the windowpanes. "Papa took me out of school when I was eight-years-old, Rosario, eight years old, because none of you bastards had the guts for the business. I was the one who did *not* want it. You and your brothers wanted it; but none of you could handle it because you were all cowards. You blamed me for everything that went wrong! Every time you and your brothers did something and things went wrong, you, all of you, put the responsibility for it on me. Papa hollered at me. All of you enjoyed that, seeing Papa do that to me." He points a thick forefinger in Rosario's direction. "I wish on you and your family all the tragedy you and your brothers brought to me and my family."

"You don't mean that, Cheech!" Even with the madness, the sadness of his Joey's death, Cheech's unreasonable charges sting.

Cheech grabs Rosario by the throat with one hand and pulls him onto the table. "Don't you ever forget what I say today, Rosario. I wish on you and your family the same burden of tragedy that you placed on me, both you and all of your damned brother's families! I mean every word I say. I curse you all for the rest of your lives!" Without effort, he flings Rosario back into his chair with enough force to make the chair legs screech and slide on the wooden floor. His voice and face change from demon to damned. "Give me your gun. If you want to do me one favor in your worthless life, give me your gun. For once, do something for someone other than yourself, do something for me!"

Touching what feel like bruises on his throat, Rosario says, "I don't have a gun, Cheech. I would *never* have a gun in the house. We don't live like that here."

Cheech sneers. "That's because you're a fucken coward like your no good brothers. That's why Papa took me out of school, and that's why he ruined my life. He knew none of you could do it, so it was up to me." Turning his face upward, he throws out his arms and cries, "And look at what came of it!" Fingers intertwined with his hair, he pulls at it and groans in pain. "Rosario, don't say one more goddamn word until O'Mally gets here. I'm a dead man. I could kill you for nothing. I don't want to hear your miserable voice. I must have been out of my mind, crazy out of my mind, to come here." Holding his aching head, he grimaces. "I don't understand. I don't feel so good." He collapses in his chair banging his head on the table. His arms slide off the edge of the table. He is unconscious.

Rosario gingerly wipes his face and fills the glasses one more time. He must calm Cheech down when he awakens, or his brother might take on the whole police force when they arrive. He might be killed or hurt someone else. In a few moments, Cheech opens eyes and cries.

"Okay, okay, Cheech, I'm sorry. Come, have a drink with me. Drink, to show you can forgive me."

"Shut the fuck up, I'll never forgive you!" Cheech shouts. He winces as his head throbs. He clutches his head and moans. "Be quiet and sit still. Sit still! Madonna mia, my head hurts! Sit still or I'll make you still! I just want quiet, no noise. Quiet."

"Okay Cheech, okay, I'll be quiet!"

Cheech crosses his massive arms in front of him on the tabletop and rests his forehead on them. "I just want to be quiet, Rosario. I haven't slept in weeks."

Horrified at the wild menace Cheech has become, Rosario does not know what to expect next from his brother. Like this, Cheech could easily kill. Rosario fears for his life for the first time. He hears an automobile pulling up onto the gravel parking area and come to a stop in front of the apartment building. Looking at Cheech, he slowly rises from his chair and edges over to the window pulling the curtains back to look out. "Cheech," he says quietly. "I think they are here. Is that O'Mally getting out of the car?"

Cheech joins him at the window. They look below as four men in overcoats climb out of a car. One turns to the others and makes hand motions as if to say, stay calm. Looking up, he waves to Cheech and Rosario. The other men look up. Rosario asks, "Is that O'Mally?"

"*Cie*; he is the one who waved."

A little later, Rosario rises to answer O'Mally's knock.

Cheech calls, "Come on in, O'Mally."

Rosario opens the door and O'Mally walks in without hesitation. Rosario tenses, not sure of what to expect from Cheech after his ranting and threats. O'Mally approaches the table. Cheech smiles and steps toward him as the two men reach out for each other and lock in an embrace.

"I am so glad you came, O'Mally, so happy to see you," Cheech says, "Thank you my friend."

O'Mally thumps his back. "I'm glad you asked for me. It gives me a chance to pay you back. Are you okay?"

Cheech wipes his eyes as he steps back a pace. "I will never be okay again, Piason; my life is over. Joey is dead. Soon I will be dead too." He gestures to the table. "Come on, sit down with me, have a glass of wine and we talk. I have something I want to speak to you about." As Cheech fills the two glasses he and Rosario used earlier, he tells Rosario, "Rosario, bring a glass for my friend."

O'Mally pulls back one side of the curtains and waves to the officers at the car. He shouts, "I'm okay; I'll be down in a while."

A faint answer rises on the sharp winter air, heavy with coal smog. "Don't be too long, and stay in view." As he turns back from the window, O'Mally inspects the injury to the back of his friend's head. "Be Jesus, Cheech, do you know what you've done?"

Cheech ducks away from the touch of examination, but he answers in a heavy, low voice. "*Cie*, I know what I did. I killed the no good bastard that killed my son. Joey told me he was dying. I didn't listen. I trusted the damned doctor, that good for nothing bastard. He killed my beautiful little boy. Now I don't have Joey no more."

O'Mally rubs the blood on his fingertips together after touching Cheech's scalp. "What the hell happened to your head, Cheech?"

Rosario tells him, "I tried to clean it for him, but he won't let me help him."

"Bring me a basin of water and a rag," O'Mally says, "and I'll take care of it."

Cheech rubs the back of his neck and looks baffled. "I don't know what happened. I can't remember. I can't remember a lot of things." Looking around with heavy eyelids, a gaping yawn ends in a grimace. "O'Mally, my head hurts so bad I wish I was dead."

With rough kindness, O'Mally puts a hand on Cheech's back. "Put your head down so I can wash off some of the mess." As O'Mally works with the gentleness his big hands belie, Rosario fills the glasses again. "I can't believe Joey's dead, little Joey. What happened, Cheech?"

Slight movements of his head when the injury is touched shows body awareness, but in tone of voice and expression, Cheech seems barely alive. "I don't know, *Piason*, I do not know. Sometimes I can remember everything, other times nothing. I no can remember anything. All I know is I am never gonna see him again." He closes his eyes as tears roll down his cheeks. "He's gone for real."

The two men quietly continue cleaning the blood from Cheech's head while he grieves for his Joey. Handing the bloody cloth to Rosario, O'Mally tells him, "Cheech, if there's anything you have to say to me, if there's anything I can do for you and your family, now's the time to tell me. Since you asked for me, they know we're friends. They won't let me hang around the stationhouse as long as you're there. So I won't be able to help you unless you tell me now." Moving around in front of Cheech, he bends to look him in the eyes. "They're already looking at me funny. I need to know now what you want me to do for your family, Totto, anyone, anything else, you know."

Cheech raises his head, wipes his eyes, leans back and meets O'Mally's look. "If you would, O'Mally, there are a few things I need for you to do. That's why I ask for you to come."

O'Mally sat in the chair across from Cheech, back to the window. "Okay, Cheech."

"I want you to first go see Maria and see if she needs anything, please. Then, I want you to take a note to the boss." He gestures to his brother. "Rosario, get paper for a letter and a pencil." After a quick trip to the bedroom, Rosario brings a tablet and pencil to the table. Cheech shoves the writing materials toward O'Mally. "I no write English, you write for me, okay?"

Pulling the pad toward him, O'Mally straddles the chair Rosario used earlier across the table.

Cheech frowns at his brother. "Get the hell out of here. This is not for coward's ears." Rosario glances at the two men then goes into the bathroom and closes the door. "Now," Cheech says, "You write what I say:

Boss, the man who brings you this paper is my friend. He is my brother. He is not Sicilian, but he   is a man of his word, an honorable man, a man of respect. Help him. Protect him. Because he helps me, he is not safe anymore. I ask you to watch him, his   wife and children. Before the law kills me, I would like to speak to you one more time. There are things I want to say to you. I will not forget you. Do not   forget me. Do not bring attention to yourself by helping me.

"That's all, O'Mally." O'Mally pushes the tablet and pencil over to Cheech. At the bottom of the page, Cheech signs his name in Sicilian. It says, your *Piason* Cheech. He folds the paper with deliberate moves of his huge hands. "Make sure no one sees it except the boss, no one!"

O'Mally leans on the table, looking troubled. "That part about me— you don't have to do this, Cheech."

"*Cie*, I do. Do you know what's gonna happen to you, now that you are here? Now they know you're my friend, that I asked for you? You will need the boss's help. He will make sure nothing happens to you while you walk the neighborhood. Let me do this for you my friend, my brother." Cheech clasps his friend's wrist and states with urgency, "Understand? *Gabish?*"

Jaw set, O'Mally nods. "Yes, *cie,* I do. Thank you, Cheech, I *Gabish.*"

"Good." Cheech passes a heavy hand over his face. He glances toward the bathroom door and lowers his voice. "Now I tell you what to do. Go to Brooklyn, to Giovanni's. You know Giovanni's?"

"I'll find it."

"When you enter the restaurant, go to the back of the club and look for the biggest table in the corner of the restaurant. Tell the men sitting there that you are Cheech's friend and that you have a message for the boss. They will understand, but they will look at you crooked because they don't know or trust you. Now this is important." Cheech leans forward and speaks with emphasis. "As long as you stand still you are okay. Be nice, on your best behavior when you speak to them. Only say what they ask, no more. They will help you." Cheech leans even closer. "Even if somebody says to, *don't* give the note to anybody but the boss. When you are with him, give him the note." He lifts a hand in caution. "Make sure you tell him that you are reaching for the note, slow. Sometimes you act Sicilian, but, my friend, you are not. You are Irish."

"I know, Cheech," O'Mally tells him with an effort at a smile, "I'm Irish, but I'm no fool."

"I know you are not, my friend. Good. After he has read my note, introduce yourself and tell him I thank him for everything he did for my family, my friends and me. Tell him that I don't want him to become involved in this, no matter what happens to me. This is a personal matter; he should not get involved."

O'Mally shakes his head. "You'll need all the help you can get."

"It's too late for help." Cheech rubs his forehead, looking days past exhaustion. "Tell him that I'll be okay. Tell him I want to die. I am tired and I want to die. I want to go home. I want to be with the people I love. Tell him if I can see him one more time, I'll take care of all of our business."

Shifting on the hard chair, O'Mally grunts. "I'll tell him for you."

"After you see the boss, go see O'Hanlon in my building, you know O'Hanlon on the second floor. Tell him to do as we said when I was there and spoke to him; everything will be okay. Tell him to use his daughter as we said. He'll know what I mean. I tell you one more time. Do *not* let anyone see this note. If you have to, eat it." Cheech points to his mouth, "*Manja!* Eat!"

O'Mally holds out a hand. "No one will see it. You have my word." Taking the folded paper, he unbuttons his tunic and tucks it into an inside pocket.

They are silent for a moment. Cheech says, "Thank you, O'Mally. Thank you for your friendship. I will never forget you, not ever. You have been the friendship of my miserable life, my only friend. I hope you know that I would give up my life for you. Thank you my Irish *Piason*. I love you."

O'Mally's eyes mist though his gaze remains steady. "I've always known that, *Piason*. It wasn't necessary for you to tell me."

Cheech sighs, makes a wide gesture and lays both hands on the tabletop, "*Basta*, that's all, finish, *finito*. Let's go." O'Mally takes out a set of cuffs as he comes to his feet. Lurching slightly as he stands, Cheech asks, "Can you put them on in the front?"

"Sure." O'Mally's expression is troubled as he turns the cuffs awkwardly. "It bothers me that I have to put them on at all . . . but I do."

"I know, *Piason.*"

As if delaying the inevitable moment, O'Mally walks to the bathroom and taps on the door. "Rosario, we're going. You can come out now."

As his brother opens the door and steps out, Cheech's expression tightens from the camaraderie of the last few minutes into a threatening snarl. "Don't forget what I said: Do *not* come to the trial!"

Though he takes a step back, Rosario shakes his head. "I can't do that. I can't stay away from my brother's trial."

Cheech makes a rude gesture. "You're not my brother, you son-of-a-bitch. I will die soon, but you are already dead."

Turning a shoulder against Rosario, Cheech gazes at O'Mally with liquid dark eyes that show warmer emotion. His friend blushes deep red as he stares back, cuffs dangling from his hand. Cheech steps toward him and extends his wrists.

His head down, O'Mally places the cuffs on Cheech and snaps them closed. Then he wipes his eyes and turns away, muttering, "Holy Mother of God." Leaning out the window, he shouts in a loud voice that cracks with the first word. "We're coming down now. He's handcuffed and unarmed, so don't do anything stupid!"

At the door to the passage, O'Mally stands back for Cheech to precede him. Rosario hurries to the window to watch. Down the dark hallway and stairs, O'Mally and Cheech walk side-by-side. At the building's entrance, O'Mally moves ahead. "Let me go first." As they step into the cold winter daylight, Cheech bows his head and squeezes his eyes shut. O'Mally takes his arm to steady him. From the back of the buildings on both sides, four of Staten Island's finest come to grapple Cheech away from O'Mally. "Wait a damn minute," O'Mally growls, pushing them back as Cheech stumbles under their rough handling. "The man's hurt; he's injured, easy!"

Cheech holds up his cuffed hands with palms out. He speaks quietly to his friend, "It's okay, I'm okay."

The four cops march Cheech to the waiting car with the detectives from Brooklyn. O'Mally follows. Reaching the car, a Staten Island cop announces in an officious tone, "We're surrendering the prisoner to you for the trip back to Brooklyn."

Two of the Brooklyn detectives step forward to bracket Cheech, with a quick nod for their fellows. Never letting go of his arms, they push him into the back seat. O'Mally must sit up front with the other two detectives. The doors close against the pervasive rotten-egg stench of burned coal heavy in the air. Despite the tight fit of six men in the car, the air bites as sharp inside as out. The engine grinds to life and the car pulls away, heading for the Staten Island Ferry and the trip back to Brooklyn.

O'Malley knew Cheech was not himself back at Rosario's place. The injury to his head did not look good. Cheech had acted with the usual trust and respect toward him, but his behavior toward his brother was strange. Finally, O'Mally puts his arm on the back of the seat to glance back at Cheech. "What was going on between you and Rosario back at the apartment?"

Staring at his hands, Cheech barely moves his head. He looks ill, as if he can hardly sit erect. The detective on one side elbows him. "You better learn to speak up when a cop asks a question!"

His head falls back from this slight jolt, but his expression does not change from its withdrawn stoicism. With his head leaning back, Cheech speaks to the headliner, sounding as if someone has simply turned on his thoughts. "I have six brothers. My father knew that out of his seven sons, I was the only one who had the fortitude to run the family business. Against my wishes, my father took me out of school at the age of eight so I could learn the family business. My brothers all stayed in school. As the years went by, I grew in stature in our family and the surrounding towns. My brothers, they resented it. When Papa wasn't around, they did things to make me look foolish. I think Papa knew, but nothing they did bothered him."

"Tough luck," the driver says, downshifting as he slows for a trolley. "You think anybody here grew up in a rose garden?"

Cheech doesn't hear him. "One day after delivering a shipment of products, my brothers and I headed home in the wagon. We stopped at a lake to water the horses and take a dip. While I swam, they left with all of my clothes, the horses and wagon. They left before I could get out of the water. They left me there alone in my skin, with nothing. By the time I knew what was going on, they were leaving. I heard them laughing as they rode off down the road."

The driver snorts, "What's horseplay among brothers? What does that have to do with the mess you're in?"

Life returns to Cheech's strong frame. He surges forward on the seat. "You don't know what I'm saying. The bastards hope I never get back alive! Because of them, my papa, he died!" The detectives on either side yanked him back against the seat. Despite the cuffs, Cheech clenches his fists and thumps his wide thighs. "I was three hundred miles away from home with no clothes, no food, no water and no horse. During the day, I had to hide because people stopped at the lake to rest. With sunset, I looked for clothes. I found clothes left out to dry on a line. But I could not find shoes."

Apart from O'Mally, the detectives stare out their respective windows. Cheech does not seem to notice or care. He talks like a radio in an empty room, for himself and O"Mally, not for an audience of police officers. "The first night, I ate fruit and slept in a barn. The next morning the man that owned the barn found me sleeping in the hay. After I told him what happened to me, he fed me and gave me a pair of old boots. I thanked him and started walking home. That night I took shelter in another barn. Just before dawn, I stole one of the farmer's horses."

"The start of your life of crime," the driver muttered.

"By this time, I was so angry I could kill. I rode all day long and only stopped to water the poor horse. Finally, on the forth night, tired, angry and hungry, I arrived home about mid-night. Everyone was asleep. I went to the barn and got a bunch of rope. I took it to each of my brother's bedrooms, gagged and tied them up. I beat each of them until my hands were so sore I couldn't hit them anymore."

O'Mally was no stranger to violence and cruelty, but the bitterness in Cheech's tone surprised him.

"Then I left them like they left me and I went to bed. The next morning I awoke to Papa yelling and pulling me out of bed. He dragged me down to the wine cellar and beat me with a board until I was unconscious. The last thing I remembered before I passed out was Papa telling me that he wished I was dead and that he never wanted to see me again." Cheech covered his eyes with the palms of his cuffed hands. "When I came out of it, Mama and my sister were taking care of me. The next day I went to stay with my older sister and her family until I could decide what I was going to do. I knew I would not be welcomed at home anymore."

The driver lights a cigarette, kneeing the steering wheel as he fumbles with the matches. The car swerves slightly. O'Mally braces himself against the dash. Cheech sways with the car's movement but keeps talking. "I decided to join the Sicilian Army. One night out in the wilderness, the enemy ambushed us and killed everyone but me. I was hurt bad and left for dead. My personal things were returned to my family." Cheech closes his eyes. His voice is thick with tragedy. "As soon as my father saw them, he had a heart attack and died. He died with my things in his hands. Mama said his heart was broken because of what he said to me when he beat me. She said he spoke of me all the time after he sent me away. I was on his heart all the time, even when he died."

O'Mally notices that the detectives are listening and glancing at Cheech as he talks. Cheech is always able to hold a crowd's attention, whether he is talking or singing.

"I didn't know my father died until months after I was well enough to return home. I rode into town on my horse, only to learn of my father's death. People looked at me as if I was a ghost; I didn't know why." Cheech grips his hair and cries out, "He died with my belongings in his hands. It was too much for me to take. I ran. I knew I could no longer live on the farm or anywhere in Sicily, so I came to America."

O'Mally wanted to talk freely; he would have said more to his friend. "Cheech, you've had your share of trouble, haven't you?"

The driver sounds less abrasive as he tells the prisoner, "Troubles, they've just begun!"

"No, Mr. *Policia*-man, you are wrong." Leaning forward, Cheech speaks with conviction. "My troubles, they are over. It is over for me. This is the easy part. I go to jail and they kill me. No more troubles."

The driver shakes his head. The officer on Cheech's left shifts his back toward the door and asks, "Can you tell us what happened, I mean in your apartment? Why did you kill the good doctor?"

Cheech nods ever so slightly. "I will try to remember. Some times I can."

The officer asks casually, "But you remember killing the doctor, don't you?"

O'Mally raises his hand from the seat back and frowns at Cheech. "You shouldn't be telling all this before you talk to a lawyer."

The officer beside Cheech glares at O'Mally. "You forget you're a cop?"

"Don't worry, *Piason*, It doesn't make any difference. I did it. I'm not sorry. I don't want to live anymore. I'm already a dead man. How can they hurt me more? Please, its okay." He looks at the detectives on either side of him. "I answer any and all questions. What I did, any man had to do . . . and I did."

The cop beside O'Mally gives him a warning look. "Let the man talk.

He needs to get it off his chest." He twists to nod at Cheech. "Never mind the questions, you just tell us in your own way why you had to kill the doctor."

Cheech nods. "My precious son Joey was sick a couple weeks, getting worse all a time. I go looking for help and stop at Pendola's Drugstore."

"I know the place," the cop on the left says in an encouraging tone.

"The doctor's brother, the drug man told me his brother was a doctor. He would get him for my Joey. When the doctor came, he gave my boy a shot in the back. Then he gave me a paper for medicine from his brother the drug man. I brought the paper to Mr. Pendola. He said it is too strong for a little boy. He tells me, 'My brother should not do things like that.'" The driver cursed just under his breath. "But he gives me the medicine anyway. I run home to take it to Joey. The doctor, he is still there when I get back. When I tell him what his brother said, he tells me his brother doesn't know what the hell he is talking about. But Joey gets worse." Cheech's dark eyes fill with tears. "Joey, he died in my arms, my beautiful little boy. Joey looks just like his grandpapa, golden hair like the angels. Before he dies, he says to me, 'Papa, the doctor he kills me with the shot, I'm dying. Please don't let me die. Papa help me.'" Cheech sobs aloud, unashamed of his grief.

Looking around the vehicle, O'Mally sees a couple of tough cops sneaking a wipe at their eyes.

"My Joey, he grabbed my arm with his little hand. He looked at me and stopped breathing, eyes open, in my arms he died. I feel the life leave his little body. He's gone . . . no more Joey. I squeezed his little body in my arms and looked at Maria. She's crying, but there's no noise, her hands on her mouth, she cries with no voice. I kiss Joey, kiss Joey and hug him. He's getting cold. I grabbed a sheet to cover him, to keep him warm, but I do not cover his face, that beautiful face."

The officer to Cheech's left fumbling from the confined space pulls out a handkerchief and blows his nose. O'Mally notices that he also wipes his eyes. He turns back to the front as the car inches along in the line of vehicles waiting for the next ferry.

Cheech continues. "I didn't listen to my son, I trust the doctor." With tears bathing his cheeks, Cheech bares his teeth, "The bastard!"

Throat tight with sympathy, O'Mally turns to give Cheech a handkerchief. "You okay?" He tries to put a warning into the look he gives his friend. "You don't have to say anymore if you don't want to."

His seatmate elbows O'Mally in the ribs, hard enough to elicit a grunt. O'Mally knows he will pay for the consideration shown to a prisoner in spite of the fact that the atmosphere in the vehicle has changed from judgment to sympathy.

The cop behind O'Mally says with sincerity, "I'm sorry for your loss. I got a couple of fine boys myself."

In his pain, Cheech hears sympathy no more than derision; the car, his fellow passengers and the ferry, all fade out of existence as he relives his son's death. "I was sitting on the floor holding Joey's little body in my arms. Maria ran around the house as if she was crazy, crying and yelling. She held the other children and then straightened the house. She ran to the door, opened it and shouted to the neighbors in the hall to 'call the wagon, call the wagon, Joey's dead, he's dead. Cheech is killing himself, please help, please help!' She left the door open and ran back to me. We held Joey together." Cheech's shoulders and arms appear to curve protectively around a small body. "The neighbors heard the noise and were looking in to see. Maria told them that I'm trying to kill myself, something like that, and then she ran back to the door and slammed it closed." Cheech reached toward the back of his head, comprehension following a frown of concentration. "I banged my head on the wall. That's what happened to it. I couldn't believe what happened. Everything was so sad. I don't know how much time it takes for the wagon to come, but in time they come. Maria brought them to Joey. I had him wrapped up in a sheet. I put him on the cot in front of the oven to keep him warm."

Gooseflesh crawled along O'Mally's arms under his tunic and shirt. *Poor Cheech*, he thinks, *his son's death has deranged him. He knew the boy was dead, yet he acted like he felt the cold.*

"The wagon man, he checked Joey and said something. Then he said someone would come soon to check the other children. He asked if Maria and I wanted some time with Joey before they took him away." Cheech rubbed his forehead, and O'Mally remembered his headache. "Maria prayed for Joey. I told her to pray for us. I said his problems were over; living without him would be our problem. I just couldn't think. Then they took my sweet boy away. Maria and I sat at the kitchen table and cried and cried. Some neighbors came to the door and knocked, but we didn't open the door. When Joey died, I died."

Looking into the depths of Cheech's shadowed eyes, O'Mally sees the deadened spirit of grief. The man no longer cares about himself.

"I told the neighbors we were okay, that we just wanted to be alone." Hands cupping into claws, Cheech's voice rises. "Then there's a knock at the door, a loud knock. I thought it was the man to check the children, so I go open the door. There's the doctor, the bastard. I was so mad, I couldn't think. The blood in my head felt like it was cooking. I was hot all over. The beating of my heart hurt my chest and my eyes; they felt like they are pumping. I let him in, closed the door and locked it. I told him it was too late. 'He's gone, Joey is dead.' I told him the shot he gave Joey in the back was poison. It killed him." Cheech's expression transformed from grief into anger as he talked. "The doctor, he turned to me with a smile on his face, a goddamn smile! 'It's not my fault,' he says, 'I did what I could. He was too far-gone when I got here. Why did you wait so long?'" Cheech turns his hands up in supplication and wails. "Like it was my fault my son is dead—like I could have saved him . . . not the doctor. I told him, 'You poisoned my son when you stabbed him in the back with that shot! Your brother was right. The medicine you sent me for was too strong for a little child." The cop next to O'Mally gives him a look, lips tight. "Then the doctor told me to go into the bedroom where we could talk. I followed him into the bedroom. He put his bag on the floor and smiled at me. He said, 'Mr. Caruso, if you will not say anything to anybody that I was here, I will pay you for your loss. I know you're upset, but we can work it out.'"

"Son-of-a-bitch!" said the detective behind O'Mally.

Nodding at him, Cheech continues. "I said to him, 'First you kill my Joey, then you gonna pay me to not say anything?' I was so mad I felt like I was crazy. My eyes felt like they were on fire. I stood between the doctor and the door, told him he was crazy. Then he punched me in the face." Cheech sways with the action of the account as he goes on. "I yelled, 'you son-of-a-bitch.' I grabbed him by the throat and punched him over-and-over again. We fell on the dresser and broke the night table. We knocked over the plant stand. I grabbed him and threw him across the room. Then I picked him up and threw him on the floor. I kicked him and punched him. He said, 'Please don't kill me, I have a wife and little child. It's my brother's fault!'"

Face distorted with rage and grief, Cheech cries out, "He has a little child still. I tell him my child is dead! I jump on top of him, grab him by the throat with both hands and squeeze until he stops breathing. I do not let go of him until his legs stop moving. Then I know he is dead. Maria saw it and screamed from the door. She saw everything. I went into the kitchen and got a butcher knife. I went back to the bedroom, grabbed the doctor by the hair and said, 'Now, you bastard. I gonna do a good job! I stick him in the throat. Then I slit his throat. I drag him into the kitchen, to the exact place where Joey died and I drop him on the same spot."

As silence thickens the air in the police car, Cheech's labored breathing resounds. O'Mally realizes how mad with grief Cheech has been, and he understands his friend's desire to kill the doctor repeatedly.

"Then I tell Maria that I go, that I will see her in court." Exhaustion hangs heavy in Cheech's tone.

At this time, O'Mally does not care what his sympathy might cost him. "I don't know what I would have done if it was my little boy. I'm so sorry, Cheech."

The ferry bumps against the pilings at Brooklyn, bringing the other cops out of various poses of thought. The atmosphere as they pulled away from Rosario's apartment was one of satisfaction over an apprehension. Now the mood is somber. To a man, they can identify with a father's feelings over the death of a child, exacerbated by the callous offer of a bribe from his killer. The vehicle makes its way through the Brooklyn streets and pulls up to the Hamilton Avenue Station. The officer in charge meets them at the curb. While the detectives help Cheech out of the back of the vehicle, the officer meeting them sidetracks O'Mally. "The commander wants to speak to you right away."

The four detectives escort Cheech into the station house while the police car pulls away from the curb. O'Mally heads for the commander's office, knowing what to expect. He takes a last look at Cheech, wishing he could do more to protect him. The cops who heard his story in the car have a changed view of his friend, but Cheech will pass into many less sympathetic hands from here on in. Standing at the commander's door, O'Mally waits to be waved into the crowded office.

Waving him into his office, the commander abruptly slaps his desktop. "You will not step foot in this station house again until Caruso is transported to Sing Sing Prison."

O'Mally stands to attention, hat under his arm. "I understand my duty and responsibility to the force, Sir, and I will carry on as usual without making a presence here."

The commander stands behind his desk. He leans forward on his hands. "Do—I—make—myself—clear? You will not appear around here until the prisoner is sent to Sing Sing!"

Grimly, O'Mally realizes he can do nothing more for Cheech here. "Yes, Sir," he replies.

The commander drops back onto the cushion in his wooden swivel chair. "Now get the hell out of my sight."

Chapter 3

The loud noise from the fight between Cheech and the doctor brings neighbors to their doorways and out into the hall. It sounds like, yelling, feet scuffling, furniture and things falling and things breaking. While some scurry to the safety of their own closed doors, the nearest neighbors decide to call the police. They explain to the dispatcher that earlier in the day, a little boy in the same family had died, and they are worried about the family in that apartment.

A police car from Hamilton Avenue Station arrives at the same time as a hospital ambulance. Up the street, Cheech sees them arrive as he heads for the Staten Island Ferry.

In the four-room apartment on the third floor at 36 Third Street, Brooklyn, New York, Maria sits in the back bedroom. How is she to console the children as they cry and cling to her, especially when she can find no consolation herself? Somehow, she has to find the strength to quell her agonizing fears for Cheech and contain her insupportable loss of little Joey. Only then might she focus her sore heart and grieved mind on the children still left to her: Lena, her dependable eight-year-old helper; Josephine, whose wits don't always seem to match her present seven years of age, pretty Anna at three and quiet little Salvatore at two. They all sit huddled around her like chicks with a hen. Maria pats three-month-old Ida, swaying with the infant in her arms to quiet her. How like Cheech to name the baby after the song "Ida" by Eddy Canter. He is always full of the music. Now his beautiful music seems dead. *Not that word, God, please, Holy Mother, deliver us from the evil of more deaths.* She knows that today Cheech is full of loss, rage and despair. He is out of his head with grief for such a horrific thing to have befallen them. Despite the dark places in his soul, the secrets in his eyes that he does not often share, she knows Cheech has an indomitable spirit that breaks forth into music like sunlight on an overcast day. *No,* she thinks, *I must not allow my thoughts to stray toward the inconceivable events of this black day. The children are too disturbed already; they need me to be calm.* Clasping Ida in one arm, Maria sways, touching each precious remaining child in turn. *Dear God, keep Cheech safe somehow and bring us back together again. Holy Mother of God sustain us for that better time.*

* * *

Arriving at number thirty-six on Third Street, police officers and detectives tramp the stairs to the third floor. The ambulance crew follows, ready if needed. Neighbors point at the door of trouble, and then duck their heads back in like turtles. Reaching the designated apartment, the police officers get no answer to knocks and break in the door. They enter the flat, guns drawn, shouting commands to submit.

Already suffering and in shock, Maria pulls the children still closer to her. All except Lena cry in terror and hold onto their mother. Leaning against Maria, Lena stares without blinking. Her heart bangs in her tiny chest so hard that her mother feels it where her daughter's chest touches her. No matter what new tragedy befalls them on this intolerable day, she will protect her children.

Clomping boots and loud male voices set the children screaming louder. Two uniformed officers appear in the doorway to the bedroom and point guns at them. Shaking her head violently at the men as her heart pounds to her throat, Maria shoves the children behind her, giving Ida into Lena's thin arms to hold. "No," she cries out, "Don't hurt my babies."

"Stay where you are, Ma'am," an officer says; "hands up."

"Got a woman and a crowd of children in here," the other cop yells.

Maria spreads her arms wide, shielding her children with her will and her body. She cannot loose anymore of her family. God could not be so cruel.

The ambulance crew waits in the cold passage outside the Caruso flat for the coroner to turn the body over to them. They are in no hurry to deal with the bloody mess in the kitchen and hallway among this nest of immigrants.

Inside, a cop stands by a dead male body on the kitchen floor. He has orders not to allow anyone near the dead man except the coroner when he arrives. A couple of officers try to separate the mother from the children, setting off howls and screams of terror from them all. Other cops shut off the remaining rooms. The body lays in congealing blood on the linoleum floor. Bloody footprints lead to, around and away from the ghastly form, from the kitchen, through the hall and into the front bedroom. Splattered blood is on the kitchen floor and wall close by the stove. From low on the wall, it ascends in a fan shape all the way to the ceiling. Nearly dry blood smudges are on the walls of the front bedroom, bed and floor. The bedroom furniture has no livable arrangement. Drawers hang out of the dresser. The nightstand is broken, chair turned over in the corner of the room. The iron plant stand lays broken and on its side, foliage and dirt spilled everywhere.

Dr. Abbato, the coroner from Holy Family Hospital, arrives and enters the apartment for the second time that day. Grim-faced, he walks into the kitchen, the very same room where earlier he had viewed a boy's lifeless body. Brows rising, he stands and stares at the blood splashed all over the wall, the ceiling and the floor. His gaze follows the trail of blood from the body of the dead man in the kitchen as it disappears into the front bedroom. He asks the police officer guarding the victim's remains, "What the hell happened in here? Is this the only casualty? Who did this?"

"I don't know, Sir, but they have a woman in the bedroom. She's the wife. No one knows where the husband is." Without looking down, the officer gestured toward the body. "A neighbor said this is the doctor who was caring for a little boy who died here a short while ago."

The coroner stands gaping. "Jesus Christ, It's Pendola. I know about the boy. I was here earlier to certify the child's death." He walks around the body and then kneels down to look at the deep slash to the dead man's neck. Glancing up at a detective who has followed him into the kitchen, he intones in a brisk voice, "Severely severed jugular vein, damn near decapitated. Only the spine and muscles in the back of his neck are holding the head on the body. He has a broken nose, broken jaw and most likely more than one broken rib. This man was viciously beaten. He has marks of strangulation." He gestures at the wall and ceiling. "You realize that pattern indicates he was still alive when his throat was cut."

* * *

A detective separates Maria from her children against the joint pleading and terror of them all. A friend of Maria's from a nearby apartment has volunteered to stay with the youngsters in the back bedroom. The kindly woman's presence does not stop them from crying, or ease Maria's fears for them.

One group of detectives stays with Maria while others go into the room with the children. The questioning of Maria begins. She wraps her hands in her apron's skirt, partly to keep them still and partly because they are so cold. She sits on the edge of the chair in the sitting room, too frightened to lean back. Listening hard, she struggles to comprehend not only the English that still sounds strange to her ears after all these years, but to understand if her answers could make matters worse for Cheech. Normally, her English is better than his is. Her family was already in America when she arrived. They helped her with the language. However, under the conditions, her mind is not clear and her word selection is even worse.

One of the detectives asks her, "What year did you come to America?"

"1913, we come to America, my family, 1913."

With men clumping all around the apartment, it is difficult to think straight or focus on one matter at a time. She tries to remember and tell the officers that even though she cannot speak correct English that she was an educated woman, prepared to be a teacher at Sicily. For Cheech and her children, she tries very hard to cope with the situation. The dreadful scene in the kitchen explodes in her mind repeatedly. She gulp's several times in an effort to keep from gagging. That floor will never be clean again. The fetid stench of blood will never wash out of her home or her nostrils.

"Mrs. Caruso, I will ask you one more time," the detective shows little patience in his voice, "What triggered this murder?"

Eyes gritty from lack of sleep except for small naps, Maria closes her eyes as she cautiously searches for the best words and manner to describe the terrible events. "My little Joey was sick. Someone put a quarantine sign on the door. Nobody came so my husband went for help. Mr. Pendola at the drug store sent his brother who is a doctor and he gave Joey a shot. Joey got worse and died."

The officer interrupts. "That's the doctor who's dead on the floor in your kitchen?"

Nodding, she touches her apron's hem to her lips. "My husband went crazy when our boy died. He loved his little boy more than his own life. He's a good man."

The detective looks scornful. "Oh yeah, a good man who went crazy enough to kill the doctor who tried to save your child? You trying to excuse what your husband did by saying he's crazy?"

Maria feared they would twist her words. Between exhaustion and grief, she is no match for the police. She decides its best to say as little as possible.

The detective leans back like he has weeks to shred her precarious composure. "Tell me how he did it." Pursing her lips tightly together, she sits mute. "Did he use a knife of his own or a knife from your kitchen?"

Shaking her head, Maria stares down into her lap. "Maybe you handed him the knife yourself?"

The man's shrewd eyes watch her like a falcon ready to swoop, sharp clawed, on any mistake she makes. Pressing her lips even tighter, she forces her fidgeting hands to be still. "You need to be reminded of what we're talking about here, Mrs. Caruso."

He stands and opens the door. Waiting for her to follow him, he motions to the frightened Maria. Wordless, she rises. Feeling lightheaded and removed from this place in body and spirit, she follows the detective. Out in the hall, he pushes her toward the kitchen. When she draws back on the threshold, he pushes harder.

Inside the nightmarish space that had been the family's gathering place, she steps to one side of the door and looks down at her shoes. The scene, permanently etched in her mind requires no reminder, no visual view. The gory scene will not scare her into speaking against her husband. Maria looks up and points to the wall near the stove. "That's where Cheech held his dead boy in his arms. He rocked back and forth; back and forth bashing his head against the wall until it ran with blood. The blood from the back of his head splattered everywhere. I thought he was going to kill himself. I ran to the door, looked out into the hallway and shouted to my neighbors to call the ambulance. I ran back and tried to stop him from hurting himself, but I couldn't; he was too strong." She catches herself, and makes short shaking movements with her hands, as if shaking water from them. She searches for words. Clenching her hands, she stops the motion that might look like nerves or guilt. "After a while he lost his senses and just sat there holding Joey and crying. The police and the death wagon came and took Joey away. Cheech wouldn't let them touch his injury, though he was bleeding badly. He said, 'Maria, don't touch me,' like I hadn't tended his wounds for the last ten years."

The detective says with impatience, "The doctor, when did the doctor come?"

"Not until after they left with our Joey." If she keeps talking, it will sound like she is telling them more than she means to. By appearing to cooperate, she might protect her husband best. "Cheech and I sat at the table in the kitchen and talked over a glass of wine. I hoped it would ease his heart to speak of Joey. We cried. Then there was a knock at the door. Cheech got up to open it. It was the doctor."

"What did your husband say to the doctor?"

Maria picks the English words with care. "Cheech closed the door and told him that it was too late. Joey was gone. Joey was dead."

The detective leaned against the wall, "Nice and calm, like that, huh? Bet he gave the doc a chance to answer, too."

"The doctor said that he did the best he could, that Joey was already too sick." She believes the next part will show them the truth behind both deaths here today. "Cheech told him what his brother at the drug store said, that the medicine he ordered was too strong for a child and that he, the doctor, shouldn't do things like that." She hurries on before the detective can ask another question. "The doctor said his brother didn't know what he was talking about. The doctor smiled and laughed at my husband. Cheech was all excited. The doctor shouldn't have laughed at him."

"Bet that made your husband mad as hell. Mad enough to kill the doc on the spot."

"No!" she yells, "Cheech swallowed the insult." She feels her pounding pulse in her ears and wonders how can she make these detectives listen to reason? "The doctor said they should speak in private. They went into the front bedroom and closed the door. I cracked the door open to listen and see. He told Cheech that no one had to know that he was here. If Cheech promised to keep quiet to everyone about him, he would pay him for our loss. Does that sound like a blameless man?"

The detective dismisses her point with careless abandon. "Sounds like a doctor who didn't want to be muddied by a nuisance lawsuit."

Was this man determined to discount every provocation, no matter how severe? Maria bit at her lip, controlling her growing frustration. "The doctor hit Cheech when he wouldn't take the money. Then they started to fight. There was a lot of noise and then it was quiet."

"Is that when your husband killed the doctor?"

Exasperated, Maria cries out, "No, no, no, no, he didn't do that. He did *not* kill the doctor. Cheech is a good man; he loved his son. He beat the doctor; he did *not* kill him!" She knows these detectives are determined to make no allowances for circumstances. She also knows they will take Cheech away from her and the children forever and maybe put him to death. She cannot allow that to happen, not to her Cheech. She cannot bear to lose both son and husband; it will kill her. For the first time since reentering the room, she steps away from the wall.

"I did it!" Gesturing in a pantomime of events, she adds details. "I ran over to the kitchen drawer and got the biggest knife I could find. Then I went over to the doctor lying on the floor and cut his throat."

The detectives look at each other and Maria.

"What did you say, Mrs. Caruso?"

Maria stands straight, smoothing down the unsuitably bright print apron. She repeats in a calmer tone, "I killed the doctor. I cut his throat with a kitchen knife."

The detective who had forced her into the kitchen asked another detective, "Do you believe her?"

The man shrugged. "She confessed. If the guy was laid out cold on the floor, she could have slit his throat."

The first detective nodded. "Could be they killed him together." He turns back to Maria. "Where did you put the knife, Mrs. Caruso?"

Lips trembling in confusion at their assumption, she says, "In the trash."

He tells the cop, "Send a couple men to check out the top layers of garbage in the trash chute." To Maria, he says, "Mrs. Caruso, you're under arrest for the murder of Dr. Pendola."

Maria closes her eyes in defeat. At least the ordeal is over and the questions will stop. "Now may I see my children?"

The detective puts his hands in his pockets and rocks back on his heels. "You don't seem to understand how this works. You're under arrest, headed for the Hamilton Avenue police station. You don't talk with anyone on the way."

"What about my babies?" Maria put her hands together as if praying. "They're already upset by their brother's death. I can't leave them all alone."

"They're not your biggest problem right now." Taking her arm, the detective pushes Maria ahead of him out into the hallway. Catching a glimpse of her children, Maria cries out. At the sound of her voice, the children start toward her, calling to her. Her friend stands to follow them carrying baby Ida in her arms. The police officer guarding their bedroom closes the door before the children reach it. Maria is hauled back by two detectives as the muffled shrieks draw her toward the shut door. Tears blind Maria as she is led out of the flat, down the passageway and stairs. Though people crowd the space, she does not see or care who they are. In her effort to protect Cheech, she has lost her children and her freedom.

They pass police officers interviewing neighbors. Police are talking with some residents on the porch in front of the apartment building, on all floors, the basement and on the roof. On the second floor, a young girl steps out into the hall. Hurrying after them, she calls, "Pardon me, sir!"

Pulling Maria to a stop, the detective says, "Yes?"

The girl glances briefly at Maria but speaks to the detective. "My name is Florence O'Hanlon" —she points— "I live over there in that apartment with my father. Cheech Caruso is a friend of my father. He came into our flat a while ago and told my father that his little boy was dead. He said he killed the doctor responsible for killing him. He had blood all over himself, on his hands, his chest, shoes and on the back of his head. He washed his hands at our sink. We gave him some clean clothes. He thanked my father for his friendship, said goodbye and left, but we don't know where he was going."

"Frank!" The detective motions a cop in uniform over. "This girl has a statement to make. Get a detective and have him get it down in writing with names and addresses."

To Florence, he says, "Thanks for your help. You'll probably be called as a witness when the trial takes place. Let's go," he tells Maria and his partner.

Back in the Caruso flat, a police officer tells the neighbor watching the children to leave. She object's, but a detective hustles her out. Seeing Lena take charge of the younger children, the detective concentrates on her. "You're a regular little mother with your brother and sisters. "I'll bet you're sharp enough to know everything that goes on around here."

Holding the baby on a little bony hip, Lena stares at him with her huge brown eyes. She is pasty-faced despite her olive skin. She looks like a gust of wind would knock her down.

"Can you tell me about today?" he coaxes, sitting down so he doesn't tower over her.

"I don't know. Joey was sick." She keeps an eye on the other children as she speaks in a flat tone with her childish voice. "Mama and Papa took care of him for a long time. Joey died. Mama and papa were crying and then people took Joey away."

"What about after that?" he asks in a casual way. "What happened when the doctor came back?" Lena looks uncertain fussing with the baby's dress. "It's okay to say what really happened," he assures her. "You've been taught to tell the truth, haven't you?"

She nods a yes. "He laughed at papa and papa was crying and angry because the doctor laughed. They went into the bedroom and started fighting. I peeked out of our room when I heard the noise. Everything was shaking, even in our room. I heard whispering and then shouting. One voice was laughing, and then scared. The other was scary, angry, that was papa. There were noises and things hitting the walls. I heard wood break and furniture moved. All of a sudden it was quiet."

"You really do notice and remember things," said the detective with admiration. "Did you see anything unusual?"

Lena jogs the baby up and down when she whimpers. "I looked down the hall and saw Papa drag the doctor out of the room and into the kitchen. I think he was dead." Her commonplace tone belies her strained face, haunting look. "Then Papa sat on the doctor. Then he told Mama that he was leaving. He put on his coat and hat and he left." Her face crumples. "I want him to come home. I miss him, my papa."

"Do you know where he went?"

"I don't know."

"Is that what happened, Josephine?" another detective asks the next younger sister.

"Yes, I think so, I don't know for sure what happened," Josephine says sliding closer to Lena. "Papa didn't like the doctor laughing at him. Is Joey dead?"

Lena frowns at the detectives and pats Josephine's shoulder. "He's okay, he's okay, Josey."

The seated officer smiles at her. "Lena, if I leave you here alone with your brother and sisters, can I trust you to take care of them for a while?"

"Yes, Sir," Lena whispers rather seriously, "That's my job, except now I will have to do it alone because Joey's gone."

The detectives leave the room and head for the kitchen. Later, a nurse comes into the bedroom where the children are. When she begins a quick examination of Anna, Lena asked, "What are you doing?"

"I am checking to see if you're well enough to take a ride in a car." Lena stays quiet while the nurse looks at the other children. She submits to a similar exam without protest. When the nurse is finished, she asks the children "Are you ready to leave?"

"Are we going to Mama?" Lena asks hopefully.

"Yes," the nurse lies. "Come along now."

A sense of foreboding settles over Lena as she helps the other children into wraps and out of the apartment. Everything has been wrong and bad all day, maybe its over, she thinks.

Downstairs, the children climb into a waiting police car without protest. Little Salvatore is enthusiastic for the ride. He says, "Go fast!" as he clambers onto the back seat to look over into the front. Lena makes him sit down properly. Josephine has shadowed Lena down from the apartment, nearly walking on her heels. In the car, she makes Anna sit on her lap so she can scoot against Lena. She stares at the nurse and police officer with an expression of fear and sullenness, saying little. A short drive later, the car pulls up in front of the Kingston Avenue Hospital for Contagious Diseases. Escorted inside, they are met by another nurse.

Lena eagerly asks, "Where's Mommy?"

The stiff and starched woman says, "Keep quiet and come along."

Getting Anna and Salvatore to hold Josephine's hands, Lena carries Ida. Keeping up with the nurse would have been easier if she was not loaded down and tired. At the end of a long corridor, they stop in front of a desk. Another nurse peers over at them and asks, "Are these the children of Dr. Pendola's murderer?"

Lena does not like the tone of that remark. Their escort nods. Still bothered by the question, Lena is not sure what it meant, but the nurse's tone of voice makes her feel dirty.

The sour-faced nurse looks at them as if they smell bad. "Bring them along." Baby Ida grows heavier as they follow the nurse back down a long hall to a little room. In a quick glimpse, Lena reads the sign on the door. It reads *Closet*. The nurse places a blanket on the floor. "You'll sleep there."

"Thank you," Lena says doubtfully. Mama would expect her to show good manners . . . no matter what. Brooms and mops hang on the walls. Trashcans with waste and cleaning supplies line the floors.

The sour faced nurse says, "This is your home away from home. I hope you enjoy your stay."

Lena does not think she means what she said, but from the way she said it, Lena wonders. She politely asks, "May I have milk and a change of diapers for my little brother and baby sister?"

The woman stares at her as if she is a cockroach. "You're lucky to get heat during the night." She turns off the light and closes the door.

The younger children cry and cling to Lena and Josephine in the dark. Josephine cries too. Even Lena gives in to tears herself. They do not understand what is happening to them and Lena cannot explain it either. Finally, Lena mops her eyes with the hem of her dress and tells her brother and sisters that as soon as they stopped crying, she will try to reach the light switch. When they quiet to sniffling, she searches but cannot find it. Anna and Salvatore wail louder than before when she admits failure. Josephine whispers to Lena, "Why did they put us in a closet?"

Though Lena wonders about that herself, she says, "They don't have enough rooms."

As they huddle together on the blanket, the little ones finally fall asleep. When her eyes adjust to the total darkness, Lena covers them as best she can. In time, she, too, falls asleep. They constantly awaken during the night out of hunger. They had little to eat during the long day before. Waking up in darkness in a strange place just adds to their nightmares.

* * *

After leaving the Hamilton Avenue Station, O'Mally heads for the Caruso flat to see if he can do anything for Maria and the kids. Climbing the steps to the third floor, he knocks at the door of their apartment. He knocks repeatedly but to no avail. No one answers. Heard throughout the third floor with its thin walls, some of the neighbors peer out. They recognize O'Mally as a frequent visitor to the Caruso's and call to him.

O'Mally introduces himself to a few of the neighbors. "I'm looking for Mrs. Caruso. I thought she might need some help."

A young woman speaks up. "I'm a friend of Maria's. I stayed with her children until the cops ran me off. The fools arrested her for the murder of the doctor and took her to jail, but I don't know which one. Maria couldn't kill a mouse, let alone a man!"

Stunned, he asks, "What about the children?"

"My husband got information." She nods at one of the men. "They were taken to the Kingston Hospital. When I was with them, I didn't see signs of the illness that took Joey."

Her husband says with a nod toward the stairwell, "You should stop at the second floor to speak to O'Hanlon. He was up here right after all the police went away the first time, but Maria and the children were already gone."

"Thanks," O'Mally says, "I'll do that right now." Making a hasty leave, he runs down a flight of steps to the O'Hanlon flat.

The door opens in response to his knock and O'Hanlon invites him in. "Jesus, O'Mally, Cheech really did it this time! They're gonna kill him for this. If the cops don't do it first, the doctors will. Do you know where Cheech is?"

O'Mally nods yes, taking off his headgear and leaving it on a table by the door. "I was with him earlier. He is in jail at Raymond Street, gave himself up to the police. Do you know where Maria and the kids are?"

"Yeah, I do" O'Hanlon says, frowning. "I can't believe it, but Maria confessed to killing the doctor and they arrested her. Can you imagine that? Why would she say that? She couldn't hurt a fly!"

Still in shock over Maria's confession, O'Mally shakes his head. "I don't know. She must been out of her mind with grief. Cheech is, that's for certain. I've never known him to be out of his head like this."

O'Hanlon looks anxious as he offers O'Mally a seat on the divan. "Cheech stopped in here. He was blood-covered, said he had killed the doctor. After he washed his hands and cleaned up, he said he didn't want me to get involved in his mess." He patted his chest. "He was worried about my ticker. Cheech is a real friend when he cares about you." O'Mally nods in fervent agreement. "He said my daughter should go out into the hallway when the cops came by to tell them he was here and left, and that we don't know where he went. Anyway, after he left, the cops did come. They questioned everyone and spoke to Flora. I heard one of the detectives say they took the kids to the contagious disease section of the Kingston Hospital, and they hauled Maria off to Hamilton Avenue lockup."

"Damn," O'Mally says. *Cheech and Maria are sitting in cells in the same jail, neither likely knows the other is there,* he thought. "Cheech asked me to see if Maria needed anything. I can't get near her in there. They banned me from the station house since I know Cheech. I'll run over to the hospital to see if I can do anything for the kids. I doubt they will let me have them, but I'll ask. They must be scared to death with all they've been through today . . . then to see their mama taken away."

O'Hanlon sighs heavily. "If I can do anything to help Cheech or Maria, let me know. Either Flora or I will do it."

O'Mally thanks him and leaves. He heads for the Kingston Hospital and stops at the hospital's main desk. He tells the duty nurse, "I'm a relative of the Caruso's. I'd like to see the children."

"I'm sorry; they aren't here."

Biting back an oath, he asks, "Do you know where they are?"

"No," she says disinterested. "I wasn't on duty when they were brought in. I have no idea where they are now. You should go home and wait anyway. They're in isolation wherever they are, until it's known if they're contagious or not."

Without a clue to the children's whereabouts, O'Mally returns to his home to think. He tells his wife about Cheech's situation and about his efforts to find Maria and the kids.

Her pretty nose crinkles at the bridge as she frowns at him. "Honey, I want you to stay out of this. Please don't involve yourself, please."

O'Mally thought she would not understand. "Cheech is my best friend. I could never turn my back on him or his family."

The next morning, he awakes early and cleans up. "I'm going out," he tells his wife. "Don't expect me back until later in the day."

Walking to the subway, he buys a newspaper from the corner newspaper carrier and enters the underground subway station for the ride to Brooklyn. As he settles onto seat, he opens the paper. The front-page headline reads; *Physician Slain by Crazed Father as Boy Patient Dies*

O'Mally mutters to himself, "Be Jesus, Cheech, what the hell have you done?" He folds the paper and places it under his arm. He stares out the window at the blur of walls and columns going by. As the subway rocks from side to side along its rails, he recalls a happier time, several years before, a time when he and Cheech first met on 182nd Street. Part of the beat he walked back then was through the Italian neighborhood; little Italy. Soon, many of the Italian families knew him and his love for Italian cooking. Constantly invited into someone's apartment for lunch or dinner, He gladly accepted. Even if a warm meal was not offered every day, food was plentiful from street wagons and stores along his beat. Many shopkeepers invited him to sample their merchandise on the outside sidewalk. He had heard of a Cheech Caruso before he met him, a man who was quite a singer, who entertained the folks on the block.

Summer nights in the city are hot, often without a breeze stirring. Outside of spending money to see a show or movie, money that most people do not have, the only other entertainment poor folks have is the radio. Many of the Italian immigrants are talented, especially when it came to music. They are accustomed in their home countries to entertaining themselves because there are no radios in Sicily. They sing and play instruments. In the Italian neighborhoods of New York on hot summer evenings, it is normal to hear singing accompanied by mandolins, accordions and other instruments. Their harmonic strains draw crowds. The music enlivens the slums.

On Friday nights after work with the sky getting darker, they congregate on the porches in front of the buildings and Cheech and other men sing with the support of a small group of musicians. Often Saturday evenings bring a repeat performance. Some women look on and listen from the front windows of their flats, while others join husbands and brothers in the street. Some folk bring blankets from their apartments and spread them on the pavement or sidewalk. Others sit on orange crates and benches. As soon as people file into the street on a block, People place wooden sawhorses at both ends of the street to stop through traffic. Sometimes they move them to allow a car to go through. There are not that many cars in poorer neighborhoods.

On other occasions when the children are in bed, the entertainment takes place on the rooftops under the evening stars. People from the surrounding rooftops bring out chairs or orange crates to sit on. The music is mainly Italian love songs. Occasionally someone asks for Al Jolson or Eddy Cantor tunes.

As evenings wear on, women bring out their Italian specialty dishes capped off by Italian red wine. The music and food brings pleasure until the early hours for people who would not be able to afford these kinds of entertainment elsewhere.

The popular O'Mally rarely refuses these invitations. Though an Irish cop, he is highly respected and well liked on this Italian block. Any time Italian cuisine is at hand, so is O'Mally.

O'Mally remembers that Cheech extended the first Italian welcome to him. It was one evening when Cheech is walking home from work. He stops to speak to O'Mally on his beat. "O'Mally, my name is Cheech Caruso," he says with the ready charm that draws you to him at once. "I know you're the *policia*-man on our block. I heard you love Italian food. I'd like to invite you to our street party this Friday night."

O'Mally grins and takes the offered hand. "That's nice of you, Mr. Caruso, but don't you think I'd be out of place? My red cheeks shine in a crowd."

"I see what you say," Cheech says, rubbing his smooth olive-skinned chin. "But if I invite you, you will be accepted. I will announce you. All will know you so it no makes any difference you are Irish. Why, you no think you are safe?"

O'Mally laughs and tells Cheech, "No, that's not it. It's just different for me here."

"What's different, O'Mally? Good food, good wine, good music and good friends." Cheech spreads his arms wide and leans back in an expansive gesture. "And you are invited, no excuse. I will remind you Friday when I come home."

Reluctant still, O'Mally tells him, "I'll think about it, Caruso."

On his beat that Friday evening, O'Mally runs into Cheech again. Cheech greets him and says, "No forget tonight, O'Mally. Go home; change your clothes; come back comfortable. My apartment is 3B. No forget!"

O'Mally smiles and thanks Cheech. On a whim, he says, "I'll be there."

As they walked past shops, merchants call out, "Will you be singing tonight, Cheech?"

"I'm sure," he responds, "and guess who is gonna be there?" He whacks O'Mally on the back. "That's right, Sgt. O'Mally."

They smile, laugh, and come out to greet him. They pat O'Mally on the back and tell him, "That's nice, good for you!"

Later that evening, O'Mally is welcomed with open arms by everyone present on what is the first of many beautiful nights when he enjoys of the Italian culture.

As the years pass, O'Mally and Cheech bond in a friendship that seemed improbable that first time Cheech approached him on his beat. Cheech and O'Mally know each other so well that Cheech can tell one night that his friend has something heavy on his mind. On this night he sits by O'Mally and sings *O Sole Mia*, the song often called the Italian national anthem. He finishes and excuses himself after the applause. He tells the people he will be back in a while. Placing a hand on his friend's shoulder, he says, "Come on, O'Mally, let's go and talk for a while." As they stroll away with ribbons of music trailing them in the darkness, he speaks in a serious tone. "*Piason*, you look like the clouds of the world are raining on your shoulders. Now, before you get drunk and have to sleep at my place, tell me, and talk to me. It will make you feel better. Even if I can't help, talking will help." Cheech cannot help but see O'Mally's eyes watering under the streetlight.

As he wipes them, O'Mally says, "I think my wife is cheating on me. No, that isn't true. I *know* she's cheating on me with some guy who fights in front of our building, a boxer, a good one."

Cheech quietly asks, "How do you know this for certain?"

"I was down in the street watching the fight. I saw them waving to each other." O'Mally blows his nose and pockets his handkerchief. It would shame him to be so emotional around other people, but Cheech is different. "He's younger than she is. I think I will loose her. All we do anymore is argue and fight over nothing. The kids know something is wrong. I don't know how it's going to end up, Cheech."

Nodding, Cheech kicks a trashcan, sending it clattering down an alley. "People make mistakes all the time, sometimes big ones, sometimes small ones. This one is big one. I know you to be a good man. Never in all the time I know you, do I hear stories about you running around on your wife.

I would be proud to call you, Brother."

O'Mally glances at him and replies, "Me, too, Cheech." The words sound weak when O'Mally feels like family with this man.

"If your wife keeps doing this, he will leave her in the end. Then she will lose you and the children. She will be alone." Cheech sighs. "She cannot win. If he is a good fighter, he will have many women, but she will lose everything."

O'Mally agrees. "I'm halfway to retirement. I cannot do anything that might cost me my pension. Besides, if I did, and she found out, she would leave me anyway. No matter what I do, I lose. I can't win."

Cheech puts his arm around O'Mally's shoulder and hands him the bottle of red he brought. "Is he Irish or Italian? What is his name?"

O'Mally drinks deep and returns the bottle. "He's a good-looking young Italian fighter named Guido."

Cheech stops and faces him. "I am not gonna ask you if you want me to take care of this, because I know you say no. So I no ask. I take care of this, and your wife never knows. Your problem goes away. I can't save your marriage, you have to do that, but I can help it. Just remember, we never talk like this. *Gabish*?"

Tempted by the offer, O'Mally cannot put his friend in danger like this. "I can't let you do that, Cheech. He is a professional boxer. There's no telling what might happen."

Holding up a broad palm, Cheech stops his protest. "Don't say more, *Piason*, not one more word. You no want me to do anything. Good! We never have this talk. Let's get back to the *musica.*"

No more is heard from the young boxer after that night. In time, O'Mally's pretty wife settles back into her role as mother and wife of the O'Mally clan. She even becomes a regular to the Italian neighborhood on its musical evenings. The bonds grow still stronger between the two friends.

Coming back to the present from his reminiscing, O'Mally gazes across the subway car's isle and out its windows as columns instead of walls zip by the slowing subway windows. Brooklyn, Clancy Street, is the stop. Leaving the car in a crowd of passengers, he passes through the turnstiles up the steps and out of the underground station. In the sunlight, he stares up the street and spots the sign: Giovanni's Italian Restaurant.

Not knowing what to expect, he opens the door slowly and steps inside. In an instant, he feels out of place. The stares all imply the same thing: You are not Italian. Uncomfortable, he walks to the nearest table and sits down. A small man comes over with a menu. O'Mally asks in a low voice, "Are you the owner?"

The man nods, adjusts his apron, "*Cie.*"

Leaning forward, O'Mally whispers, "I'm here on behalf of Cheech Caruso. It is important that I speak with the Boss. I have a message from Cheech."

The owner studies him, turns around and walks to the back of the restaurant. A few minutes pass. Some men come out from the back and surround O'Mally and the table. He does not budge or speak. They sit down and one of them calls to the owner to bring out a bottle of wine and some glasses. Tensions tighten O'Mally's muscles while they wait for the wine, but still he does not break the silence. When the glasses are full, the men raise them. The leader who first looked him over proposes a toast, "To absent friends."

Raising his glass with them, O'Mally looks directly at the leader and says, "To Cheech."

All of them drink deeply of the wine. O'Mally is glad to find he can still swallow. As he sets down his glass, the leader speaks in a quiet tone.

"Where do you know Cheech from?"

Without moving a muscle, O'Mally replies in the same low, neutral tone. "I've been honored with Cheech's friendship for years. He would only give himself up to me when he had his brother call Brooklyn's Hamilton Station to pick him up."

"You are a cop?"

"Yes I am."

The men look at each other not saying a word. The leader nods. "And why are you here?"

"I have a message from Cheech that I can only give to the Boss," he says with emphasis, "It's very important to Cheech."

The man stares at O'Mally and after a while says, "Stand against that wall and spread out." Without hesitation, he complies. After the search, he says, "Follow me." O'Mally trails him closely to the back of the restaurant. At a big corner table occupied by a few diners, the man who leads him gestures to a chair and they all sit down. "Tell us what's happened with Cheech."

Briefly, O'Mally relates the details of Joey's illness and death. He repeats Cheech's account of the doctor's murder and his request for O'Mally to be with him when he surrendered.

The men seated at the table listen carefully, smoking and drinking as they watch him. When he finishes his account, the leader tells him, "Feel at home here. It will be a while until the Boss can come. In the meantime, take your choice of the menu. Giovanni's food is excellent."

Glancing over the entrees quickly, O'Mally chooses a favorite dish from the familiar Italian specialties. Giovanni and the leader exchange approved nods at his ready replies to the owner's questions about accompaniments. O'Mally senses he passed another test. While he waits for his food to be prepared, curious diners and friends of Cheech come by to ask him about him. They all claim a long friendship with him. They ask how their friend is doing. O'Mally does not quite relax, but he begins to accept that this might not be his last meal after all.

Chapter 4

A well-dressed, stocky man enters the back room accompanied by six others. He sits across from O'Mally, facing him. The others take seats around the table. All eyes scrutinize O'Mally.

The leader calls to the owner of the restaurant, *"Patroni, wana ca! Come here!"* He promptly arrives wiping his hands on his apron. Asked to clear the table, he complies.

O'Mally says, "My name is . . . ."

A deliberate, defined tone interrupts him. "I *know* who you are." He orders O'Mally to place both of his hands on the table. In a stern, calm voice . . . almost a whisper he says, "Do not remove your hands from the table until I tell you too! *Gabish?*"

The otherwise tough New York cop feels fear. *"Cie."*

The man nods. *"Bene,* I have but one question to ask of you. Your life depends on your answer. Are you a member of the Irish mob?"

Without hesitation, O'Mally responds, remembering that Cheech said, 'Be honest.' "Yes I am."

The man smiles at O'Mally and asks for Cheech's message. "What have you come here to give me?"

"It's in my jacket pocket. Can I remove my hands from the table?"

With a penetrating look, the man says, "No!" Then he tells one of his men to get it. He reads the note, looks at O'Mally and places it on the table. "And so we meet. Do you know who I am?"

To which O'Mally replies, "No."

"Good, a long time ago Cheech came to me about you. He told me he had an Irish brother with a problem. No matter, I will honor the wishes of my *Piason.* He is my brother . . . you are not. As my brother wishes, you and your family are under my protection for as long as I am alive. No one will bother you because of what you do for Cheech, not even your superiors. If you or your family have any trouble, if Cheech needs anything, come here and speak to Antonio." He points to O'Mally's contact sitting on the other side of the table. *"Gabish,* Antonio?"

"Cie, e' gabish, Patroni."

O'Mally's tough features soften as he implores the man in front of him, "May I ask that you not listen to Cheech? He needs all the help he can get. He is giving up on life. I don't want to see him die."

With a stern and direct look, the Sicilian boss warns, "You have no right to ask anything of me. You are not Italian. You are not Sicilian. You are not my Piason, you're not my brother and you are not my friend." He reaches across the table and grabs O'Mally's hands. He whispers, "If I need your help for anything, I will reach you by Antonio, *Gabish*?"

"*Cie*. Thank you."

"You can remove your hands now." The two men shake hands. He tells Antonio to take care of O'Mally. Then he leaves.

Antonio speaks, "We'll have a glass of wine. Give me your address, the names of your wife and family, your station number and your badge number. Then you can leave. If I need you, I will reach you. If you receive a message from Joey, it will be me. I will tell you what I want. If there is no message, you are to come here, understand?" O'Mally nods his head yes. "Good, then we drink up and you go. Joey!"

* * *

It is the morning of February 14th and the morning edition of the New York Times reads:

Slayer of Doctor Not Sorry For Deed

* * *

Spending last night in a cell at the Hamilton station house under suspicion of stabbing the doctor due to her confession to detectives, Maria awakens from a guard telling her she must be in court in an hour. Not having slept most of the night, in a state of shock and on the verge of nervous collapse, Maria feels faint and confused. The guard enters the cell to help her to her feet.

Being arraigned at the Fifth Avenue Court, Magistrate Dale tells Maria that her husband is caught and that no one believes that she, weighing a mere one hundred pounds, could be the killer of such a big man as Dr. Pendola. Maria says nothing, just listens, not fully understanding the judge.

When asked for an explanation as to why she claimed such an ostensibly impossible claim that she could have successfully overpowered and slain such a strong man as Dr. Pendola, Maria closes her eyes and refuses to answer. Magistrate Dale explains to Maria that he is going to release her. He says that she will be a witness against her husband and will be required, under oath, to recount the events that had happened at their flat on Sunday February 13. He asks if she has a place to go. Her court appointed attorney tells the Magistrate that she will be staying with her parents in Fort Lee, New Jersey.

In the lobby of the courthouse, her attorney places a call for her to her parents at Fort Lee to tell them she is free and awaiting their arrival. He tells her that her children were held overnight at the Kingston Avenue Hospital for observation to consider the possibility of a contagious disease, and that they are cleared to leave.

In about an hour, Maria's parents Mr. and Mrs. Privitera and her older brother and sister, Louis and Florence arrive by train at the courthouse. Released to her parents, she is told by her attorney that the court will call her at the appropriate time.

Maria sadly tells her mother that she has not seen the children since Sunday afternoon and that she wants to get them before they return to New Jersey. Louis flags down a taxi to takes the family to the hospital. A rude nurse tells them, "The children are not available. They have not been checked yet." Maria is troubled and frightened by the cold, calculated and cocky attitude of the attending nurse. She shouts for her children in Italian. The nurse nervously insists that she does not know anything about the children.

Louis, who has been silent, walks behind the counter and grabs the nurse by her hair. He grips the nape of her neck and says in a stern voice, "We have been told by the Magistrate that they *are* here. Tell my sister where her family is in ten seconds or you are going to need the police more than I do. Do you understand, *Bastia!*"

Her eyes are wide open with fear. Bending over the Counter, she promises Louis, "I'll get them for you."

"No, you won't! You will take us to them, and you will do it now! Do you understand?" He orders her to lead. Cheech's family follows the frightened nurse down a long hall. She stops at a door with a closet sign, opens the door and turns on the light switch.

Maria rushes into the closet. The children yell and cry for their mother, eyes squinting from the brightness of the light. She sits on the blanket clinging and crying with them.

Louis and his father are seething with anger. Papa Privitera yells, "Is this the way you take care of Children? You put them in a closet?"

Louis abruptly grabs the nurse by the throat and shoves her into the corner of the closet causing her to fall over covered trashcans. Not knowing what to expect of him next, she lays still looking up at him, eyes wary. Louis, wiping sweat from his brow, tells his father to take the women and children out into the hall. "Shut the door." Maria's mother asks Louis not to do anything rash. He assures his mother that he wants to talk to the nurse alone. As they leave the closet, Louis's father gives Louis that 'With my Blessing look' and shuts the door.

Standing over the nurse Louis rasps, "You want to know why people don't trust doctors and hospitals? They are reasons like this and people like you. How can you treat children like this? You have no right to do this. You keep them trapped all night long in the dark with no food, no water and no place to sleep. They smell like trash! You treat them no better than yesterday's filthy garbage in this greasy, grimy, stifling hot closet. You should be ashamed of yourself!" He grabs a trashcan one at a time and empties the contents on the woman. She is pleading on her knees, crying and sobbing like an abandoned child, like the Caruso children. Next, he throws all of the mops and brooms on her. He kneels down next to the smelly trash-covered woman and whispers gently but firmly, "Understand me well, *descasiadsa*, one word, one scream, one cop and the next time we meet, you won't know it. It will be all over for you—like lightning—you won't know what happened!" He grabs her by the throat. "I will never speak to you again. Look at me!" With his left hand, he makes a slicing motion across his throat. "Do I make myself clear?" In total fear for her life, she shakes her head. He squeezes her throat causing her to choke for air and pushes her back into the pile of trash gasping for air. Louis stands and places a foot on her abdomen. He whispers, "Remember what I say." He straightens his collar and tie, exits the closet and the hospital to the waiting cab. He gives the address and directs the cabby to take them to his home.

They are silent in the cab. Back at Louis's apartment, they discuss everything. Once the children are clean and fed, they leave for New Jersey in Louis's car.

* * *

The morning of February 16 finds Cheech at the King's County Court, before Judge Franklin B. Taylor. When asked by the judge if he killed the doctor he replies, "*Cie,* I did, but not with a knife. I kill him with my hands first. No need for a knife, but then I decide to do a good job. I cut his throat. He kill my boy, I kill him."

Court appointed defense attorneys Hector McGowen and John B. Johnston in response to the judge interpose a 'not guilty' plea.

In this pre-trial hearing, the prosecution presents Dr. Gregory Robillard, Deputy Medical Examiner. He states that the previous day's autopsy on Caruso's 6-year-old son clears Dr. Pendola of any blame in the child's death. He also states that the Doctor gave the dead boy the appropriate medication for his illness that he had diagnosed as diphtheria.

When he hears the opinion of the medical examiner, Cheech snaps his ankle chains to show his extreme dissatisfaction. Everyone in the courtroom turns and looks at him. Cheech stares long and hard at the doctor causing him to glance at him and quickly redirect his gaze.

Dr. Herman T. Beck, the Health Officer in charge at Brooklyn, is the next witness for the prosecution. He takes the customary oath and solemnly tells the court, "No one at the Health department was ever notified of the case of diphtheria on the third floor of the building at 36 Third Street. We were aware of a case on the second floor with a quarantine sign reported by the police, not the third. It is our policy in contagious disease cases for a nurse to go to the address and place the sign on the entrance of the dwelling. Only she or the attending doctor has the authority to remove it. The reports of the sign on the Caruso the flat are incorrect. We would have serviced him if we knew about it. No one notified us."

Cheech yells, *"Bastia!"* The Judge threatens to have him removed from the court if there are any more interruptions.

Cheech bangs the tabletop and shouts, "Did the doctor call you and tell you that he was at my home? No, he did not! He knew he did wrong. He killed my boy and died for it!"

The judge bangs his mallet and orders the detectives to remove the prisoner. There are no more witnesses. He adjourns.

The detectives transport Cheech in cuffs and ankle-shackles to the Raymond Street Station in preparation for his trial appearance.

* * *

On February 16, the newspapers headlines read:

Slain Physician Buried

Mrs. Pendola Overcome at Church

Body of Caruso Boy Unclaimed

Funeral services were held today for Dr. Pendola who was killed last Sunday by the crazed father of a six-year-old boy who died of Diphtheria whom he was caring for at Brooklyn.

A requiem mass was celebrated by Father Otavio Sivestri at the Roman Catholic church of Saint Joseph Suydam Street and Central Avenue Brooklyn. While a crowd stood outside the church, friends and family participated in the mass.
Mrs. Pendola fainted as she entered the church and had to be revived and assisted to a pew by relatives. The Pendola's were married for two years and have a daughter of eighteen months.

Joseph Pendola, brother of the slain doctor, was also overcome by grief. He is the proprietor of the drug store in the Caruso neighborhood. He summoned his brother for the Caruso child when there were no physicians available from the neighborhood. The body of the slain doctor was interred at St. John's Cemetery, Queens.

At Kingston Avenue Hospital, a morgue spokesman said no claims have been made on the body of the dead boy by the Caruso family. If the family makes no claim, the boy will be buried at the expense of the city.

* * *

On February 21, a hearing is held at the request of the defense. Attorney David Price tells the Judge, "Your honor, I need more time to prepare my case for trial. The present date is not sufficient." After a brief discussion, the judge sets April 5 as the new date.
Mrs. Pendola, wife of the slain doctor suddenly stands up and yells out, "This man murdered my husband and it was a cruel, cold blooded murder. He should be killed! Instead, he gets an adjournment!"

The friends and relatives with Mrs. Pendola try to comfort her. They quickly escort her out to the hall where she continues to shout and verbally harangue the defendant. Defense attorney Price thanks the judge when he closes the hearing. When Price leaves the building, the Pendola group jeers him. They are at the top of the steps looking down at him. One of the men with the group clenches a fist in rebuke of the attorney for requesting a delay. As Price drives away from the curb, he looks in his rear-view mirror. Several people and Mrs. Pendola are standing at the curb shaking their fists at him.

* * *

On April 5, 1927, the New York Times headlines read:

Caruso Trial Begins in Doctor's Slaying

Father Charged With Killing Victim Called To Attend Dead Child

Eleven Jurors Obtained

Vigorous Prosecution Urged by Physicians Who Want Safety Assured in Patients Homes

Yesterday, the trial started with the appointment of George A. Voss as defense attorney for the trial. Jury selection was completed. Voss replaces David Price as Caruso's court appointed attorney.

* * *

The Jury is selected in one day. Sitting quietly in the back of the courtroom is a tall, thin man with a pencil mustache. Dressed in a three-piece pin striped suit, he sits with a cane and hat on his lap. He will sit through what proves to be a travesty of justice. He prepares to listen to the proceedings.

Although a few of the prospective jurors are turned away because of their strong opinions on the death penalty, most are feared by Attorney Voss to be relatives or friends of the dead doctor, yet there is no objection by the defense. At this early stage, there is a feeling in the air that the

Medical community has exerted its pressure on the court. Letters and petitions written by persons of authority in and about the medical community are circulated for doctors and nurses to sign. Articles in local newspapers try to influence the opinion of the public to ask for a speedy trial.

On this morning, everyone stands as Judge Alonzo G. McLaughlin enters. The jury is ushered into the courtroom and the trial begins. The judge tells the court, "This will be a fast trial. I will not tolerate stall tactics by either counsel." Then he tells prosecutor Assistant District Attorney Joseph V. Gallagher to proceed with his opening statement.

Gallagher stands and proclaims that he will prove beyond a doubt that Francesco Caruso willingly and wantonly murdered Dr. Casper S. Pendola. He points to Cheech and tells the jury, "I will prove to you that he knew what he was doing when he murdered the good doctor. I will show you that on two previous occasions he admitted that he went into the kitchen for a knife to kill the doctor, and in fact did just that. There was no reason for the terrible beating sustained by the doctor, much less his brutal death. I will prove to you that Dr. Pendola did nothing wrong in the treatment of the sick child. I will prove to you that this was a cold-blooded premeditated, calculated murder. This is a murder worthy of a first-degree murder charge and the death penalty. Anything less will be a travesty of justice! Thank you."

Defense attorney George A. Voss stands and starts his opening statement. "Lady's and Gentlemen of the jury, have you ever done something you wish you could undo or lost something you knew you could not ever, ever get back? Have any of you ever had your child die in your arms? That is what happened to my client on February 13 of this year. It is my intention to show and convince you that Francesco Caruso acted out of rage. He did not consciously intend to murder Dr. Pendola. This was a tragedy, but most certainly not premeditated murder. It is not worthy of the death penalty. Thank you all. I'm finished your honor."

At the judge's request, the prosecutor begins. "Your Honor, I would like to call our first witness."

"You may precede, Counselor."

"I'd like to call Florence O'Hanlon."

Miss O'Hanlon, all of thirteen-years-old, walks down the isle and is administered the oath. "Please hold up your right hand. Do you swear to tell the whole truth and nothing but the whole truth, so help you God?"

"I do."

Gallagher begins, "Please tell us your name and address."

"My name is Florence O'Hanlon. I live in the same building as Mr. Caruso, at 36 Third Street, Brooklyn, New York. My Dad and I live on the second floor."

The prosecutor asks her to tell the court how the events of February 13, unfolded as best she knows.

The 13-year-old girl begins. "About 12:30 mid-day, we heard screaming and hollering coming from the third floor. They were so loud; you could hear the terrible sounds coming down the stairway. My dad and I, and some of our neighbors, opened our doors so we could hear it better. Then we heard a lot of banging noise and people on the third floor running around. Some woman yelled out that Joey was dead, and that Cheech, Mr. Caruso, was killing himself. She yelled for someone to call the wagon. She screamed and screamed. I think it was Maria, Mrs. Caruso. We don't have a telephone. One of our neighbors said he would call. When everything got quiet, we all came out of our apartments and stood out in the hall talking and wondering what had happened."

There was a pause as she sipped some water. The judge gave Gallagher a look. Gallagher asked, "Then what happened?"

"In a few minutes the ambulance wagon came and went into the Caruso flat. On the way out one of the attendants told us that a Child in 3b had died of Diphtheria. We were all sad for Mr. And Mrs. Caruso. We all knew Joey. He was so nice. Everything got quiet after the ambulance took Joey away. My Dad and another man from the second floor went up to the third floor and knocked at the door of the Caruso apartment. My Dad said there was a quarantine sign on the door. We Knew Joey was sick, but not that sick. He said no one answered the door when he knocked and called to Mr. Caruso. They left and came back down to the second floor. About an hour later, we saw a doctor climb the stairs to the third floor. We heard a door open and heard Mr. Caruso tell the doctor to come in and the door shut. After the door closed, it was quiet for a while. Then we heard all kinds of noises. We heard two men yelling, one was mad and the other sounded afraid. Then we heard fighting and things being broken. It was terrible; everyone was afraid. We heard the noise all over the building. You could feel the ceiling vibrating. Then it was quiet again. The neighbor who called the ambulance ran back into his apartment to call the police. We all went back into our apartments. We were afraid."

Again, she pauses to sip water and clear her mind. She wants to make sure she remembers exactly what to say. She takes her time. This time, the prosecutor does not push. He knows Children need some patience. She sets the glass down and continues, "In a minute or so after the noise stopped, someone knocked at our door, so my Dad answered it. It was Mr. Caruso. Dad told him to come in. Mr. Caruso told him that the doctor killed Joey and that he killed him. He asked Dad if he could wash his hands. Dad told him that he could. Mr. Caruso thanked my Dad and left. Later, the police came. We heard people running all over the building, a lot of people, doctors and police. We saw all of the children in the Caruso family taken out by nurses and we saw Mrs. Caruso taken out in handcuffs. We didn't know what to think. Then the excitement was over, except for the talking. The people on the second and third floors got together to talk about it. Everyone felt so bad for the Caruso's and for the doctor."

Gallagher asks the young witness if Mr. Caruso said anything about how he killed the doctor. She replies, "Yes he did. He said they fought and he killed the doctor. Then he went into the kitchen, got a knife and cut his throat."

Cheech sits quietly not looking at the witness. He stares down at the tabletop in silence. He is pleased with the girl's story.

"Did you say that he washed up? What did he wash? Did he have blood on him?"

"Yes he did; he washed his hands and arms in the kitchen sink. He had blood on the front of his shirt and pants. There was blood all over the back of his neck from his head."

Gallagher asks the girl if he said anything else to her father. "The only thing he said was he killed the doctor and he wanted to wash up. After that, he left."

"Do you know why Mr. Caruso chose your apartment?"

"I don't know. I guess because he and Dad have been friends for years?"

Gallagher says, "No more questions, Your Honor."

The judge tells the defense attorney, "Mr. Voss, Do you have any questions? If so, keep it short."

Mr. Voss says, "Yes, I do, Your Honor. I'll keep it short. Thank you. Miss O'Hanlon, tell us how long you have known Mr. Caruso and what kind of person he is."

The girl hesitates, "I think for about four years. He is a nice man. The kids all like him. He likes to sing, and he makes us laugh."

"Thank you, Young Lady. I have no more questions, Your Honor, thank you."

The judge tells the witness to step down. As she walks past Cheech their eyes meet. He gives her a little half smile unnoticed by the court.

The prosecutor calls his next witness. "I'd like to call Mrs. Helen Pendola to the stand." After she is sworn and seated, Gallagher asks, "You are the widow of the slain doctor?"

"Yes, I am."

Do you have any children? "Yes, I do; I have a daughter eighteen months old. I am left with a child, and she has no father."

Gallagher says, "I know this is difficult. Please tell us what you can about your husbands death."

"Last Saturday, the 12th of February, Casper received a call from his brother Joseph in Brooklyn about a boy in his neighborhood ill with Diphtheria. He grabbed his bag, jumped in his car and left for Brooklyn. When he got back home, he told me that it was the worst case of Diphtheria he had ever seen. We had to disinfect all the clothes he wore to the Caruso home."

"Mrs. Pendola, please tell us about your husband."

She wipes her tears. "Cas was a good man, only twenty-seven-years-old. He graduated from Fordham University. We bought a house at Queens after we got married. Now he is dead, my daughter will never know her father. I don't know how long I can keep the house that we live in. My daughter and I have lost everything. Cas used to sit by her crib and sing little songs to her until she fell asleep. She will not remember him. She'll never know her daddy, never!

She looks with hatred toward Cheech. He is not looking at her. She continues, "Last February Medical Examiner Dr. Robillard's autopsy findings cleared my husband of fault in the little boys death. He said that my husband died from the stabbing. That man," —pointing at Cheech— "murdered my husband in cold blood . . . and for nothing. He deserves to die in the electric chair!" Cheech sits without expression although his heart is sad for the young woman.

Gallagher turns to the judge, "I have no more questions, Your Honor."

"Very good, Counselor, do you wish to question the witness Mr. Voss?"

"No, Your Honor, I do not. Thank you."

Judge McLaughlin asks Gallagher if there are more witnesses for the prosecution. Gallagher stands and says, "The prosecution is finished your honor, but I would like for you Your Honor and the jury to know, that according to this documentation, Francesco Caruso has a police record. In 1918, Mr. Caruso was arrested and convicted for carrying a weapon. He was jailed and fined a hundred dollars. He has used aliases. We believe there are other arrests. We will submit the documentation as soon as we have it."

"Thank you, Counselor. Please submit what documentation you do have to the clerk. Do you have witnesses you would like to present on behalf of your client, Mr. Voss?"

"Yes, I do, Your Honor, thank you."

The only witnesses that Voss calls are friends and neighbors of Cheech. They tell the jurors that Cheech is a devoted father and husband. He loves children and they love him. They speak of his singing and entertaining on summer nights and how much he loved his little boy. When a friend attempts to tell the court that he cannot imagine how it came about that Cheech murdered the doctor, Gallagher objects. Judge McLaughlin shouts "Sustained!"

Voss tells the judge that he is finished with the witness, and he would like to call Mr. Caruso to the stand. Judge McLaughlin nods his head and tells Voss to proceed.

Chapter 5

"**P**lease take the stand, Mr. Caruso," Voss says. The court is silent as Cheech walks to the stand and takes his oath. Voss approaches the stand. "Mr. Caruso, What is your age?"

"I am thirty-five-years-old."

"Would you please tell the court your name and address?"

"My name is Francesco Caruso, I live at 36 Third Street in Brooklyn flat 3B."

Voss asks Cheech to describe Joey to the court. Prosecutor Gallagher objects stating it is not relative to the crime.

The judge declares, "Sustained!"

In the back of the court, the man in the three-piece suit shakes his head at the travesty of justice unfolding before him. The jury is leaning forward to hear it all.

The judge says, "Mr. Voss, continue and keep it short.

"Yes, Your Honor, I will." "Mr. Caruso, Please tell the court about your son's illness, how you came to find Dr. Pendola and how you feel about losing your little boy."

"Joey was sick for about a week with a runny nose and fever. We didn't let him go to school. He got worse. I went to the drug man to get medicine. It don't work. One day I open the door to go to work see a quarantine sign on the door. I closed the door and told my wife Maria that we have to stay in the flat until a nurse or doctor comes for Joey . . . nobody came, never! We waited and we waited. Joey, he got worse. Maria and Me, we were up day and night with very little sleep. We slept here and there. I took care of him the most because Maria was with the other children sometimes. I swabbed his throat every half hour. He still got worse, it don't help. We tried to give him soup, but he can't eat. He choked and threw up all the time."

Cheech pauses as he fights to control his emotions and block the horrible memories of his dying son's suffering.

"Saturday came, nobody comes. I knew I must do something or Joey would die. I left to look for a doctor. All the doctors were closed because it was Saturday. I did not know where else to go. On the way back home, I stopped at the drugstore again. I thought the drug man could help. I told him that Joey was worse, dying, and that I couldn't find a doctor. I begged him to help. He told me his brother was a doctor. He called his brother and gave him my address. He told me to go home and get ready for him, and I did that. The doctor, he came and gave Joey a shot in the back. It made Joey cry. The doctor gave me a paper. I ran to the drugstore. Mr. Pendola told me that the medicine his brother prescribed was too strong for a little child. He gave it to me anyway. I don't know about medicine, so I paid for it and took it home. I told the doctor what his brother said. He told me that his brother should mind his own business that he did *not* know about what he was talking. He was fresh to me, not nice. He gave the medicine to Joey and threw the box in the stove. He told us he would be back the next day on Sunday about ten o'clock in the morning; then he left."

Voss notices that Cheech is growing distraught from reliving it all. "Mr. Caruso, you can take a drink of water if you need it."

Cheech nods and pours water into the glass. He drinks it all before continuing. "We were up all night Saturday with Joey. He got worse and worse all night long. About eight O' clock on Saturday morning, I knew I must find another doctor. Joey, he didn't want me to go. He held on to me. When he fell asleep again, I ran to find a doctor. I couldn't find one so I ran home. When I got home, Joey said to me, 'Papa, I want to come to you!' I took my child up in my arms and had him look out at the backyard from the window. He looked around the yard a couple minutes. Then he said to me, 'Papa, I want to go to sleep again.' I said, 'All right, Joey, I will put you down to sleep.' He didn't sound like a little boy anymore, my Joey. I didn't understand him too much. Maria understood Joey better than me. He grabbed my hand and looked at me. He said, 'Papa, I don't feel so good. I'm dying, Papa!'"

Cheech breaks down and cries. The courtroom is silent except for the quiet sobs. He takes out his handkerchief and wipes the tears away before continuing. "Joey said, 'Papa, help me. I don't want to die. That shot the doctor gave me is killing me. Please don't let me die, Papa. Help me, Papa." I didn't believe my son that he was dying. Stupid me, I trusted the doctor. He fell asleep again. I sat near. He woke up, 'Papa, I am going to die!' I say, No, you no die, Joey. You no do this to papa. You no die! I help you every time. At that same time the child was sick crazy. He looked and acted crazy! He didn't want to stay anymore inside. All I could do was hold him inside my arms from 4 o'clock until 8 o'clock in the morning. After eight o'clock in the morning the child, the poor child, got even worse in the morning."

Once again, Cheech stops his testimony while he composes himself.

"Then what happened, Mr. Caruso?" Voss asks.

"Joey said, 'Papa, I want to go to sleep.' I said, 'All right I will put you in the bed.' A little later, he wakes and says, 'Papa, I have to go to toilet.' I said, 'Okay, Joey, I take you to toilet.' When I held my child, he started to shake in my arms. My wife knew better than I did. I cannot see too good myself, so she told me what kind of shakes he had, she said, 'Listen, Frank, the child has died already.' I told her not to cry, that there was no harm because she scared the child. I went right away and put the child on the bed. Before I put my hand to the pillow, Joey, he said to me, 'Goodbye, Papa, I am going already.' Joey let go of my hand and looked away from me. He looked up to the ceiling, breathing slowly. Then his lips moved and his little body got soft. He took one deep breath—then he was still—he did not move anymore! Please, my Joey, don't do this to Papa, not again. You no die on papa, no die please!"

The courtroom is hushed as Cheech covers his face with his hands for a few moments. Once composed, he continues. "So I said, 'my child, he is dead! Jesus, my child is dead! Why you do this to me again, *Dio*?' I said that nobody would put hands on my boy again! I looked at Maria on the other side of the cot. She was crying with no noise; it hurt me; my heart was so sad. Both her hands were on her mouth. It was so quiet in the kitchen. I said, 'Joey is dead, Maria. What have I done to my baby? Why did God do this?' She bent over and held his little feet. She said, 'I can't believe Joey is dead.' I cried too. My heart died. I grabbed a blanket and wrapped my Joey in it. I picked him up and held him. His body was getting cold, so I held him tight to keep him warm. I sat on the floor and rocked him back-and-forth, back-and-forth. I thought I was crazy because sometimes I couldn't remember what I did. Maria straightened her housedress. She ran around the house straightening things up and comforting the children in the back room. They knew something was wrong. They were crying. I didn't know what to do. My son was dead. Joey was gone. My wife ran to the door and shouted to the people on the floor that Joey was dead, that I'm killing myself. She told them to call the wagon. The other children ran out of the back bedroom and sat with us as I held Joey in my arms; we all cried together. Maria held the children. I held my boy. In a little while, the wagon people came. They looked at Joey and asked some questions. They told us that someone would come to check the other children. Then they took him away. I will never see my boy ever again. *Finito*, Joey is gone, buried. I don't know where."

"Do you need a little time, Mr. Caruso?" Voss asks. There are a few wet eyes in the courtroom, mainly from those who cannot fathom losing a child.

"No, I go on. My wife and me, we sat at the kitchen table. We drank wine and talked. We could not believe we lost Joey. I was getting mad at the doctor. Why did I listen to him and not my boy? His brother was right; the medicine was too strong." Cheech looks out over the courtroom and sees the druggist sitting with his head in both his hands, crying softly. He looks around the courtroom. He does not see Maria or any of the other relatives. He sees only relatives and friends of the doctor.

"My neighbors came by and knocked and called for us, but we didn't answer the door. We wanted to be alone. Then I heard a loud knock at the door. Nobody spoke. I looked at the clock. It was after one O'clock. I knew it was the doctor. I told Maria to go to the back bedroom with the children. I got up and answered the door. I let him in. He asked me what bothered me. I told him, 'Joey is dead. My boy is dead.' With a smile on his face he said, 'It's not my fault, I did everything I could!' I told him his brother was right! He said he wanted to talk to me in private. We went into the front bedroom to talk. He closed the door and told me if I did not tell anybody that he was there, he would pay me for my loss. My face got hot. I felt like I was gonna blow up. I yell, you gonna pay me for Joey? How much you gonna pay, you *Bastia*? Your brother was right. I should not have trusted you. He got mad and punched me. I moved between him and the door. I told him, 'You killed my Joey. Now I am gonna kill you, you son of a bitch!' He dropped his bag and hit me again. I grabbed him by the neck and punched him again-and-again-and-again. He yelled that it was his brother's fault, not his. I grabbed and threw him across the room. He fell on the floor. I picked him up and threw him on the bed. I jumped on him and grabbed him by the neck. I squeezed and squeezed. He punched me; I squeezed harder. I let go when his legs stopped moving. I threw him on the floor, kicked him over-and-over-and-over. He no longer moved. I told him, 'Now I will do a good a job you, *Bastia*!' I went into the kitchen for a knife. I went back to the bedroom, grabbed him by the hair and stabbed him in the throat. Then I cut his throat with one slice. I dragged him into the kitchen and I dropped him on the exact spot where my boy died. I told Maria that I must leave. I put on my hat and coat and told her,

'I will see you in court, and I left.' Later, the *policia* arrested me. The doctor killed my boy—I killed him. That's all, *finito*."

Judge McLaughlin asks, "Are you finished, Mr. Caruso?"

"*Cie,* I am, Your Honor."

The judge turns to the prosecutor and tells him he can cross-examine. Gallagher walks to the stand and addresses Cheech. "Mr. Caruso, you testified that when you went into the kitchen to get the knife, you were going to do a good job. Is that correct?"

"*Cie,* yes."

"You knew you were going to kill him; is that correct?"

Cheech shakes his head and grits his teeth. "*Cie,* I wanted to kill him like he killed my Joey."

"The prosecution has no more questions for this witness, your Honor."

Judge McLaughlin say's, "If there are no more witnesses, you may start your closing statements."

The man in the back is astounded that the judge is plunging ahead without a recess.

Gallagher rises from his chair and steps over to the jury. "Lady's and Gentlemen of the jury, I told you in my opening statements that I would prove to you that Francesco Caruso was a cold-blooded murderer. That he knew exactly what he was doing when he murdered the good Doctor, Casper Pendola. You heard him admit twice that he was awaiting his arrival, that he knew he would murder the good doctor. He admitted it once in his own statement and another time when I put the question directly to him. He knew exactly what he was doing when he went into the kitchen and got the knife from the drawer. He knew he was going to kill with that knife. What you don't know is that when he was arrested at his brother's home on Staten Island, he admitted it twice more to the arresting detective's during his return to Brooklyn. He not only admitted it numerous times; he showed a complete lack of remorse. It has been found and presented to Judge McLaughlin that in 1918, Caruso was convicted for carrying a gun. There are other finds and fines pending with more arrests using aliases. Your civic duty makes it imperative and justified for you to determine and come to a decision of first-degree murder in the death of Doctor Casper S. Pendola. First-degree murder carries the sentence of death, very appropriate for this cold-blooded, premeditated and brutal murder. If you do not find the defendant Francesco Caruso guilty of first-degree murder, the word will go out all over this country.

No doctor will feel safe anywhere in America. Once that happens, most doctors will no longer make home visits. Poor people and immigrants will suffer. The Lord only knows of the size and scope of coming epidemics. I would hope that you would let your conscience and good sense be your guide, and make this be a moral judgment in this case. Anything else would be a travesty. Thank you, Lady's and Gentlemen." Gallagher returns to his seat amidst applause and cheers by the majority of people in the courtroom.

The judge does not declare them out-of-order for the outburst. He merely tells the defense attorney, "Your turn, Counselor, please!"

Standing besides his client Voss looks toward the jury. "Try to imagine what it must have been like for this man to lose his child after over two weeks of caring for him, of that beloved little boy dying in his arms. Try to imagine what it felt like for the attending physician to laugh about it to his face. Lady's and Gentlemen, imagine having this laugh compounded by a bribe for your silence after all of this. Try to imagine your state of mind when you feel driven to kill. Try to imagine the state of your mind at that point. Surely, you can find it in your hearts to understand that this crime took place under extremely stressful conditions. Francesco Caruso was out of his mind with grief on February 13 of this year when he took the actions he did. Can you say that under no circumstances would you kill in the same situation if it were your child? I ask of you, Lady's and Gentlemen, in your wisdom and compassion to find that my client was temporarily insane at the time he committed the murder of Dr. Casper S. Pendola. Thank you."

With the final statement finished, the judge instructs the jury. They leave the courtroom to deliberate.

Once again, as he was each day of this trial, the man in the three-piece suit makes notes before he stands and leaves. The murder trial lasts a mere four days. It takes the Jury only five hours to reach a verdict. At 11:51 p.m., Judge McLaughlin is notified. His pages notify Prosecutor Gallagher and defense attorney Voss. Cheech is brought back into the courtroom. Most of the visitors left earlier when the jury went into deliberation.

Judge McLaughlin tells the bailiff to bring in the jury. The jury returns. The judge tells the members of the jury, "I understand that you have reached a verdict."

The jury Forman speaks out, "Yes, your Honor, we have reached a verdict." He hands a note to the bailiff who carries it to the bench.

Looking at the note, Judge McLaughlin asks the jury for a show of hands to make sure they agree with the verdict. Each of the members raises their hand.

McLaughlin tells the Forman, "You may read the verdict, Sir."

He stands, opens the paper and reads. "We the jury, find the defendant, Francesco Caruso, guilty of the murder of Doctor Casper S. Pendola."

In the silence of the moment, the Judge looks at Cheech and then at the jury, "I wish to thank each and every one of you for the verdict you have rendered. Anything less would have been a travesty, an injustice, an insult and a slap in the face of the good doctor's family. Very well then, I set the date of April 18 for the sentencing. Jurors, I thank you, dismissed. Guards, remove the prisoner. Thank you all, court adjourned."

Cheech is ushered out of the courtroom and driven back to the Raymond Street Station to await sentencing before going to Sing Sing.

* * *

The New York Times April 8 front-page headlines read:

Caruso Convicted of First Degree Murder

Doctor Killed After Death of Little Son

* * *

The next morning, April 9, the family of the convicted Cheech approaches the Kings County Courthouse steps. Rosario, who came in from Staten Island, greets them. They all walk up the steps and into the courthouse. They approach one of the guards. Louis speaks, "Pardon me; my name is Louis Privitera and I am here with the wife and family of Francesco Caruso for his trial. Could you tell me what room it is being held in?"

Court Officer Joseph L. Fair shows his surprise. "I'm sorry. It is all over. It ended yesterday late. Who told you to come today?"

A frustrated Maria starts crying. The children cry with her. Her sisters Josephine and Florence console Maria and her children while Rosario and

Louis try to make sense of it. Louis tells the Officer, "We were told to be here today. A man called and told us to be here today."

Officer Fair says, "I don't know who told you, but it's all over. He's behind bars awaiting sentencing for killing the doctor." Mr. Voss is walking down the hall. The Officer calls him over and explains the situation to him.

Voss agrees to speak with the family. "I am Mr. Voss. I represent Mr. Caruso. I don't have good news for you, but it's not over yet. In any death sentence, there is an automatic appeal. I assure you that I will do everything in my power to fight for Mr. Caruso. It will take time. I feel confident that we can win." He assures them that he will help Cheech. He tells them there is nothing they can do for now and suggests they go home and wait for him to notify them.

Rosario returns to his home at Staten Island while Louis drives Maria, the children and his sisters back to Fort Lee, New Jersey. In the car, he explains to Maria how serious the situation is for Cheech.

* * *

Mr. Privitera answers a knock on the door. He opens it to find a woman standing there. "Can I help you, Miss?"

"I'm Mrs. Snyder. I'm here to speak to Mrs. Caruso about her husband Francesco."

"Come in; I will get my daughter. Please, come in." They all gather at the dining room table. As Maria enters the dining area, Mr. Privitera introduces Mrs. Snyder to her and the rest of the family.

Not knowing her or understanding why she came, they allow her to start the conversation. Her focus is on Maria. "I am working with a gentleman by the name of Alexander Marky. He started an organization named the Francesco Caruso Defense Fund. The purpose is to raise enough money through donations to get a better lawyer for your husband. It is the opinion of Mr. Marky that your husband should have been acquitted of the murder of the doctor. He believes the doctor was wrong in the treatment of your boy, and that the murder of the doctor was an act of passion. He believes that your husband was so upset with the death of his son that he did not know what he was doing. He wants you to know that we can help you; we hope you will allow us to try. Will you allow us to help you?"

Maria tells Mrs. Snyder, "Yes, we want your help! We need help!"

Mr. Privitera says, "Josephina, make coffee for Mrs. Snyder, and we will talk." Taken in by the sincerity and kindness of Maria and the Privitera's, Mrs. Snyder stays for the rest of the day getting to know everyone. As time goes by, Maria explains to her and the family how everything happened. It is the first time Maria's family hears the whole story. The hours turn into dark. Mrs. Snyder tells them that she and Mr. Alexander Marky will soon visit them. He will tell them everything at that time. She kisses the children and hugs everyone as she bids them good night. She tells them to try not to worry too much, that Mr. Marky will help them. It will be all right. Waving good-bye, she gets into her car and heads for New York.

Feeling hopeful for the first time, they all prepare for bed and call it a night. Maria's father, Giovanni (Pepi) lies in bed reminiscing. He thinks back to a day many years ago when he first met Cheech. He wonders how this all will end for his daughter. He reminisces back in time to a summer night on 108th Street Harlem, New York.

* * *

In the back of the apartment building, sit a group of men playing cards. Sitting on orange crates around a makeshift table, they speak in Italian. Approaching the men playing cards is a young twenty-four-year-old man. Some of the men call out to him. "Cheech, *wana ca*, come here. Sit here and play. Come on, sit!" one of the men say's, "Cheech, *gonad, gonda,* sing, sing. Sing a song for us!"

Cheech smiles and sits on an empty crate. "Not tonight, next time for sure, but not tonight." He shakes hands with his friends. Later, he changes his mind and tells them to include him in the next hand. As the men are playing their hand, Cheech tells them, "I just saw a beautiful young girl with red hair on 107th street. Someone called her Josephine. Does anyone know who she is and where she comes from?"

Very softly, a man say's, "Uh oh, good night." The table grows quiet. Some of the men look at Cheech, others at Pepi sitting next to him. Pepi peers at Cheech over his eyeglasses and tells him, "Her name is Josephine Privitera. She lives on 106th street." Cheech smiles. Pepi continues, "I know her parents. I could introduce you to them."

Cheech is thrilled. "If you would do that for me, I would be grateful to you for life. *Bene, it's good.*" He stands to shake hands.

Pepi says, "Sit, we will talk later."

Looking around, Cheech notices that some of the men are trying to hide their smiles. "*Qui, qui*, what did I say? What's so funny?"

One of the men tells Cheech, "Nothing, lets play cards."

The card playing goes on all night until the sun's morning haze appears. Everything is gathered and put away. Cheech turns to Pepi and says, "Pepi, when can you introduce me to Josephine's mother and father?"

"Today is Sunday, *Dominica*. They will be home. Meet me on the steps of St. Iqnatius Church at twelve o'clock today. I will take you to them."

"Thank you, Pepi, I owe you. All you have to do is ask. If I can't do it, I can have it done. Thank you, *Gradcia*."

"What can you do for me Cheech? Do you know someone?" Cheech stops short and looks at Pepi. "First introduce me, and then you can ask."

The grin on Pepi's face disappears. After a pause, he tells Cheech, "Just meet me in front of the church at twelve o'clock."

They shake hands, say their goodbyes, and go their way. Cheech rushes home to clean up and change his clothes for the introduction. As noon approaches, Cheech finds himself waiting by the church steps with a warm morning sun sparkling off the colored cellophane wrapping on the basket of fruit he bought. He is dressed in a three-piece pinstriped suit with tan spats over gray shoes. He turns to see Peppi approaching. "*Choa, Pepi*, good day. You look like me . . . the same clothes. Next time I bring my cane."

"*Choa,* Cheech, you look wonderful. I like your shoes!" The men laugh as they match clothes. They look like a brother act.

Pepi tells Cheech, "If I was a woman, I would not walk with you because you have my dress on."

Cheech laughs and says, "*Gabish e' gabish.*"

Along the way, Pepi stops to pick up some Italian bread, pastry and the Italian newspaper. They enter a building and climb to the second floor. Reaching the apartment door, Pepi opens it and invites Cheech to enter. "Come on, Cheech, come go in, go in. It's time to eat; I'm hungry!" Cheech has a confused look on his face. He wonders why Pepi barged in without knocking.

A woman's voice calls out from the kitchen, "It's about time, Pepi, where have you been? We're all starved!"

"I had to meet someone. He was hungry, so I brought him home with me." Cheech places the basket on the dining room table as a woman comes out of the kitchen wiping her hands on her apron. "Annette, I want you to meet Cheech Caruso. He is a friend of mine. Cheech this is my wife Annette." Cheech is more confused, but he smiles and they exchange greetings. Behind Annette, out of the kitchen come two beautiful girls. One of them has long red hair. "These are my beautiful daughters, Josephine and Maria. Later you will meet my son Luigi."

With a shocked look on his face, Cheech turns to Pepi and say's, "*Senior Pepi, scusa me,* I didn't know. I meant no disrespect to you!" Now he understands why the men at the card game were smiling.

"We can have a glass of wine. A little bit of wine before we eat will be nice. Maria, bring us a bottle and two glasses. Come on Cheech, let's sit in the parlor." Pepi asks Cheech when he came to this country as the two walk into the parlor and sit on the couch. They converse for a while.

Maria enters the room with the wine and two glasses on a tray. "Here, Papa, here is the wine. Shall I pour it for you and your friend?"

"No, Maria, I will do it. Thank you, *gradcia.* "You were very respectful all night long, Cheech. If you were not, you would not be here now." Maria leaves the room, trying not to look at Cheech who is watching her. Pepi pours the wine and the men sit back. "Cheech," Pepi say's, "You must understand that it won't be easy or fast when you will be allowed to be alone with my daughter."

"*Cie, e' gabish.*"

"*Senora* Privitera is small, but a very hard woman. I will tell you, because I like you, that she does not trust you. So choose your words carefully. I like you . . . I love her.

Gabish," Cheech nods his head in understanding.

"It will take you sometime to be welcome in my house, so be patient.

"I will be patient, I promise."

Josephine walks into the room. Cheech tries not to be too attentive. "Papa, can I get you something?"

As her father attempts to respond, she says, "Hello, Cheech, my name is Josephine."

Pepi's head snaps toward her. He tells her in an angry tone, "*Basta Josie,* enough, now leave the room!" Not upset by her father's admonishment, she smiles and looks at the young man one more time as she leaves the parlor.

"*Femina* . . . they don't listen anymore." My wife is the ringleader. Cheech takes another sip of wine and smiles at him.

"Cheech, I hear you have a beautiful voice. Would you sing for us after lunch? Maybe you will stay for dinner too?"

Cheech tells Pepi that he will be happy to serenade them if he can find an instrument for him to play. A guitar, accordion, concertina or mandolin will be fine.

"That will be no problem," Pepi replies, "Many people in the building play musical instruments."

Annette calls out that it is time to eat. Everyone sits; she does the honor of saying grace before they eat. They do not say much. Glances are exchanged from all sides of the table. As the meal finishes, Cheech says, "*Senora* Privitera, you are a wonderful cook. Thank you. Everything was *bellisimo*."

Annette scrutinizes them both. "Did you two plan on wearing the same clothes?" Cheech and Pepi look at each other and burst out laughing. Maria and Josie clear the table.

Pepi tells his wife, "Cheech is a singer. If we can find an instrument for him to play, he will entertain us."

Annette looks surprised. Josie peaks around the doorway going to the kitchen. Pepi sees her smile at Cheech. He looks, but Cheech has his head down. Annette smiles, says "*scusa* me," and goes to the kitchen.

With the kitchen clean, Josephine leaves the apartment. She borrows a guitar from a neighbor. She enters the flat and walks with a big smile over to Cheech. "Sing, Mr. Cheech, sing." Pepi looks at his daughter with a very stern look but does not speak.

Cheech sits on the edge of the couch, tunes the guitar and closes his eyes. Strumming, he sings softly at first. As he goes from song-to-song, they applaud. As the music fills the hallway outside the flat, people invite themselves into the little apartment and soon it is full, so some neighbors sit out in the hall to hear the music. When he takes a break, people introduce themselves and congratulate him on his singing. Some of the other tenants tell Cheech they play instruments. He invites them to get them and join him. Because it is crowded inside, Cheech suggests that they all go up to the roof. As the entertainment goes on, people bring food and drink to share. The musical songfest continues until the stars shine brightly in the dark summer sky. A young man and pretty girl begin dancing. The people move to the edges of the roof to make room for the dancers.

During a break in the music, Pepi signals Cheech. "The dancers are my son Louis and his beautiful wife Anna." He motions to the dancers. "Louis and Anna, I want you to meet my friend, Cheech."

Louis shakes Cheech's hand and asks him what he does for a living.

"I'm an ironworker."

"That's a shame, Cheech, you have a beautiful voice. What's your name?"

"Francesco Caruso" he tells Louis.

Louis chuckles. "You must be joking, huh?"

"No, it's not a joke."

Louis tells Cheech that he just met Enrico Caruso, the famous tenor. "Have you ever heard him sing?"

"Yes, Caruso and I remain friends." Louis asks Cheech to explain. "Caruso is a fine gentleman. He knows there are poor people who will never hear him sing, who don't have money for tickets. Often, he buys tickets and hands them to people in the alley in the back of the Metropolitan. I know because he hands me one and asks me what my name is. I tell him it is Francesco Caruso. He shouts, 'Can you sing?' I say, 'Sure!' He says, 'no go away, wait for me.' He gives away all the tickets and asks me to come inside with him. He pours wine for the two of us. We drink a toast; he asks me to sing . . . so I sing."

Louis looks skeptical. "Just like that, you sang for the Great Caruso?"

"Just like that I sing for him. Then he stops me and wants to know if I would like to sing on the stage of the Metropolitan Opera. I say, 'Ma sure!' We leave the room and we stand on the stage, a big stage!" Everyone in the room is listening. Cheech continues, "He leaves me on the stage and sits in the first row of seats." He says, '*Gonda, gonda*, sing, sing!' and I sing! Then he comes on stage with me. We sing together. Musicians at the foot of the stage join us. We sing many songs. I can't believe I sing with Enrico Caruso. After we finish, he asks if I would like to study opera. I have to say no. We talk for a while, embrace and say goodbye. I return to see him sing on stage, but I no bother him no more; he is a busy man. But I never forget that I sing with him."

Louis astonished, but believing the story, asks him to sing again for them. After the first song, Louis tells Cheech that he has a beautiful voice and asks why he refused Enrico's offer to sing opera. Covering the truth, he tells Louis that he likes to sing, but not for a living. When retelling this story, he never tells people the real reason he cannot accept Caruso's offer is because, if he is recognized, he will be deported as a felon and a non-citizen.

He goes back to singing, and the crowd chants and claps to the Italian love songs. As the sky grows darker, the party ends. They all want to do this again. He tells them he will if the Privitera's invite him back. He thanks Pepi for having him and asks if he can come back. "Ma sure, Cheech, You are welcome, Ma sure!"

* * *

Brought back to his senses by a poke to his ribs, Pepi lies quietly remembering and smiling.

Annette asks, "What are you smiling about?"

He looks over at his wife. "I was thinking about the first time we met Cheech. This terrible thing happens to him and Maria. A terrible thing happens to them. What will happen to him, Annette?"

"I don't know, but he is in my prayers. My worry is what will happen to Maria and the children; go to sleep, *Amore' Mia*."

Chapter 6

It's April 18 1927, Monday morning 9:00am. Sitting in the courtroom waiting for Judge McLaughlin to enter is Prosecutor Gallagher, Defense Attorney Voss, Pendola family members, Cheech, several guards and a few close friends of Cheech from the neighborhood. There are no Caruso family members because no one notified them of the sentencing. The judge calls his court to order and the proceeding starts. "Will the defendant, Francesco Caruso, please stand?" He asks Cheech if he knows why he is present.

Cheech turns and looks at the widow, then focuses his attention on the judge, "*Cie.*"

"Very well, I, Judge Alfonzo G. McLaughlin, sentence you Francesco Caruso to be put to death in the electric chair at Sing Sing Prison located at Ossining, New York during the week of June 6, 1927."

In a quiet courtroom, the widow applauds. Joseph, the murder victim's brother, who gave the medicine to Cheech for Joey, grabs his sister-in-law's hands to stop her. The courtroom is once again silent.

The judge asks Cheech, "Do you have anything to say?" Cheech closes his eyes and shakes his head no. "Very well then, sentence dispensed; the prisoner will be removed from the courtroom and prepared for delivery to the Sing Sing death house for execution in the prescribed week of June 6 of this year." The guards escort Cheech out the side entrance of the courthouse and take him to the Raymond Street Station where he will await his transportation to Sing Sing.

The next morning, Defense Attorney Voss submits the routine appeal at the Kings County Courthouse, a normal procedure in any death sentence.

* * *

On April 19, the newspaper headlines read:

Caruso Convicted of First Degree Murder After Death of Son.

The AMA, doctor groups, nurses and other medical groups applaud and support the verdict of the court.

* * *

A man sitting behind his desk at his office on Broadway picks up the newspaper and reads the headlines about Cheech facing the death sentence. He shakes his head and calls to his secretary, "Mary, have my car brought around." He makes some phone calls, buttons the jacket of his three-piece pin-stripe suit and flicks some lint off his derby.

His secretary calls out, "Mr. Marky, your car is out front!"

Before he leaves, he tells Mary he will not be back for the rest of the day.

* * *

The Privitera family in New Jersey still talks about Mrs. Snyder's visit. They feel hopeful about Cheech and his outcome. They are unaware of his sentence since they have not seen the morning newspapers.

Maria does not let her family know of her concerns. She has a strong premonition that something is wrong. Not everyone notices how her younger sister snubs her. Her mother Annette, in a moment alone with Maria, tells her that Josephine cannot help herself because she is still very much in love with Cheech, even though she is now married to Nunzio. Annette tells her oldest daughter that she knows that Josephine cannot help herself . . . and that she is almost glad that Cheech will not come back. She tells Maria that after all these years, "Josephine still can't get over the idea that Cheech married you instead of her. She knows Papa brought you and your husband together. She also knows that when he first came to our home, he was looking for her and not you. I know these thoughts are awful of her. Still, my heart hurts for her."

Maria tells her mother, "Thank you for telling me the truth, Mama. I understand. I know how my sister feels. I know her heart is broken. I knew it before Cheech and I were married. I know that if she could, she would take him away from me. Unless a miracle happens, Cheech will die for what he did. Then, maybe I will be a friend to my sister again. I also know that you don't like Cheech. I know why. It is because he reminds you of Papa when he was young. I understand, Mama. I know how much you lost to have your Pepi. You left your whole family back at Sicily for him. I'm lucky. Only two people in my family don't like my Cheech."

Annette looks at her daughter with tears in her eyes, "My little Maria, I love you. You have always been a joy to me. If all of my daughters were like you, I would have a perfect life. I knew when you were born that you were special. I wanted the best for you because I knew you were different. You were kind, sweet and smart. I wanted better than Cheech for you . . . and I was right. Look at my poor daughter's life, at what happened. I was cursed when I fell in love with your father, and you are cursed with your husband. You and your sister will never be friends again. Her heart will never heal."

"Mama, would you give up your curse for a fresh start?"

Annette thinks for a moment and tells her daughter, "How can I, Maria, when he owns the best part of me, my heart."

"Mama, please try to be happy for me. You know how I feel about Cheech. I'm about to lose him. He loved Joey more than he loved me. I know that; it's okay. I'm the one who gave Joey to him. Now he doesn't care if he dies because he doesn't have Joey, but I do, I care. Please pray for him, Mama."

"I will. First, I pray for you. Then I pray for Joey, and if I have time, I pray for your husband."

"Thank you, Mama. I love you so much. I know Papa loves Cheech. He wanted me to marry him because he knew he would take care of me. I love Papa, too."

A loud knock at the front door interrupts their conversation. Pepi opens the door to see a tall, dapper man with a derby in his hand. "Yes?"

"My name is Alexander Marky. I'm here to speak to Mr. Francesco Caruso's wife about his case. Mrs. Snyder spoke to you last week."

"*Cie, Cie*, I remember Mrs. Snyder. *Cie*, come in, Come in!" He calls to his wife, "Annette, *wana ca*, come here, look who's here. It is Mr. Marky. You remember Mrs. Snyder told us about him. *Wana, ca* quick! Come on in, Mr. Marky; please come in." Annette and Maria hurry into the parlor off the living room. They see Pepi shaking hands with the tall stranger. Pepi introduces his wife to Mr. Marky. He nods to Maria and says, "This is my daughter, Maria. She is Cheech's wife."

Marky tells Maria, "I am very sorry about your little boy Mrs. Caruso. He should not have died of Diphtheria in this day and time. What the doctor did was wrong, and what your husband did, although just as wrong, was understandable. It was a crime of passion. I want you to know there are many people who want to help your husband. I must ask you; do you want us to help him?"

Maria glances at her parents and focuses on Marky. "Mr. Marky, Ma sure, Of course I want you to help my husband. We do not have money, nothing to give you. We didn't even have money to bury my son. He was buried by the state; how awful."

Pepi leads the way to the living room where they settle around the table. Marky says, "Mrs. Caruso, we don't want your money. We will have the money." He hesitates; he doesn't want to tell them the bad news, but knows he must. "There are very powerful organizations out there that want your husband killed for what he did. They feel he must be executed or no doctor will be safe anywhere again. Do you understand me?" They nod yes and he continues. "I was in the courtroom every day of your husband's trial. I listened to all of the testimony. I noticed that none of Mr. Caruso's family was there to support him."

Maria interrupts him to say that someone gave them the wrong date, and they showed up after the trial. "We went there the next day and were told to go home because it was over. My poor husband was all alone. I don't know what happened, what they said about him, or what they did to him. We all felt so bad."

Marky say's, "I see, I was wondering why no one was there for him. I understand now, Mrs. Caruso. The people I told you about, those who want him killed. They gave you the wrong date; they did not want your husband represented in the courtroom. It also means they knew beforehand that the trial would take only four days. Apparently, they misled you twice. Yesterday, they held his sentencing. Now, I must tell you the bad news. He's at the Raymond Street Station. Tomorrow he goes to Sing Sing Prison's death row to await his execution."

Maria gasps. Her eyes roll back as she collapses.

Pepi carries her into the living room. "Maria, Maria," he calls out as he lays her out on the couch and places a pillow beneath her legs. "Mama, get a rag with some vinegar and water; bring it here."

Mr. Marky feels responsible for Maria fainting. "Mr. Privitera," he says sadly, "I'm so sorry. I had no idea it would affect her like this. I'm truly sorry."

"How could you know? There is no good way to say something like this. How could you know? Don't feel bad."

Annette returns to the living room carrying a damp rag with a mixture of water and vinegar on it. She applies it to Maria's head. Maria opens her eyes and glances around the room. She cries out, "Papa, they're gonna kill my Cheech. Don't let them do that!" It strikes her that Joey spoke those same words before he died. She breaks down completely. "Mama, I sound like Joey! That's what Joey said to Cheech when he was dying. He told his Papa not to let him die. Now I say it to my Papa. Oh God, help my husband, Mr. Marky, please help Cheech!"

Taken aback by Maria's words, Marky asks, "Is that what your boy said?"

"Yes, Mr. Marky, he knew he was dying. We didn't listen to him. We trusted the doctor, a stranger. God paid us back."

"No, Maria," Marky says, "God doesn't pay people back when we make a mistake. We do that to ourselves all on our own."

Maria calms down a bit and asks him again to help Cheech.

"Of course I will help him, Maria. I could leave you alone with your family and return tomorrow if you like. It would be no trouble."

Maria wipes her eyes and looks at Marky. "No, Mr. Marky, please stay. I want you to help us. I am so sorry for acting this way. I *will* be strong; I *will* be fine; please don't go. I want you to stay."

Pepi tells Annette, "*Mia amora*, my love, please make some coffee for us." He asks Marky, "Would you like a bit of wine instead?"

"No, no wine please; coffee is fine, thank you." Maria sits up. Marky asks, "Are you sure you're okay, Maria? We can put this off if you aren't."

She assures him she is okay. "Please, Mr. Marky, let's talk. I need to talk."

"I am working on behalf of your husband. I started a Caruso Defense Fund. Its primary function is to raise money for expenses incurred while working for an appeal and new trial for your husband. It includes expenses for you and the children. The biggest expense it will take on is the search and purchase of the services of the best attorney possible to take over your husband's case. The next thing we are going to do is find a place for you to live in New York. You should be closer to where everything is going on. The contributions we receive through the fund will take care of all of your expenses, anything you need. Now comes the hard part. It will be a lot of work. At times, it will be humiliating for you and your family. We must win the sympathy of the public by showing them you and your children are destitute."

Pardon me, Mr. Marky, Maria asks, "I no *gabish* what is destitute?"

"It means you cannot live on your own since your husband was arrested. It means you are poor and need help. We want you to ask for help. You must make your situation look worse than it really is. You must win the sympathy and financial assistance of the public, people who feel bad for you and the things you are going through. You will apply for welfare . . . even if you do not receive it. Your effort to gain assistance must be noted by the public."

"Mr. Marky, I may be poor, but I'm proud. I don't accept charity from people, especially people I don't know. I won't go before strangers and beg for their money."

"I understand, Maria, but if you refuse to work with me, I will not be able to help your husband, and he will die. The medical community in New York is very powerful. They have many politicians in their pocket. Your husband will die for what he did to one of them. I was at the trial every day. The AMA paid for everyone of power in that courtroom. It was shameful, a crime no worse than your husband committed. They knew what was going to happen to him ahead of time. The jury was handpicked. The court handpicked Mr. Caruso's attorney. Your husband had no chance. It was a conspiracy. I don't know what kind of man your husband is, and I don't care. I do know his was a crime of passion . . . not premeditated murder. No one in the courtroom cared about what your husband said. They didn't care that the pharmacist said the medicine was too strong for your little boy. They said there was no quarantine sign placed on your door. "Your husband does not deserve to die for this. There are laws to cover this kind of killing, Mrs. Caruso. I simply cannot help him without your help. I cannot raise the amount of money I need to save your husbands life without your help. Think of your husband. Think about your children. They will be fatherless. I promise to help you with everything. I promise to be with you when the prison releases your husband. Mrs. Snyder and I will work with you everyday until we win. Please, Mrs. Caruso, please help us to do this for you, your husband and your children. Forget the charity; this is your husband's life."

Maria crying softly places her head on her father's shoulder. Pepi says, "Maria, listen to me. I love you very much; I also love Cheech. I don't want to lose him this way. I don't want your children to be without a father. Enough people have died. Beautiful little Joey died and then the doctor. His daughter will grow up without her father. Is that what you want for your children? You know you must do what Mr. Marky is telling you. I know you will do it. Mr. Marky, thank you for helping my daughter. Maria will do it. Tell Mr. Marky you will."

Maria straightens herself up and wipes her eyes. "Mr. Marky, whatever you ask of me, I will do."

Marky smiles, "Maria, You won't regret it. You'll meet many people who expressed concern for you, your husband and your family. You'll receive many offers of help, but do *not* accept anything without my consent. People and groups are already forming all over New York and New Jersey. They will be there for us when we need them." Maria asks him what she will do and say to people. He gives her examples. "You will do a lot of public speaking. You will meet with some very important people. When we can afford it, you will speak to a radio audience. You will speak to the newspaper reporters. You will have a lot of help and support; however, you must lead the fight for your husband's life."

"Papa, I don't know if I can do it, but I will try."

Pepi tells the apple of his eye, "Maria, you don't have a choice. Your husband's life depends on it. Of all my children, if I were to ask one of them to do this for me, it would be you."

Maria hugs and thanks Pepi for being a good father. "Mr. Marky, I will do my best to do what you ask."

Marky pats the back of Maria's hand, "Good, Maria, I know you will. Together we will help your husband."

"Mr. Marky, his name is Cheech. Please call him Cheech. He likes to be called Cheech by his friends."

"I will, Maria. Cheech it is."

Now I have a lot of work to do and people to meet with, so I will say goodbye for now. I will get in touch with you soon. If I need you to be somewhere, I will send Mrs. Snyder to get you and drive you around. We have a number of very important people involved in helping your husband, powerful people. If you see something in the newspapers that isn't good, try not to pay attention to it. In the end we *will* win."

* * *

The police are preparing Cheech's transfer to the Sing Sing Prison Death House to await execution in the electric chair. The commander asks the Sergeant, "Are Caruso's papers ready to go?"

"Yes, Sir, they are, since yesterday."

"Good, let's get him the hell out of here. Get the transportation ready."

"Yes, Sir, I will get right on it." The sergeant makes a quick call and leaves the Commander's office.

In a short while, two armed guards come into the station house. "We're here for Caruso. Is he ready to be moved?"

Sergeant Kelly walks up to them. "This is the paper work on Francesco Caruso. His classification is dangerous, so be cautious. Follow me." They walk to the back to the holding cells where Cheech awaits them. Kelly stops in front of Cheech's cell "There he is! Caruso, these men are here to take you to Sing Sing." The men enter the cell. One of the guards searches and handcuffs Cheech.

The other guard remarks, "You don't look so tough. Are you as tough as they say you are?"

Cheech is hesitant, but says, "Tough is stupid. Are you stupid?" With his hands cuffed behind him, the guard strikes him in the stomach with his Billy club. He doubles over in pain and receives a blow on the back with the club. In intense pain, his fear and anger take over. He kicks the guard in the stomach sending him flying out of the cell and across the aisle into the bars of the cell across the way.

"You goddamn Dago, you're never going to make it to the big house!" The guard runs back into the cell with his club raised. Kelly steps in front of him and the other guard. "Enough! You had your fun. Raise one more hand to the prisoner, and I will file charges against you."

The other guard tells Kelly, "I Give you my word, sergeant; the prisoner will not be touched again." He turns to the other guard, "right, Asshole?"

The guards place Cheech into the secured back section of a prison truck with two other prisoners. They enter the cab of the vehicle and drive away. The guard who handcuffed Cheech laughs. The other guard asks, "What the hell you laughing for?"

"I never thought I'd see the day when you got your ass kicked by a man with his hands tied behind his back. You're lucky you didn't try that before Caruso was handcuffed. I think you met your match, Asshole! I can't wait to tell the guys!"

"He hit me while I wasn't looking! Fuck you, Murphy!"

"Yeah, right, Asshole! You weren't looking because you were running—the wrong way!"

The rest of the ride is quiet. The vehicle enters the prison grounds. The truck backs up to a loading platform. The guard Cheech kicked heads to the office. Murphy unlocks and enters the back of the vehicle. He glances at the other two prisoners and sits in front of Cheech. "I read about your boy in the newspaper, Caruso; sorry you lost your son. Are you as tough as people say you are?"

"I lost everything important to me. I have nothing to live for. I will die for the few things I have left to believe in, including defending myself. Don't confuse not being afraid to die with being tough. There is a big difference. You look like a nice man. I give you some advice, Mr. Guard; get rid of your partner before he cost you your life."

"Mr. Caruso, You shouldn't be here. With a good lawyer you will be returned to your family."

"Thank you, but for me that is the worse thing that can happen, like a living death for me."

Murphy leads the prisoners onto the platform and into a waiting area. His last words to Cheech are, "Good luck, Caruso." Cheech looks but doesn't respond.

Searched and examined, head shaved, issued a prison uniform, hands and feet shackled, Cheech is lead to the cell on death row from which he will be led to his electrocution.

He lies on the cot of his cell and thinks about Joey. He smiles when he thinks back to last summer when, at age five, Joey sang with him at one of the neighborhood musical sessions.

No one close, since O'Mally, has spoken to Cheech. Losing contact with his world helps him find inner peace. He hopes it will sustain him until the first week in June. He has no idea of efforts by Salvatore D'Aquila, Marky and a number of private citizens, friends and groups to have his trial overturned. A guard interrupts his thoughts. "Caruso, the warden wants to see you. You will have hand and foot shackles. There will be two guards with you at all times. Do you understand?"

"*Cie,* I understand, Mr. Guard."

The guards lead Cheech from his death row cell down the long corridor and to the door of the warden's office. The warden calls, "come on in," when they knock. The guards stand on each side of him as Cheech stands in front of the warden's desk. The warden says, "Very good; remove Mr. Caruso's shackles please."

A guard warns, "Warden Lawes, I suggest that you not allow the prisoner that much freedom."

The warden gives him a penetrating look, and repeats, "Remove Mr. Caruso's shackles. Then you can wait on the outside of the door. Do not enter my office unless I call you. Do I make myself clear?"

"Yes, Sir, we will not enter unless you call." They remove the shackles from Cheech's hands and feet. On the way out, the guard says, "We'll be right outside, Sir." Warden Lawes waves them out with the back of his hand.

Chapter 7

The warden walks around to the front of the desk and sits back on it. "Cheech, Francesco, sit down. Sit down, please." Cheech is puzzled. He sits on the chair in front of the desk. "Francesco Caruso. What a beautiful name. Can you sing like Caruso?"

Unsure how to respond, Cheech says, "I sing well, but Enrico is better. I do not want to sing now."

Warden Lawes smiles, "I was only joking. Are you serious? Can you really sing?"

"*Cie*, I can sing."

"Perhaps you will sing for me sometime. I'm Warden Lawes. This is my prison. I know every person here. We have killers, robbers and rapists. Then there are the prisoners who are here because of events beyond their control. Of that group, none of them deserves to be here less than you do. I followed your case ever since it appeared in the newspapers. I am fully aware of the circumstances that bring you to death row and me. It amazes and confuses me that you are here. I cannot help but wonder about the power brought to bear on the justice system to bring your case to this point. Do you understand me, Francesco?"

Cheech nods yes. "I cannot read or write the English language, but I understand very well."

"That's good. Mr. Voss, your attorney, what kind of attorney is he; did he try to save your life?"

Cheech shrugs his shoulders. "I don't know American court system. I don't offer him help; he don't ask. It is not important, Warden Lawes. Why fight to live? When I lost my Joey, I lost the will to live."

"May I call you Frank?"

"*Cie*, Frank is fine."

"Frank, let me tell you something about the law in America. A man brought to death row gets an automatic appeal before he takes that last walk. The purpose of an appeal is to re-evaluate the original sentence. Do you understand what I am saying?

"*Cie,* it means that they want to make sure."

"Right, they hold court to see if there is reason to have another trial. If they decide there is enough reason, a date is set for the new trial. I do believe you will get a new trial and be released a free man on an insanity plea."

"Thank you for believing in me, though it is for nothing. I am thirty-five-years-old, and feel like an old man. I have seen enough hardship in my life to cause a heart to die and that is what I want. In Sicily, I lost my childhood sweetheart Valenta. Her husband, by arranged marriage, killed her because she would not accept him as her mate. My father died because of something that I did. I left Sicily and my family because I could not live there anymore. I came to this country and married a girl I could never truly love. She gave me a son who looked like my father. He had blond hair and blue eyes just like my Papa. I named him Joseph after Papa—now he is dead too. I am not new to violence, Warden Lawes. I saw my share of death. You are right about me being crazy when I killed the doctor. Still, I cannot remember things. It's not important because I have nothing to live for. My will to live died when Joey died. It was my last chance. I do *not* want anyone's help. There are lots of people who need help; help them."

"I knew nothing about you before you killed the doctor. I'm telling you, you don't belong here; you belong with your wife and family. What the doctor did was wrong. What the AMA did for that doctor is worse. You will have lots of time to think about it, Frank. I must lock you in a cell on death row. That does not mean I can't make you comfortable. Tell the guards if there is anything I can do for you until you leave. I will do what I can. In the meantime, is there anything I can do for you now?"

"Yes, Mr. Lawes, there is something you can do for me if you would. When arrested, I had sixty-five dollars. If you could, I would like to have that money sent to my wife."

"How can I do that for you, Frank" Is there someone who you trust enough to deliver it to her?"

"Yes, Sergeant O'Mally works at the Raymond Street Station. He's a good friend."

"Okay, I'll locate O'Mally and have him take the money to your wife."

"Thank you. You're a nice man."

Warden Lawes calls for the guards. He instructs them not to use hand or feet shackles on Cheech whenever he comes to or from the Warden's office. "You can remove him now." The guards have Cheech walk directly in front of them as they return him to his cell.

Later, Cheech is lying on his cot when a guard stops at the bars of his cell, "Caruso, how do I reach O'Mally?"

Cheech sits up. "He works at the Raymond Street Station. If he isn't on duty, speak to Murphy; he will tell you how to reach him."

"Thanks, Caruso, I'll find him. I need to tell him to come and see Warden Lawes." Cheech asks if he will be able to see O'Mally. "Usually the only visitors the warden will allow on death row are relatives. Caruso, the warden asked us to see to your needs. My wife wonders if you would accept a sandwich once in a while when she makes me lunch?"

Cheech gets up and walks to the bars. "What is your name, Mr. Guard?"

The guard chuckles at the formality. "Just call me, Donald."

"Donald, thank you for your kindness; tell your wife that Cheech will not forget her kindness and ma sure, it would please me. Thank you, Donald."

The days pass, and then one day Donald awakens Cheech with an announcement. "Hey, Cheech, I reached O'Mally last night. He meets with Warden Lawes today. He knew he couldn't meet with you, so he gave me a message, a private message. Cheech walks to the bars. The guard hands him a sandwich wrapped in waxed paper. "Here put it away for later, but don't wait too long to eat it or it will spoil."

Cheech thanks Donald and tells him to thank his wife. "I will eat is as soon as you tell me what O'Mally told you."

In a low voice Donald say's, "O'Mally said he went to see Sal and everything is okay. He said that I should thank you for him. He tried to find Maria, but wasn't able too. He met with your neighbor O'Hanlon. He said there is a Mr. Marky who has started a Caruso Defense Fund. He is working with your wife to help you. He said to tell you many people believe the AMA wronged you. They are working to overturn your conviction. They are not only looking for a new trial, but a reversal of your conviction. Mr. Marky will take O'Mally to meet with your wife this week. She is staying with her parents at their home at Fort, Lee New Jersey. He said to tell you the reason Maria and her family didn't come to your trial is because someone deliberately gave them the wrong date so they wouldn't be there for you. I'll have more news for you when O'Mally meets with your wife this week. I'll let you know."

Cheech's eyes are welled with tears. He reaches through the bars and pats Donald on the cheek, "Thank you, Donald, you a good man. Bless you."

* * *

At his home at Brooklyn, O'Mally picks up the phone and calls headquarters. "This is O'Mally, I won't be in today. See if you can get someone to take my shift; I'll make it up to him later. I will be in tomorrow. Thanks."

As he hangs up, his wife sharply asks, "Where you going today? Why don't you take a day off and stay with me?"

"Not today, Hon, can't do it today, but I will soon. I promise."

An hour later, O'Mally arrives at the entrance of Sing Sing Prison. A guard checks his identification and has someone escort him to the warden's office. He knocks on the door. "Sergeant O'Mally is here, Sir." The warden opens his door. "Come on in Sergeant O'Mally." They shake hands. "Please be seated."

"Thank you, Sir."

"I understand that you and Frank have been friends for a long time."

O'Mally looks puzzled. "Frank? Oh! You mean Cheech! Yes, we've been friends for over fifteen years."

"Is that what he's called?"

"Yes, Sir, that's Italian for Frank. His friends all call him Cheech."

"I see. Does he have many friends?"

"I've never met a man with more friends than Cheech. He is like a god in his Brooklyn neighborhood. They look to him for many things. Italians trust him more than they do the authorities. He can never make it from the subway station to his home without some merchant or friend stopping him. The merchants usually hand him a paper bag with a piece of fruit or a vegetable, just a gesture of kindness. The kids help him bring his tool bag home. He loves to sing. I don't know anyone who doesn't like him. There are all kinds of groups forming to help him try to win an appeal. Kids are running around asking for signatures on petitions. Anyone who can afford it is donating money for the cause. He's just special in his neighborhood; they miss him a lot."

"He seems very important to many people. How does he help them?"

O'Mally tells him of the times Cheech has helped people who are down and out or have no place to live. "He stops young hoodlums from hurting people and generally just takes charge of a situation. If they can't deal with a problem, they look to him. He knows people who can help him do things for people in need. He's just a good man."

"Has he helped you, Sergeant O'Mally?"

"Yes, Sir, he has. I'll never forget it."

"Well, O'Mally, now you have a chance to help him."

"Just tell me how."

Warden Lawes reaches for an envelope on his desk and hands it to O'Mally. "Cheech was arrested with sixty-five dollars on his person. He asked me to make sure it got to his wife. That is where you come in. He asked me if I could find you for him. Would you see that it gets to Maria?"

"Of course; I'll take care of it. I haven't seen her since I helped Cheech in his arrest, but I understand that she is at her parents place in New Jersey. I'll go there as soon as I can."

The warden looks surprised. "Did you say you helped Cheech in his arrest?"

"Yes, Sir, after he killed the doctor and fled to his brother's at Staten Island, he was nearly out of his mind. He called for me to be part of the arresting party. He needed a friend. It was my pleasure to be there for him. Besides, I knew that an Italian arrested by Irish cops could be trouble. Italians and Irish have always had a love hate relationship except for us. Sometimes I can't tell if he's more Irish or Italian and the same I guess for him. May I see him?"

"I'm sorry; the law prohibits it since he's on death row. You'll see him when he returns to Raymond Street. There will be an appeal. His spirits are very low, not feeling good about life. I believe he'll be all right, especially since you told me about him. In the meantime, see that this money gets to Maria."

"Thank you, Sir, I will."

As they head for the door, the warden tells O'Mally. "If you have to return for any reason, call me at this number, and I will clear you for entry."

"I will, Sir, thank you! By the way, would you allow him to have this note I wrote to him?"

"I thought he couldn't read English?"

"He can't, but someone will read it for him, maybe even by you, Sir."

"I'll go see him when you leave. He'll want to hear from you."

"Thank you again, Warden Lawes."

As O'Mally drives away from Sing Sing, Warden Lawes heads for death row and Cheech's cell. He reaches the guard desk at the entrance to the death row cells and speaks to the guard on duty. "I need to be let in. When I approach Caruso's cell, unlock it. Do not lock it until you hear my order to shut the door."

"You are going in by yourself, Warden?"

"That's correct; you'll know when I'm finished by the slam of the cell door."

"Sir, the man is a murderer!"

"I'm aware of the charge. You don't know the circumstances. He shouldn't be here. While he is, I'll have him treated with respect or at least understanding. Now let me in."

"Yes, Sir."

The gate opens. The warden walks down the long corridor. On the way, he stops to speak to some of the prisoners. He reaches Cheech's cell and finds him sitting on his cot with his head in his hands. He slides the cell door open and walks in.

"Cheech, I just had a visit with your friend Sergeant O'Mally. He holds you in high regard. So does your neighborhood. Everyone is asking for you. There are groups forming to help raise money for your upcoming appeal. He did everything you asked, except speak to Maria. He went by your place after he left you, but they had the apartment taped closed. He said a friend of yours from the second floor told him everything. He hasn't been able to get her address. Your neighbor told him she went to Jersey to stay with her parents. I gave him your envelope. He said he'll take it to her as soon as he can."

Cheech stands. "Warden Lawes, I don't know how to thank you."

"Cheech, if I may call you Cheech, I told you before that you shouldn't be here. Many people want to kill someone. Something stops them. Most likely, they haven't suffered a loss like yours. I have a letter from Sergeant O'Mally for you. Sit down and I will read it to you if that's okay?"

"*Cie*, please read it for me."

The warden tears the envelope open and prepares to read the message to Cheech. It is the first time he has heard from anyone since O'Mally and the other detectives brought him back to Brooklyn. The warden reads:

"Cheech, my friend, I can't begin to tell you how much I think of you. Everyone does. I took care of all your business as you asked, except Maria. I went by your place. The police closed everything up. I stopped by O'Hanlon's and spoke to him and his daughter. They told me everything that happened. They told me your wife is with her mother and father in New Jersey. I haven't been able to get their address because no one knows it, but I will. I will go see her and help her with anything she and the kids need. There are all kinds of groups getting together to help you. Even the kids are running around begging for change. I heard that a defense fund was set up for you by an Alexander Marky who is a Broadway agent. I will find him this week. The command at Raymond Street has changed. When you come back, I'll spend some time with you. Mr. Voss filed an appeal. So take heart, my best friend; we all want you back."

Cheech is sitting with his head down trying to hide the tears. He takes a deep breath to compose himself. "Thank you, Sir, *Gradsia*."

Warden Lawes gives Cheech a long look, deep in thought. "I know what we're going to do with you. Before you leave here, you will learn to read and write English."

Cheech gives the warden a direct look. "You're a good man, Warden Lawes. I am lucky. I found one more friend."

The warden walks to the cell door. He turns and says, "I heard that you have a knack for making friends out of strangers. They all want to do things for you." He smiles, walks through the entrance and slams the door shut. At the sound, the guard flips the switch to lock the door.

Before he walks away, Cheech asks the warden if he can have the letter. The warden passes him the letter through the bars.

Cheech sits on his cot and holds the letter. He examines his reasons for wanting to die. He knows the most difficult thing will be living without Joey. He lies down on his cot and closes his eyes. He thinks of the warden's promise about learning to read and write English. The idea pleases him.

* * *

At dinner, O'Mally tells his wife. "I'm going to see Maria this week to deliver an envelope for her from Cheech."

"I hope you know what you're doing," she responded rudely. "The last time you helped him, it got you transferred! He's just another wop, good with a knife."

"Mary, if you ever say anything like that again . . . ."

She interrupts, "What will you do? Will you hit me? No wonder you two are friends. You're both alike!"

"Just shut up, Mary, shut the hell up! I'm going out." He grabs a jacket and leaves the apartment.

On the way down the steps, he decides to look for Alexander Marky. He picks up a New York Times on his way to catch the subway. He settles in the train and opens the newspaper. He reads an article about Cheech. It mentions that Broadway agent Alexander Marky is running the Caruso Defense Fund; it lists his address. O'Mally makes note of it as he prepares to get off at 42nd and Broadway. He leaves the train and heads for 1.133 Broadway where he enters the building and climbs the steps to the space listed for Marky. The door is unlocked so he walks in.

"May I help you, Sir?" the girl at the desk asks.

"I'm Sergeant O'Mally, Miss. It's important that I speak to Mr. Marky."

"May I ask what it's about Sergeant?"

"I'm a close friend of Francesco Caruso; I need to speak with Mr. Marky."

The girl knocks on a door and enters. She and Mr. Marky come out. Marky shakes hands with O'Mally and says, "Sergeant O'Mally, please come into my office." Marky offers him a seat and asks, "How can I help you?"

"Cheech is my best friend. I just left Sing Sing where Warden Lawes and I spoke about him. At Cheech's request, I visited with him prior and accompanied him at his arrest and transfer to Brooklyn. I tried to find Maria, but no one knows her parent's address. I have a message for her from Cheech. I saw your name in the Times and came looking for you. Can you help me?"

Marky is cautious, unsure about O'Mally until he shows him his badge and the envelope with Cheech's name on it. The two men discuss the circumstances that led to the murder, and what they can do to help Cheech.

"Well, Sergeant, tomorrow is Saturday, and I have to pay a visit to Mrs. Caruso. Would you like to join me?"

"That would be great. What time?"

"Can you be here at 9:30 sharp?"

"I sure can." They shake hands. As he leaves, O'Mally says, "See you in the morning, Mr. Marky."

The next morning the sun comes up. O'Mally rises and heads to the bathroom to prepare for the subway ride to Broadway. Mary cries out, "Where you off to now so early?"

"Don't start again first thing in the morning, Mary. I really do *not* want to hear it. I have to go see the Caruso family." To avoid an argument with his wife, O'Mally skips breakfast. He stops at an Italian pastry shop to pick up some Canoli and pastry for Maria and the family. He eats a roll on his way to the subway. In a short while, he enters Mr. Marky's office.

"Good morning, Sergeant O'Mally, you're right on time. You beat Mr. Marky, but he should be here any moment."

"Yes, Mary, I wouldn't be late for this meeting."

Marky walks in. "Good, O'Mally, you're on time. We can get going as soon as I get some things straightened out with Mary. Would you mind waiting for me in my office?"

"I can do that." O'Mally walks into the office and shuts the door.

Marky tells Mary to set up all of the meetings they spoke about previously that include groups, newspaper reporters and radio stations. He tells her to delegate people to have the banners painted, the posters, letters and notices printed. He calls for O'Mally and asks him to join him for breakfast before they leave for New Jersey; O'Mally responds positively. The two men leave Marky's office and walk to a Broadway deli.

* * *

The medical community is satisfied with Cheech's sentence. They express their opinions in all of the newspapers and on radio. Aware of the appeal requested by Voss, they do not stop trying to swing public opinion to their way of thinking. More-and-more people, both professional and nonprofessional citizens, involve themselves in the case that divides Brooklyn in so many ways. The lines between those who want the penalty carried out and those who want it overturned are firmly drawn. The more information the public receives, the deeper the lines go between the two groups.

* * *

At Sing Sing, the guards get to know Cheech better. As usual, he affects them in a positive way as he has so many others. Some guards are surprised to hear a different version of events than those printed and on the radio.

The warden keeps his word to teach Cheech how to read and write English. A small desk is set up in his cell along with paper, pencils and books. Many of the guards, without being asked, help him. Mail arrives at the prison for Francesco Caruso. At first, there are a few letters and postcards, but as the days go by it multiplies many times over. Many include cash for the appeal and any other purpose that his family needs. The guards volunteer to read them for Cheech. At first, Cheech does not want to see the greetings from all over New York, New Jersey and

Connecticut, but Warden Lawes convinces him that he will eventually owe them a debt of gratitude. Because he trusts the warden, Cheech allows the guards to begin reading the growing pile of messages for him. They leave his cell open, and sit at the little desk to read.

From time-to-time, Warden Lawes visits with Cheech and the guards in an effort to convince him that life *is* worth living. There is no doubt in the warden's mind that the court will overturn Cheech's verdict in appeal.

Maria has not received any messages on behalf of her husband because Marky has purposely not allowed the public to know her whereabouts. She has no idea of the support piling up for Cheech. There has been very little in the press or radio about the campaign Marky is about to unleash.

Chapter 8

Driving through the Lincoln Tunnel, O'Mally says, "Can I ask you a question, Mr. Marky?"

"You can ask, but I can't promise you an answer."

"What part are you playing in this?"

"I'm the Chairman of the Caruso Defense Fund, and I'm the Chairman of the New York Chapter. We have Chapters and Chairmen in New Jersey and Connecticut as well. Our headquarters are at my office on Broadway."

"How did you get involved? I mean did someone ask you to become involved on behalf of Cheech?"

"I can't tell you. It isn't because I don't want to; I just can't tell you." He explains that in show business people who want to keep working learn not to ask questions. He glances at O'Mally. "There is nothing illegal about anything I'm doing. I'm just trying to save a man's life wronged by the legal system. "Can I ask you a question, O'Mally?"

"Sure you can, same rules apply."

"I'm aware of the differences between the Irish and the Italians. I know they don't like each other too much. How did Cheech win your obviously strong friendship? What did he do to earn your respect as an Irish cop?"

"That I can't tell you, but I will say that in one unselfish and helpful act, he won my respect and friendship for life."

"That's a pretty strong statement."

"I can tell you one thing for sure. I've known him for about fifteen years. I know without a doubt that he was out of his mind with grief when he murdered that doctor. I know him to be smart and deliberate. I really would like to know what happened between him and the doctor to drive him to do what he did. When I spoke to him right after the killing, he still didn't have his senses about him. He didn't make much sense all the time we were together then. I never saw him that way before. You should hear Cheech sing. His beautiful voice just melts the heart. I don't know why he isn't an entertainer. There won't be any more summer night singing sessions . . . enormously talented man Cheech is."

Marky asks O'Mally, "Singing sessions?"

O'Mally nods his head, "Yea, singing sessions. Cheech's neighborhood is about the same as mine. I mean poor. We all work hard but we do *not* have any money. Summer nights we usually end up out in front of the building or on the roof. People bring food, drink and something to sit on. The musically inclined bring their instruments and voices; we make our own entertainment. Very rarely does a neighborhood have someone who can sing like Cheech, someone special. Musicians get together every weekend to play for him. Other singers back him up. Occasionally they sing so he can take a break. He sings and dances all night long. He's also one hell of a dancer." O'Mally chuckles. "Song and dance man . . . that was the Cheech we knew. I suspect with Joey gone, he will stop singing in public. It is a shame, so sad. He told me that he met Enrico Caruso and they sang together. That would have been something to hear. I believe Cheech. He brought it up on several occasions over the years, in public, but in a joking manner, because he knew that no one would believe him. I do and I told him I did."

Marky shakes his head, "Quite a man our man Cheech isn't he?" He turns off the main highway onto a dirt drive and pulls up to park in front of an apartment building. "We're here, O'Mally, let's go in."

Josephina answers the door. "Come in, Mr. Marky, come in please. Mama, Papa, its Mr. Marky!" Maria and her parents come out of the kitchen to greet him.

As soon as Maria sees O'Mally she cries, "O'Mally, where have you been?" Arms outstretched and eyes welled with tears of joy, she gives him a strong hug. "It is so good to see you!"

Seeing the affection their daughter places on this man, Mama and Papa exchange a look. Maria sees the concern on their faces. She brings O'Mally to them and introduces him. "Mama and Papa, this is Sergeant O'Mally. He is Cheech's best friend. O'Mally these are my parents."

O'Mally shakes hands with Mama and Papa Privitera. Pepi invites them into their kitchen. Maria sits next to O'Mally and asks him if he has seen Cheech.

"Maria, the last time I saw and spoke to Cheech was when the station house called me and told me that he wanted to speak to me." Not knowing anything about Cheech calling O'Mally, she has a surprised look as she listens to him. "I was ordered by the commander to get to the station house as soon as possible. After I got there, Rosario called back and I spoke to Cheech. He asked if I would come with the arresting officers. We drove to

Staten Island. I went in alone and stayed with Cheech until he was ready. Then I walked him out. He was arrested, and we drove back to Brooklyn."

Maria says, "Cheech was crazy, I never saw him like that. Joey's death tormented him. I couldn't control him when he hit his head against the wall splashing blood on the floor, wall and ceiling. He could have killed himself! He just held Joey and rocked back and forth slamming his head against the wall. I cried and ran around doing stuff and yelling for help. We both yelled like fools. The children cried; it was terrible."

"Maria, I feel so bad for you and Cheech. How did poor Joey die?"

"My little boy was so sick. The doctor gave him a shot and medicine that was too strong. The next morning he died in Cheech's arms." Maria sadly tells everyone in the room, "He told Cheech while he was holding him, 'the doctor is killing me, I'm dying, Papa, don't let me die, I don't want to die!' Cheech told Joey he wasn't dying. Right after that Joey stopped breathing, and Cheech went crazy. He wrapped him in a sheet and sat on the floor holding Joey. He wouldn't stop beating his head against the wall. I tried, but he was too strong. I yelled for help; nobody came!"

"I'm so sorry, Maria, so sorry."

No one is dry eyed. They feel Maria's agony. They haven't heard the whole story before. Now they realize why Cheech acted the way he did. Marky is lost for words because it is the first time he's heard the whole story, too.

O'Mally tells Maria, "I have an envelope for you from Cheech. I got it from the warden at Sing Sing. He hands the envelope to her. Maria opens it and sees the money. "That is the money he had on him at the time of arrest?" O'Mally nods. Maria does not tell O'Mally that she knows Cheech only had sixty-five dollars on his person. She counts off four hundred dollars. She smiles at O'Mally, turns to her father, hands him the money and says, "Here, Papa, take this." She turns to O'Mally and smiles. "You're a good friend O'Mally and a good man. Did you see Cheech while you were at the prison?"

"No, I didn't see him. The warden said only relatives could see a prisoner on death row. Tell Rosario he can see his brother."

"Oh no, that's no good. Cheech hates Rosario. I'm surprised he went to see him!"

"Maria, trust me; he will be happy to see him. He hasn't seen anyone since I brought him in."

"Oh I don't know" Maria says with a dubious look. O'Mally tells her that Cheech told him why they do not get along.

Mr. Marky speaks, "Enough of this. I have some very good news; however, if I tell you, you must promise not to tell anyone. Cheech's life depends on your silence." He looks around at everyone there. They all nod yes. "Arrangements have been made for a man to come to New York to give a speech. While he is here, I will meet with him to explain your situation and ask him to work on Cheech's appeal. He is not a New York attorney, but he won't have any trouble. His name is Clarence Darrow."

Silence—Cheech's relatives have no idea who Clarence Darrow is. O'Mally gets over his initial shock and yells out, "God Almighty, Marky, how in hell did you swing that? He's the greatest lawyer of all time!"

"It's not a done deal yet! I've never spoken to him before. Nevertheless, I have no doubt I can arrange it with him. Somewhere in this city there are some strong people working to save Mr. Caruso. All I know is that I have to meet with him while he's in the city."

O'Mally turns to Maria, "Do you know what this means, Maria? Cheech is as good as free. Clarence Darrow is not accustomed to losing a case."

"Are you sure, O'Mally? He can do this?"

O'Mally looks from Maria to her parents, "Cheech is as good as home; it's just a matter of time. It depends how quickly they can set up a new trial. Wait until the AMA hears about this!"

Marky says, "They can't know for now, O'Mally." He looks at everyone else in the room with his finger over his lips. "Nobody can say anything, nobody! Understand?" They nod their heads and make silent gestures.

Pepi says, "We *gabish*."

O'Mally in a festive voice shouts, "Let's celebrate with some Canoli. I'm hungry for them!"

They are more cheerful. An air of thankfulness permeates the little apartment. Pepi proclaims, "First, before we have the Canoli that our friend O'Mally bought, we are all going to have a bit of wine to celebrate." Annette places glasses on the dining room table. Pepi fills them and says, "We gonna celebrate and toast Mr. Darrow, Mr. Marky, Mrs. Snyder and O'Mally a good friend of the family, our Irish friend. Everyone pick up your glass and salute!"

The mood in the apartment is festive. Pepi invites the guests to stay for dinner. Josephina does not contribute to the festivity. She leaves the house and will not return until after dinner. As the evening ends, Marky compliments Annette's cooking. He and O'Mally head back to Manhattan.

They agree to work together whenever possible to help in the effort to get Cheech's conviction overturned.

Although events of the last two weeks give hope to the Caruso family and supporters, it is only the lull before the storm. At the home of the Privitera family, a new event fills every moment. Maria nervously awaits the certainty of doing what she must to save her husbands life. The newspapers cover the events as they occur. Every day people who support the findings of the first trial run stories. Radio stations air discussions of the tragedy. Maria and her family follow them and try to remember the words of Mr. Marky when he assured them these stories would appear and not to get discouraged.

Baby Ida, the youngest of the Caruso children has a cold. Maria and her mother share time caring for the baby of four months. She has difficulty sleeping through the night. Ida sleeps for short periods, but stays awake most of the night. Pepi purchases her medicines. Two weeks later, little Ida takes a turn for the worse. They fear her cold will escalate to pneumonia. Josephina is no help. She cannot stand the site of vomit or blood. She has a tendency to faint when something displeases or is uncomfortable to her. The family knows any kind of negative excitement is not good for her, so they do not ask for her help. In a cruel way, the events surrounding Joey's death cast their shadow on the Caruso family with the odor of death once more.

Annette tells Maria, "Ida is much worse. Short of a miracle, I don't know what else to do, but pray. I worry about Ida's life. It's my duty to tell you; she needs a doctor, maybe a hospital."

Maria's voice is anguished. She cries, "Oh no, Mama, I can't do that! I can't go through that again! No doctor will ever kill a child of mine again. I will do it myself first."

Pepi runs into the room and kneels in front of Maria who is sitting on the couch. She kisses Ida on the forehead and tells him, "Papa, the doctor killed Joey with that shot. Now that doctor and all of his medical friends want to kill my husband. If I bring his baby to them, what do you think they will do to Caruso's daughter? I feel like I'm in Hell. Why am I punished like this? *Mio Dio*, My god, what did I do?"

Annette takes the baby, and Pepi sits on the couch and wraps his arm around Maria. "I support you Maria; we have no choice since you don't trust doctors or nurses. We'll keep Ida home no matter what happens. If it's God's will to take her, so be it. No one will kill her!"

"Annette is stunned, "Are you crazy, Pepi? Do you know what you're saying?"

"Mama, Papa is right; if you saw and heard Joey, you would understand. Maybe we are crazy out of our heads. I will not make that mistake again. I will not trust the life of my child to some doctor who wants the father of this child killed. I will not allow that to happen . . . never again!"

Annette cries, "God help us. Why is this happening?" She is crying.

Pepi, torn between his daughter and his wife says, "Mama, pray for us all. Would you take Ida Caruso to the hospital? What would happen to her when we leave? Would you chance that? I wouldn't!"

Annette does not answer. She sits next to Maria and wraps her arm around her. She grasps Pepi's hand. "I will pray for Ida and all of us."

Little Ida's condition worsens. It is obvious to all that the end is near for the baby. Maria tells Annette that she doubts she will ever forget watching Joey and Ida die. Ida stops taking nourishment. She sips on a little bit of water. Her fever is higher. The family sees Ida's life slipping away. It is May 17, 1927. Maria holds the baby in her arms as she blows tiny bubbles. She has her wrapped in her white christening blanket. The young mother wipes away the bubbles. Then the bubbles cease. Immediately, her skin loses its flushed color and turns white like the blanket. Ida feels cold. Maria wraps her a little tighter, and then she holds the sweet little face next to her own. Once again, at the loss of a child, Maria cries silently. Another Caruso child is dead. Maria calls out to Pepi and Annette, who are sitting in the dining room drinking coffee, "Mama, Papa, Ida is dead. She is with Joey. Joey will take care of her now. She's safe with him."

Pepi and Annette hurry in to console Maria. Josephina faints and falls off a chair onto the kitchen floor. Holding Maria in this awful moment, Pepi and Annette fail to administer to Josephina in the kitchen. Due to the loss of Joey and now Ida, they pay little mind to Josephina who faints almost at will anytime something displeases her. Pepi tells Maria, "Josephina will awaken in five minutes; Ida will not." He notices that Maria has aged since she came to stay with them. "Maria, *mia Bambina*, should I call the wagon?"

She shakes her head, "No, Papa, please not yet. I want to be with her for a while. I want to be with her alone. Can I take her into your bedroom and close the door?"

Pepi wipes his eyes. "Ma sure, mia Babina, I won't call the wagon until you tell me."

Maria sits in Pepi's bedroom silently rocking Ida. Pepi goes into the kitchen to check on Josephina. She opens her eyes as he brushes the hair off her face. "Papa is she, is Ida dead?"

"*Cie*, Josephina, Ida is gone. She's with her brother. They have each other." He helps Josephina up off of the floor.

Later, when Maria returns to the living room carrying Ida, Pepi and Josephina go in to be with her. Josephina speaks softly. "Maria, I'm so sorry for you and Cheech. I do love you. I don't know what comes over me. Please forgive me."

Maria has not heard a word. Then she realizes that Josephina just spoke to her. She places the palm of her hand on her sister's cheek and cries softly to her, "Josephina, my baby is dead. That's two dead children. What did I do wrong?"

The sisters cry and embrace keeping the dead child between them. Annette asks Maria, "*Mia filia*, my daughter, shall we call the wagon?" Maria nods her head up and down. Pepi makes the call for the wagon explaining that his granddaughter has just passed away. In a short while, the ambulance arrives. The medics examine the baby and take her away.

Pepi makes one more call. "Hello, Mrs. Snyder, This is Mr. Privitera, you remember me?"

She says "yes," and starts to greet him when he interrupts.

"Mrs. Snyder, I have some bad news. My granddaughter Ida died. The wagon just came to take her away."

"Mr. Privitera, what happened to her? I'm so sorry. You poor people, what is happening to your family?"

"The ambulance man said she had pneumonia. Maria refused to take her to a doctor. She said she will never trust another doctor as long as she lives."

"That is terrible. Of course, she wouldn't trust the doctors, I understand. This is terrible!" Mr. Privitera, I have to call Mr. Marky, and then I will come to your home to speak to you and the family. I should be there in about an hour. Can I bring you anything?"

"No, Mrs. Snyder, we don't need anything . . . except God."

Mrs. Snyder calls Marky's office. "Hello, Anne, what's up?"

"Alex you'll never guess what just happened. It is so sad! I just got a call from Maria Caruso's father telling me that another Caruso child is dead. Little Ida, the infant, just died of pneumonia!"

Marky is silent for a moment. "How could this happen?"

"Her father said she was afraid to call a doctor, would never call another doctor, so it was in Gods hands."

"Anne, I know how fearful of the medical community this family is, but we're going to have to tell people what has happened here. This family if just plain terrified of asking for help from the medical community, and I don't blame them. I expect trouble from Maria with this one. I'll need your help. Go to see them and make whatever funeral arrangements necessary for the family. Tell them the fund will pay for the burial. Don't mention that we want Maria to tell people why her child died."

"I won't mention it until you tell me too. I'm going to Jersey right now; I'll call you when I return."

"Thanks, Anne; tell them I'll be by tomorrow."

Pepi answers the door when Anne arrives. "Come in, Mrs. Snyder; please, come in!" The family is at the dining room table. As Anne approaches, Maria stands up to hug and greet her.

Anne wipes away tears; "Maria, I feel so terrible I can't express myself."

They sit. Maria says, "Ida was sick all of last week. I wanted to call for help. I was afraid because her name is Caruso a doctor or nurse would mistreat her. I just couldn't trust anyone, so I left it up to God."

Pepi wipes his eyes. Annette looks worn out. Josephine goes to the bedroom and closes the door. Anne says, "I just spoke to Mr. Marky; he will be here tomorrow. He said to tell you that the Caruso Defense Fund would take care of all of the burial expenses. Maria, this is so sad to lose two children in three months. It is difficult to live through one loss. God Bless you! I will make all of the funeral arrangements for the family if it's alright with you."

"That is so nice. Thank you."

Pepi tells Anne that the McNally Brothers Funeral Home is in the neighborhood up the street. She calls, and a man from the funeral parlor shows us a short time later to make arrangements. When all of the necessary papers are completed and signed, he promises to notify them of the times for the wake and the burial. Mrs. Snyder reminds them once again that Marky will be coming tomorrow and that the funeral expenses are covered. She asks if they need money, they tell her they do not.

* * *

Anne returns to Marky's office and fills him in on her visit to the family. He says, "Arrangements for Maria's speaking engagements are nearly set up. You will be responsible for getting Maria and the children dressed appropriately. You will be their transportation until this is over. Lena, the eight-year-old, will be doing many engagements with her mother. The entire family must appear extremely poor. There may be objections from Maria, but it's so very important that they do not appear to be handling Cheech's incarceration too easily.

As evening approaches, Anne leaves Marky's office. His secretary reminds him that the Belmont Hotel expects him at seven o'clock. He tells her, "That would be very difficult for me to forget, but thanks for reminding me!"

A little later, the secretary walks back to his bathroom where he is adjusting his tie for his meeting. She tells him that she is leaving for the evening. "I put the folder on your desk, Mr. Marky. It contains every newspaper article, every magazine story on the case and all of the necessary documents and photos we have accumulated since it happened. I also included the substantiated statements made by all parties."

"Good night, Mary, see you in the morning. Tomorrow morning, I want a list of all the verified engagements we have to date and any progress on the radio stations." He puts on his jacket, walks into his office, sits behind the desk and reaches for the folder. He scans the contents and places the folder into his attaché case. A few minutes later, he walks out onto the sidewalk and heads for the Broadway deli and some supper. He rides the subway to the Hotel Belmont and his special guest. He enters the ballroom and sits in the back row. Everyone is excited in anticipation of hearing the guest speaker.

The master of ceremonies approaches the podium and makes an announcement. "Ladies and Gentlemen, On behalf of the Hotel Belmont, it is my honor to present the most famous and highly respected lawyer of our times, Clarence Darrow!"

Clarence Darrow comes onto the stage in a thunderous show of affection and applause. He shakes hands with the master of ceremonies and smiles at the audience. The applause continues. Finally, he raises his hands to quiet the audience. He thanks them for a gracious reception. "Thank you all; thank you!" Mr. Darrow speaks for nearly two hours to a quiet and attentive audience. He finishes, thanks the audience again and promises to come back to New York more often. He leaves the stage and steps down to a table to sign autographs. The line is long. Somewhere in the middle is Marky.

Chapter 9

When Marky reaches Clarence Darrow's autograph signing table, he extends his hand and introduces himself. "Mr. Darrow, my name is Alexander Marky."

Darrow's welcoming smile is genuine, "I'm pleased to meet you Mr. Marky! We need to talk about something very important. My backstage people will let you into my dressing room to wait; they're expecting you."

Surprised and a bit confused by Darrow's reaction, Marky thanks him and heads back stage. He walks up to two men and introduces himself, "My name is Alexander Marky. I'm here to speak to Mr. Darrow."

One of the men checks his clipboard. "It's good, let him in."

Marky takes a seat to wait. He wonders how much Darrow already knows about the case. He suspects someone set the meeting up ahead of time. After a long wait, Clarence Darrow steps in. "Alexander, please come to my room with me so we can talk. I must speak to you before I return to Chicago."

"Of course Mr. Darrow, it's no problem, my pleasure."
Darrow tells him, "It's going to take some time."

Marky wonders how much Darrow knows. He strongly suspects that the famous lawyer came here for the sole purpose of defending Cheech, and the speech he made was the prop to bring about this chance meeting. After speaking to the two men guarding his room, Clarence Darrow turns to Marky and says, "Come with me, Alexander. We'll do some serious talking."

Marky grabs his hat, cane and attaché case and follows, a look of confusion on his face. He feels like a fly caught in a web, as though he is not initiating the meeting. He wonders whether this secret meeting between them is really so secret.

The famous lawyer sees Marky's concern. "Don't worry, Alexander, I guess they didn't explain too much about this meeting. I will explain as much as I can. You tell me what you know about this case. I will stop you from asking the wrong questions."

Darrow leads the way to the elevator. Marky and the two guards enter with him. They head for a room on the third floor. Once inside, Darrow takes his jacket off, loosens his tie. He tells the men to brew a big pot of coffee. "Alexander, it's going to be a long night. Take your jacket and tie off. Just relax. Try not to leave anything out." Marky starts by taking the folder out of his case. "Just leave the folder on the table; I'll have plenty of time to look at it on the train when I head back home. For now, I want you to tell me everything you know about Francesco Caruso and how this case has evolved from the start."

Marky is a little nervous; he still does not understand the turn of things since he shook Clarence Darrow's hand earlier. "Well, his name is Francesco Caruso. He's thirty-five-years-old, been married for twelve years. In the last three months, he lost two of his children, pneumonia for the baby girl and an overdose of medicine for his little boy who was ill with Diphtheria. He's a man who, despite his lack of schooling at Sicily where he was born, seems to be very responsible, dedicated and enormously deliberate. He's charming, personable and extremely talented as an artist, singer and dancer. Adults and children love him. People in his neighborhood respect him. He has apparently taken on the role of neighborhood mediator. Whenever a dispute of any kind occurs, people go to him rather than the authorities. Shortly after he arrived in America, he befriended a network of people in powerful places to assist him in getting things done at an escalated speed. Although I have yet to meet the man, I feel that I know him. Apparently, he has that affect on those who meet him. I met his wife, her family and her children, as well as some of Cheech's friends; he like's to be called Cheech by his friends. I have yet to meet a person who really knows him who doesn't like, love, admire or respect him. He is truly an unusual man.

One of the guards brings in the coffee pot, cups and spoons. The other places cream and sugar on the table. They leave and Darrow pours the coffee. Once they have a few sips, Darrow says, "Please, go on."

"Because of a number of tragedies back at Sicily, most assuredly the death of his father whom he feels responsible for, he abandoned his family and country and came to America in 1911. He was married in 1917. Their second born was a blonde haired blue-eyed boy. Because of the strong resemblance to his father, he named him Joseph, after the boy's grandfather. A couple of months ago, Joseph, or Joey as they called him, became ill with diphtheria. Someone put a quarantine sign on the Caruso apartment door, but no medical person came to help the child. Joey got much worse, so Cheech broke the quarantine to find a doctor for him. Through a neighborhood Pharmacist, Mr. Joseph Pendola, he found a doctor. It was Saturday, so he had to accept the pharmacist's offer to get his brother who was a doctor. He went home to prepare. The doctor arrived, gave the child a shot and sent Cheech to his brother's pharmacy to have a prescription filled. The pharmacist told Cheech that it was too strong for a child, that his brother should not do things like this. He did fill the prescription. Cheech ran back to the apartment. The doctor was still there, so he told him what his brother said about the medicine. The doctor was indignant. He told Cheech that his brother should mind his own business; he was *not* a doctor. He went ahead and gave the medicine to Joey, and then he left saying that he would be back the next day at about ten o'clock in the morning. Joey immediately got worse. After his parents cared for him all night, he was so sick the next morning that Cheech broke the quarantine again to find another doctor, to no avail. He returned after his futile search to find his child dying. A little while later, he died in his father's arms. This is the account told to me by Maria. According to her, the death of Joey turned Cheech into a different man, changed. Maria, who went through it with Cheech, was unaware of just how much Joey's death affected him. She was not aware that she also changed; therefore, she didn't recognize the change in Cheech."

Marky pauses to accept a refill of coffee. He stirs a little cream into it, takes a few sips and continues. "Joey's body was removed about ten-thirty that morning. The Caruso's wept and talked as they dealt with their grief. About one in the afternoon, the doctor arrived to check on Joey. According to Maria, a confrontation took place after Cheech let the doctor in. Cheech told the doctor Joey was dead. The doctor asked Cheech to step into the bedroom so they could speak privately. Apparently, an argument and fight broke out. When it was over, the doctor was dead. Cheech went into the kitchen to get a knife. He went back to the bedroom and cut the doctors throat. He dragged his body out to the kitchen and dropped it on the spot where Joey died in his arms. Neither Maria nor I know why he took the next course of action, but I will ask him when I do get to meet him. He left the crime scene and went to his brother Rosario's at Staten Island. As he left the crime scene, he told Maria he'd see her in court. It was a deliberate move. He had Rosario call the Brooklyn Raymond Street Station to tell them he would surrender peacefully if Police Sgt. O'Mally accompanied the arresting party."

"Why did he do that?" Darrow asked.

"O'Mally and Cheech are best friends, have been for years. I don't quite understand the tie between the two men, but it's as if they are brothers. With O'Mally's assistance, they took Cheech to the Raymond Street Station."

Marky gives Darrow a direct look to emphasize what he is about to say. "I sat through his entire trial, never in my life saw anything like it. No one cared about anything Cheech said. He knew it, so he stopped defending his actions. It made no difference anyway because he wants to die. The judge, the prosecutor, the court-appointed defense attorney, even the jury were all bought and paid for. It took just four days to select a jury, hold a trial and have the jury find him guilty of first-degree murder. It was the most brazen, arrogant and deliberate disrespect for the law I was ever witness too. Some one called the Carusos and told them when to be in court for the trial . . . appropriately, one day late. I cannot say for sure, that at the national level, the AMA supports and condones the actions by its subordinates in this case, but with all of the publicity, they most assuredly know what's going on. There is a concerted effort to make sure that the public realizes that the doctor's safety is primary, to the extent they would willingly electrocute a man who was clearly distraught and out of his mind at the time of the killing. I come to you in hopes that you will help me in my effort to reverse his conviction. Mr. Voss, his court appointed attorney, has already filed for an appeal. I want the most qualified person available to represent Mr. Caruso in this travesty of justice. I'd like to think that your appearance and speech here at New York is by chance and a special omen of things to come. I've had the feeling from the very start that you were expecting to be asked. I'm not at all sure it is necessary."

Clarence Darrow lifts and sips his coffee and looks over his glasses at Marky. "Mr. Marky, I didn't ask on what authority you made it your business to attend the trial and set up a defense fund for Francesco Caruso; it isn't necessary for me to know. Neither is it necessary for you to know why I choose to take on this case. I assure you my being here is not an omen. All you need to know are the type of cases I defend. Usually they are cases other attorneys don't want. Many involve the poor and working people of this country who live from day-to-day, from check-to-check. There are so many obstacles that poor people have to deal with. It would surprise me if you ever thought that I would accept simply because you asked. Money is not necessary; I will defend Caruso free of charge. When I return to New York, I want to meet with Sergeant O'Mally."

"Mr. Darrow, consider it done! Thank you, Sir! Thank you."

Darrow stands and tells Marky, "So be it then. We have a deal. Voss has to go after he brings about the appeal. In the next week, an attorney by the name of Schneider will offer to assist us; accept it. I have no license to practice law in the state of New York, so he will lead the fight. I will direct it. Avoid any unnecessary publicity about me entering the case until it is absolutely necessary."

Marky stands and shakes Darrow's hand. "Thank you, Sir, no matter what your motive or involvement, I thank you. I will leave you now. Rest assured I will keep your decision secret until I speak with you about the announcement of your acceptance." Later, as he sits on the subway car, he glances at his right hand and murmurs to himself, "I shook hands with the great Clarence Darrow." He thinks about how little he knows about the involvement of so many people in this unusual case that captured the attention of the tri-state area. He wonders about his own involvement. His thoughts send him back in time to when it all started for him.

In the field of show business, for anyone to be successful be it a producer, playwright, actor, singer or even agent, a strict chain of command is always enforced. Breaking that chain can lead to blackballing and the ruination of a career. In the world of the "Great White Way", it is even tougher. The Mafia, not well known at this time, wheels an enormous amount of power in the field of entertainment. Most entertainers and business people in the field of entertainment, including Marky, are unaware of the mob's hold on the entertainment world. When people suspect something sinister, they pass it off as, "the powers that be." It is a reference not often used that refers to a small group of business people who control what will and will not be allowed to debut on Broadway's theaters. They are the authority that guides entertainment business.

As he rides the subway, Marky is still lost in his past. He remembers a phone conversation that began with his secretary. "Hello, this is the Alexander Marky Agency, how may I help you?"

"Little Lady, may I speak to Mr. Alexander Marky please?" Mary inquires, "May I ask who's calling and what your business is?"

After a pause, the man clears his throat. "No, you may not. However, if you feel it necessary, I would be more than willing to make a personal appearance at your desk."

It takes Mary off guard. "No, Sir, that won't be necessary. Please wait." Rattled and a bit confused, she walks into Marky's office and tells him about the man on the phone. He assures her its okay. She returns to her desk and picks up the receiver. "Sir, I'm connecting you right now."

"Thank you, Hon; have a nice day."

Marky answers. "Hello this is Mr. Marky!"

"Hello, Mr. Marky, this is Mr. Zigfeld. I understand you have several clients participating in my theaters." He mentions names and play titles.

Marky is amazed that Mr. Zigfeld called him. "Yes, Sir, that's correct; what can I do for you?"

"I have a favor to ask of you. I'm sure you heard about the murder of a doctor in Brooklyn. The accused is going to trial. I want you to sit in attendance at the trial that starts in four days. When the trial is over, I want you to set up a fund in his name for his appeal and re-trial. The fund covers all expenses. Clarence Darrow, the world famous attorney from Chicago, is giving a speech in Manhattan at the Hotel Belmont. You are to meet with him after the speech to request his assistance in the second trial. When you do what I ask of you, you will enjoy years of prosperity on Broadway. I thank you, Sir. I will not speak to you again. Have a nice day." With a click, the man is gone.

He leans back on his chair to go over the conversation again in his mind. Mary is looking into his office hoping for some kind of explanation. After a bit, he calls, "Mary, come in here please."

She hurries into his office and sits down. "Are you going to tell me what just happened? That man scared the hell out of me."

"Have you heard about an Italian guy from Brooklyn who killed a doctor over the death of his son? It's been in all the papers?"

"Yes, Mr. Marky, I did! It was terrible!"

"From now on, I want you to buy and keep every story, every article on the case. Outside of important business that can't be dismissed or delayed, that is what we will work on until it's over. We're involved in this story. I've heard of this happening to other people on Broadway and other places in show business, but this is the first time it's happened to me. Someone asked me to help the murderer. I intend to do as asked. You'll never believe who that was on the phone just now! It was none other than Florence Zigfeld. I will do it. When it's over, we're on easy street."

Mary eyes him, a confused look on her face. "Mr. Marky, I'm afraid I don't understand."

"I've just been asked to render my services to assist this man at Brooklyn by someone very powerful. I know he can make or break me. I've been assured that I will be well taken care of for complying. Don't ask any questions right now. Will you help me?"

"Of course I will, Mr. Marky."

"One more thing, Mary, Clarence Darrow is coming to the Hotel Belmont to give a speech. I must meet with him after the speech. Please call the hotel and ask when he will be there."

"Wow, Mr. Marky, Clarence Darrow the Chicago Lawyer? I can't believe it!"

"Neither can I. Call the court house and find out when the trial starts."

Jarred out of his reverie by the subway car screeching to a stop, Marky leaves the train. He walks to his office and collapses on a couch in the back room, too tired to drive home.

* * *

Maria's brother Louis drives Rosario to the Sing Sing prison. Rosario decided he should be the one too tell Cheech about the death of his daughter Ida. They show their identification at the gate. The guard places a call and gives them directions to the warden's office. Louis waits in the car.

The warden welcomes Rosario. "Mr. Caruso, come in. Please be seated." He shakes Rosario's hand. "I'm Warden Lawes; what can I do for you, Mr. Caruso?"

"Thank you, Mr. Lawes. I would like to speak to my brother Francesco. I have some bad news. His wife thought it would be best that I should tell him. His baby girl Ida died two days ago of pneumonia."

Taken aback by the announcement, Lawes sits back in his chair with a pained expression. "When is it going to stop? This is terrible. Please wait." He tells a guard to bring Cheech to his office.

The guard enters the locked area and stops in front of the cell holding Cheech. "Cheech, come on, the warden wants to speak to you." As they approach the warden's door, he tells Cheech, "I'll wait for you out here. Knock on the door and go in."

Cheech enters the office. The first person he sees is Rosario. Cheech is displeased by the presence of his brother, but he doesn't let on to the warden.

Rosario stands and the two brothers embrace. The warden says, "Cheech, your brother has news from home."

"Cheech, I have some bad news for you. Maria asked me to come and speak to you in person. Two days ago, little Ida died of pneumonia. She died at home with Maria and the Privetera's taking care of her. I'm so sorry, Cheech."

Cheech closes his eyes, as the tears roll down his cheeks. Warden Lawes tells him, "Cheech, sit down." He sits placing his head in his hands and cries softly.

Rosario takes a tiny hand-knitted infant sock from his pocket, one of Ida's. "Cheech, Maria wanted you to have this." He asks the warden, "May I give this to him?"

"Of course you may."

Cheech wipes his eyes and takes the tiny sock in his huge hands. He holds it against his cheek and smells it. His agonizing cry causes the guard to look in. Warden Lawes signals that all is fine and tells him to close the door.

Cheech gains some control. "You see why I want to die? No matter what I do or where I go, I cause death. Now I lost two children. *Basta*, enough, that's it, no more!"

"You had nothing to do with Joey's death or Ida's," Rosario says. "Maria was afraid they would kill her at the hospital when they found out she was your daughter. She asked her parents to help take care of her at home, and they agreed. They preferred that the baby die at home with them than with doctors and nurses at a hospital who wanted her father dead! It isn't your fault!"

Warden Lawes shakes his head. "Jesus Christ, when will this all stop? Cheech, listen to me. This isn't only your loss. They were your wife's children too. You lost your son because a representative of the medical community screwed up. Because the medical community is making an unjust example of you for making him pay, they put fear into the hearts of your family. That is what brought about the death of your baby girl. If your wife needs one thing right now, it is *you*. Only the two of you understand the pain you have been through as a family. You owe it to your wife to fight for your life. As long as you're here with me, I will *not* allow you to give up. I told you that you do not belong here . . . and you don't. You *will* win on appeal of your sentence. And you *will* be returned to your family."

Rosario looks at the warden in complete surprise, "Thank you, Mr. Lawes. I thank you very much for my brother and his family. Thank you."

Cheech asks, "Warden, is there any chance that I can attend Ida's funeral?"

The warden walks to the back of his desk, "I promise to do what I can to help you attend her funeral, but I must tell you now, the only one who can authorize it is the governor, and he believes you deserve the verdict and the death penalty."

"I would appreciate you trying, Sir." He clutches the little sock. "Please, Sir."

Rosario says, "I almost forgot to tell you Cheech. Soon you will have a new lawyer fighting for you. Louie told me that Mr. Marky, the man running your defense fund, spoke to Clarence Darrow. He agreed to represent you. Clarence Darrow is a special man in America!"

Warden Lawes smiles and says, "Do you know what this means, Cheech? You'll be a free man soon."

Not knowing about Darrow, and unimpressed Cheech shrugs his shoulders. "I need to be alone." He thanks Rosario for coming. The guard escorts him to his cell.

Warden Lawes asks Rosario to stay for a moment after Cheech leaves. He closes the door and turns to Rosario, "Don't expect Cheech to be in attendance at his daughter's funeral. I'll try. If the governor approves it, I'll notify you and you can let the family know. If you don't hear from me in the next twenty-four hours, it didn't happen."

"Thank you, Warden Lawes, I won't say anything unless I hear from you. Thank you again. You're a good man. My brother is lucky." On the way back home, Rosario tells Louis about his meeting with Cheech and the warden, but does not bring up the possibility of Cheech attending the funeral. Louis drops Rosario off at Staten Island. Then he drives to Fort Lee to tell the family about the meeting between Lawes, Cheech and Rosario.

* * *

The warden picks up his phone. A voice says, "Hello, Warden Lawes, this is an aide of Governor Smith. I'm sorry to tell you that the governor denied permission for Francesco Caruso to leave his cell on death row for the funeral of a family member."

The warden acknowledges with a thank you and hangs up the phone. He heads to Cheech's cell to tell him the news in person.

Chapter 10

Despite Marky's best efforts to keep the fact that Clarence Darrow will be joining the Caruso defense team secret, whispers and stories abound in the New York area. Soon, the New York Chapter of the AMA catches wind of it. Since the conviction of first-degree murder, the representatives of the medical community are quiet. Now, they are more concerned and vocal with the rumor of Darrow's possible involvement. The once arrogantly confident medical community knows a new trial is possible with Darrow's help. They set up an accelerated effort to thwart that possibility. At meetings and medical conferences, representative speakers express their views and defend the ruling of the court. Administrators, doctors and nurses give speeches in defense of their stand in the matter. Hospital bulletins post notices and speeches. The AMA posts their opinions on buildings, telephone poles and bulletin boards along the roads, exhibited in a manner befitting a powerful and wealthy profession to support their view.

The first of Alexander Marky's scheduled meetings takes place at the famous Pennsylvania Hotel. In the next few months, there will be many gatherings on behalf of Cheech. Friends and people, who have followed the story, come from all of the boroughs of New York, from New Jersey and from Connecticut.

Posters and painted signs appear everywhere due to the efforts of the Marky organization, and from the many people who know Cheech or those he helped.

Italian groups are involved. These include the Italian-American Club of New York and other Italian-American groups such as merchant's organizations and lawyer groups. The New York chapter of the Italian-American Lawyers Association runs stories and articles in newspapers, magazines and Journals. Their involvement is for special reasons. It is mostly to support Francesco Caruso. The death of an Italian by an Italian is a sensitive issue to them. They try to determine how such a terrible crime in an Italian community could take place. They especially fault the court system for the mockery and travesty of justice in the first trial. They campaign for a new trial with every benefit allowed by law for the condemned man. People who do not know Cheech give corner speeches on his behalf. The AMA feels the force and power of the public uproar against injustice. The strength of the Italian neighborhoods is a force they cannot deny.

Officially, the news of Clarence Darrow's involvement in Cheech's case became public information when the May 18, 1927 issue of the New York Times printed it. In homes, neighborhoods and organizations in Italian communities around the city, people are both joyous and sad at the wording of the headline. Some think both families involved suffered enough. Another death adds to the tragic story. The headlines read:

Darrow to Plead for Caruso, Doctor's Killer

Another Child of Convicted Man Dies

Clarence Darrow, the Chicago defense lawyer, will serve gratis in appealing the conviction of Francesco Caruso.

Alexander Marky, the New York chair of the Caruso Defense Fund, persuaded Clarence Darrow to represent Caruso should a new trial be set from his appeal.

* * *

The people who support Cheech are excited and hopeful. Marky is upset because he did not want the news released so soon. The medical community and the AMA are angry.

Cheech's court appointed lawyer, Mr. Voss, is upset and angry. He states publicly that he accepts Darrow's involvement. He tells the newspapers that Mr. Darrow is not a New York licensed attorney, and that he will not be able to take over the case. Voss goes on to say that, he and attorney Price have been with the Caruso case from the start; they will be with it when the court of appeals makes its decision. Voss says in his public statement, "If Clarence Darrow wants to come into court and sit with us, we don't mind. I don't know what Mr. Darrow can do to aid Caruso. He admitted that he does not have a license to practice law in the state of New York and would have to obtain permission from the court to appear on Caruso's behalf. The court appointed Mr. Price and I to represent Caruso in an appeal. I wish people who want so much to help

Caruso would speak to *us* before they make statements and decisions on their own. Governor Smith stated that he will not listen to any organization or individual until the court of appeals makes their decision in this matter."

Marky responds to Voss's stinging attack by issuing one of his own. He calls the New York Times and tells them, "I am extremely happy that I was able to get the great Clarence Darrow, who just retired from his legal practice, to come to Caruso's defense. The Caruso Defense Fund is solely interested in two things. They are to find the very best representation for the condemned man, who in my opinion did not get a fair deal at his trial. The other is to help his destitute family until there is a final resolution to this matter. We now want Francesco Caruso released from prison a free man. He suffered enough! The legal system and medical community wronged him. He just lost another child because his wife was afraid to take the child to a hospital. Enough is enough." After talking to the reporter, he hangs up the phone and sits back in his chair, pleased by the events of late.

* * *

At the home of Maria's parents, Mrs. Snyder is helping the family deal with Ida's death. The McNally Funeral Home in Fort Lee, New Jersey handles the viewing and funeral services of the baby. Mrs. Snyder is the only non-family member there. She reports to the newspapers on the funeral, purposefully kept quiet until after the burial, that the Caruso Defense Fund covered the funeral expenses of the Caruso's baby daughter.

* * *

Marky is at work on Friday morning May 20 when the phone rings. Mary answers. A woman says, "This is the Governor's office. May I speak to Mr. Marky?"

Mary transfers the call and calls out, "Mr. Marky, the Governors office is on the phone."

"Hello, Alexander Marky here. What can I do for you?"

"Mr. Marky, Governor Smith would like to meet with you regarding the Caruso case. Would you be available for a meeting on Monday at 1:30 in the afternoon?"

Marky hesitates for a moment, "That will be fine."

"Fine, I'll tell the Governor that you'll be here on Monday at 1:30 in the afternoon. Thank you, Sir."

Before Marky can respond, she hangs up. He walks out to Mary's desk smiling and shaking his head, "Can you believe that? First, I get to meet the greatest lawyer in the world. Then I get the attention of the Governor of New York. Could the president be far behind? The meeting is Monday at half past one. Don't forget to remind me.

* * *

Cracking the door open, the governor's secretary looks in and says, "Governor, Mr. Marky is here. Shall I send him in?"

"Give me five minutes; then send him in."

A few minutes later, she says, "Mr. Marky, you may go into Governor Smith's office now." She points, "You'll find it down the hall, first door on your left."

The governor greets Marky with a handshake. "Come in, Mr. Marky; please sit down." The Governor sits at his desk and begins the conversation. "It's nice to meet you."

"The honor is mine, Sir."

"We're working to the same end, Mr. Marky; I believe we should become familiar with each other since there will be times we will consult one another. An open door policy is the best way to go. From now on, when there is a need, you will have my personal phone number and I shall have yours."

Marky doesn't respond, unsure where this conversation is going. He sits quietly listening to the Governor.

"With deep regret, I just didn't know all of the facts on the Caruso case prior to the burial of his second child. Although highly unusual, if I had, I would have permitted him to attend his daughter's funeral. Yesterday, I received a number of very informative calls. They made all the difference in the world to me. Do you understand what I'm saying?"

"I believe we both do, but we don't quite understand what is at work here. For the longest time, I wasn't completely sure of it, but as this case precedes, it is more and more apparent that there are powerful forces at work here that neither of us has any idea of or should question. At first, I had many questions, but soon figured out it isn't necessary to ask. For me, I find it best to listen. I sat through the whole trial and saw what they did to this man. I've become personally involved with his family and have come to meet many people I never thought I would ever meet, much less get to know. So it is with great pleasure that I place your name on that list."

The governor leans back in his chair, "Mr. Marky, we will *not* meet again, but you will need my services until this case is settled. For that reason, I have designated one of my aids to be my contact for you. There are things you will need from this office. He will take care of your needs. Publicly, you are not to listen to anything that comes out of this office or take any statement I make seriously. Just ignore it. The next time you talk to Clarence Darrow, please have him contact me. At my intervention, the former New York Deputy Attorney General Charles A. Schneider will replace Mr. Voss. This is not public knowledge and won't be until early in June. The new defense team will be Schneider, Spellman, Pollak and Darrow."

As happened so many times before, Marky feels as though he is but a small part of this effort to free Cheech. He feels as though the ground is moving under him and he is just along for the ride.

The Governor continues, "This is a slow process. It will take time. Once the appeal is won, time is on our side and Caruso is on his way home. Do you have any questions on the matter?"

"No, I've learned not to ask, just listen."

"Very well then, I guess we're finished, Mr. Marky."

Marky stands to shake hands with the Governor, "Governor, if you care to see a Broadway play from a special seat, perhaps you and your family, call me, and I will make arrangements."

"Thank you, Mr. Marky; I will take you up on that after we are finished. In the meantime, as you leave, stop by the reception desk. My Secretary will give you an envelope with information in it that you will need in the near future. It's been a pleasure meeting you."

* * *

As Marky drives back to Manhattan from Albany, he can't help but look back on events since he first received the telephone call asking that he be in attendance at the Kings County Court house for the trial of Francesco Caruso.

His reminiscing leads him to the voice of an old friend speaking to him on the telephone, a man who has become one of the three most powerful people on the Broadway scene. He thinks of his old friend, the friend he grew up with, his childhood best friend. He thinks back to a time when they were young men, yet old enough to fight in the First World War. He hears his friend say, "I'm not going to die in some foreign country with my face in the mud. That is not part of the plan. That is for fools to do and for politicians to justify. I've got news for you. You're not doing it either. I won't let you do it. I'll kick the shit out of you first. We have things to do!"

As birds of a feather flock together, so it would seem do draft dodgers and deserters. Before Cheech's trial is over, Marky will discover that Cheech, feeling abandoned by life, not only left his homeland and family behind, but in the process became a deserter from the Sicilian army. He left without completing his service obligation of fifteen years. He served only up to the time when he left for America, for a fresh start. A fresh start was not in the cards. His father's face tortured him, even in his new country. His son Joey reminded him so much of his father that his eyes would mist sometimes when he looked at him.

* * *

It is the middle of May and a search is on for a new home for Maria and the children. Mr. Marky prefers a place in Manhattan so Maria will be closer to the activities surrounding the appeal. He knows Maria will miss her parents being around, but he believes it is necessary. Mrs. Snyder, often accompanied by Mary, does most of the looking.

* * *

On Wednesday, May 25, Marky and local politicians officially begin the campaign to save Cheech with speaking engagements.

Maria makes her very first appearance in public at a gathering at the Hotel Pennsylvania. She will not speak, but her presence will show support for Cheech. Her oldest daughter Lena accompanies her. In the months ahead, Lena pleads for her father many times. With Joey gone, Lena, the oldest of the six Caruso children and most like her father, is brave as she stands alone. She is now and will always be the strong one in the family, the one who goes face-to-face with her strong-willed father, the only one who can alter his opinion. She will be the only one he turns to. She found a special strength when, as a child of eight, she felt and dealt with the traumatic and violent deaths of Joey and Dr. Pendola. Lena defends Cheech more than anyone else including Maria who loves

Cheech, perhaps more than her own life. It is unfortunate for Lena that she is both intelligent and a beautiful child. She is the one that Marky exploits for the most beneficial result. She does everything he asks of her without complaint, even though she hates it.

Marky's job is tough. He is compelled to defend a convicted murderer with a wife that can barely speak English. He must work with a child who may not be reliable when the lights go on and the applause starts.

* * *

Maria arrives in this country in 1913 with her family. Her Father, Pepi Privitera, is an *Carabinieri*, Italian for a police officer on horseback. He is a handsome man and quite dapper in presence. In order to survive at this time, a police officer in Sicily must be willing, on occasion, to turn his back on certain things or deal with unusual happenings. By choice or not, most are associated with the Mafia or at least know about it and the people who are.

Grandma's family, the Perticone's, are a well-to-do family. They have enough land and wealth to demand how they want their children to live and what kind of work they will spend their lives doing. Some of grandma's older brothers are involved in local politics.

When Maria's parents first meet, neither one can stay away from the other. The Perticone family is very much against their daughter marrying a poor police officer. They warn her they will disown her if she marries him. She marries him anyway. Years later, with four children and no hope of winning the favor of the Perticone family back, they make a new life in America.

The plan is for Pepi to go first and earn enough money to bring the family to America. The voyage is very expensive for six family members. Almost immediately upon coming through the gates of Ellis Island, Pepi is on his way to Argentina. He stays in Argentina for little more than a year. He sends money to Annette in Sicily after a month or so. The exodus from Sicily begins. The boy Louis comes first. Annette and her daughters, Maria, Josephina and Florence, follow him. As soon as he has enough money, Pepi returns to America from Argentina to be with his family.

Back in Sicily, Maria leaves a young man she plans to marry. They have known one another since childhood. Maria is very upset about leaving Sicily for America. She is so sad that, early on, she refuses to leave Sicily with her family. She asks that her intended come with them.

The Privitera's refuse her request. Maria asks to stay in Sicily. They deny that request as well. Her grandparents insist she accompany her family to America. When her intended says he will not leave Sicily with her, she reluctantly gives in to the family's wishes. Broken hearted, she gives up all hopes of marrying and having a family. She also gives up her dream to be a teacher.

Louis, upon arriving in America works as a ditch digger. At night, he takes up ballroom dancing. He very quickly finds his perfect dance partner and soul mate. By 1927, he and his wife are world-renown tango specialists and an all around excellent ballroom dance team. They tour the states and many foreign countries dancing for the court of King Ferdinand and other national leaders. Upon retiring from the world stage, Louis instructs at the Terpsichore School in Manhattan, New York.

In 1915, Dad and Mom meet . . . not by chance. Pepi sets up the meeting without Maria's or Annette's knowledge or consent. Pepi is impressed with Cheech. He wants him as a son-in-law. He knows Josephina is the one who interests Cheech, but he wants Cheech to marry his oldest daughter Maria. He believes Cheech is the one man capable of making Maria forget her lost love. Annette takes an instant dislike to Cheech. She has some of that same stubborn and unforgiving pride that her parents showed when she chose to marry Pepi. Her opinion of Cheech is unwavering throughout her life. The only time the two enjoy each other is when Cheech sings and dances. Music from home is not common here at America. However, when the music ceases, Annette expects him to be subordinate to her; he obliges. This quality endears Lena to him. More like grandma than her own father, Lena administers. She is the one who gets things done; the one everyone calls first no matter what the problem. Marky recognizes this quality in Lena almost from the start . . . long before Cheech.

* * *

The middle of May finds Mrs. Snyder at Fort Lee more frequently to complete their work. Maria and the children prepare for the upcoming defense. The public must be informed because they only know what the press and radio have sensationalized for their own purpose. Mrs. Snyder is warmly welcomed. Italians offer their hospitality in a demonstrative manner. As a friend, she accepts it as they intend. She takes Maria shopping for a black dress, shoes, veil and hat. Upon returning, she coaches Maria on what to say, how to speak and how she is to present herself. Mrs. Snyder tells Maria she must appear destitute. This is what Maria dreads the most. Maria and Annette have a lot of pride. Annette sees her strong daughter swallow her pride and face shame, in her opinion, for the love of a man Annette doubts loves her.

* * *

Back on death row, Cheech continues his reading and writing lessons. He respects the warden. Warden Lawes meets with him several times weekly. Occasionally he brings Cheech treats from his wife. He impresses on Cheech who and what he has to live for. It does affect Cheech. The warden understands the many sad events in Cheech's life affect him, but he believes Cheech must be encouraged to understand that life is worth living. He sees in Cheech a strong change in attitude and a willingness to work very hard to learn how to read and write English.

His presence affects the guards as well. They see how gentle and sincere he can be. Some of them come in on their own time to help him with the lessons. Occasionally, they give him a cigarette or bring him a pack or carton. Cheech influences the guards on death row to look at their job differently. The warden is and always was popular with the guards and prisoners since he took the job. He is destined to be the most popular warden in Sing Sing Prison's history.

* * *

The date is May 25, 1927, and although Marky releases stories and statements to the press since the end of the trial, last night marks the official kickoff of the campaign to save Cheech's life. The New York Times article read:

One-Hundred Attend Meeting of Defense Committee Aid for Family of Condemned Man

The friends of the slayer of Dr. Casper S. Pendola will not be content to have him freed from the death house at Sing Sing Prison. There will be a concerted effort to have him freed entirely," said Alexander Marky while speaking to a group of over 100 friends and associates of Francesco

Caruso last night at the Hotel Pennsylvania. They gathered to protest the impending electrocution set for the first week in June.

* * *

Among the guests are friends and relatives of Cheech. Sergeant William O'Mally, O'Hanlon and his teenage daughter who testified at Cheech's trial are also there. Friends from the Italian Club of Brooklyn showed up. Merchants include Franco the bread man, the owners of the vegetable stand and even the iceman. Many of the people do not know Cheech, while others enjoyed his singing and dancing.

Maria, heavily veiled and dressed in black, is there with Lena and Mrs. Snyder. Although she is there, she does not speak to the group. Marky brings her to the attention of the people. He asks her to walk around shaking hands so that the people in attendance will see her there supporting Cheech. She waves and smiles at the many people she recognizes. After she sits, Marky speaks:

"Lady's and Gentlemen, my name is Alexander Marky. I will start the evening by giving you some background and some updates in this sad episode. Many of you in the audience knew Joey Caruso. He was six-years-old when he died last February 13, a Sunday morning. He was ill for about three weeks with a nasty cold that turned into a sore throat and eventually into Diphtheria. Although someone quarantined the Caruso apartment, no medical person came to help Joey. He became critical. His father broke the quarantine to find help for his little boy.

He stopped in the neighborhood pharmacy owned by Joseph Pendola. The pharmacist called his brother from long Island who was a doctor. The doctor came to the Caruso flat, gave Joey a shot and sent his father to the pharmacy for a prescription. The pharmacist told Caruso it was too strong for a child; however, he filled it. The doctor later told Caruso the pharmacist didn't know what the hell he was talking about. He gave Joey the medicine and left, said he would return the next day at three o'clock in the afternoon. The Caruso's were up all night with their son. The next day, Caruso broke the quarantine again to find another doctor. He had no luck, so he returned. Joey died in his father's arms saying to his father, "Please Papa, don't let me die, the doctor is killing me with that shot!" He closed his eyes never to open them again.

"At about one o'clock that afternoon and after the little body of Joseph was removed by the medical examiner, the doctor arrived.

Francesco was still in a state of shock and temporary insanity from the death of his little boy. They exchanged words and a fight broke out. The doctor's body was in the same room that witnessed little Joey's death.

"The quarantine sign on the Caruso flat disappeared. Professionals in the medical field testified during the trial that the quarantine was never there. It was obvious during the trial that no one paid attention to any of the testimony by the defense. The judge and everyone else intended to make an example of Francesco Caruso.

"The AMA influenced that court. Doctor and nurse groups supported the actions of the court. It mattered not that the doctor may have made a terrible mistake—it mattered not that the doctor could have been negligent—it mattered not that this poor man's son died in his arms—it mattered not that he was out of his mind with grief. They want Francesco Caruso electrocuted primarily to protect doctors who make home calls and out of loyalty to one of their own. I sat through the entire trial. Never did I see a sadder case of justice in my life, a kangaroo court. Doctors are supposed to save lives . . . not take them. What happened to the Hippocratic Oath? What is it worth now? Caruso does not want to fight this unwarranted decision because he feels he has nothing to live for.

"I ask you to consider and compare the Snyder-Gray convictions with Caruso's conviction. Snyder and Gray plotted to murder Mr. Snyder. They received the death sentence for a cold-blooded, calculated, premeditated killing, rightly so! Francesco Caruso received the same death penalty for a killing that, to this day, he cannot fully explain. To this day, he cannot explain why he murdered Doctor Casper S, Pendola. How can these cases extract the same penalty of death? I ask you, every man and every woman in this room, to think about that. How can you compare the two cases? There is another comparison. That is the case of Leopold and Loeb. Leopold and his friend Loeb took it upon themselves one night to kill a young boy just to know how it felt to kill someone. They were curious about how if would feel to take someone's life! They planned it and carried out their dastardly deed. Yet they received a lesser sentence than Francesco Caruso for a more calculated and premeditated murder.

Where is the justice? There is no justice in Caruso's case. Would he be sitting on death row if he had the wealth that Leopold and Loeb had? Well, good people, you the friends of Francesco Caruso, and those who believe in justice, can balance the scale of justice tonight. He needs the support of all of you, his long time friends. Remember the times he spoke for you and your families. For the times you enjoyed his music."

Marky pauses to drink from a glass of water on the podium. "There is one more thing you should know before I let you go. Although the law does not consider it a murder, a death occurred as a direct result of the medical community's actions against Caruso. They will not pay the penalty. Less than two weeks ago, the Carusos lost their four-month-old Ida to pneumonia. Why did she die of Pneumonia? Mrs. Caruso, Maria, was terrified to leave her baby in the hands of another doctor who would have control of her, especially knowing how the medical community is campaigning for the execution of her husband. She and her family treated the baby at home and the child succumbed to the illness. This happened because she lost all trust and faith in the medical community. What in the hell has happened to us? What have we come to when an organization will willingly sacrifice a man's life with cold disregard for the circumstances that surrounded the death of one of their own? When a mother fears for her child's life in the care of a licensed hospital? May God have mercy on us. Organize your neighbors and friends. Help us help Caruso. We need your financial support. It is up to you his friends and neighbors. I cannot stress it enough; Francesco Caruso's life is in our hands. Good night, Lady's and Gentlemen, thank you for coming."

The room is silent as Alexander Marky leaves the stage and approaches Maria. "Maria," he whispers in her ear, "It is started. Everything will be fine. Thank you for coming."

She turns from a tap on her shoulder to see O'Hanlon and his daughter. "I'm so happy to see you, Thank you for taking the time to come." She grasps the daughter's hand and thanks her for her support.

O'Hanlon says, "Maria, I feel so bad for you and Cheech. Do you know if I can send him something?"

Maria thanks him. Marky writes the address down for him on a piece of paper. O'Mally, who was sitting with the O'Hanlons, approaches them. "Mr. Marky, Maria and Lena how are you? Mr. Marky, I wish Cheech could have heard that speech. He should have, he needs it."

Marky says, "Wait until we get him back to Raymond Street, he will hear it."

Maria asks how they are doing. This is the first time since police hauled her away from her flat that Maria has a chance to speak with her neighbors and long time friends. She sometimes weeps for joy because she is so thankful to see them.

O'Hanlon's teenage daughter Florence and Lena enjoy each other's company. The girls have so much to say, they can't talk fast enough, often interrupting each other. In their Brooklyn neighborhood, Florence is the one who walked Lena and Joey back and forth to school three blocks away. Florence tells Lena that all of her friends at school miss her and are always thinking about her. "Lena, can I tell them I was with you and tell them what we spoke about?"

Lena smiles at her friend, "Of course you can! Tell them I asked for them, that I miss them so much."

"I will, Lena; it's so good to see you." They hug. Lena wipes away a tear from Florence's cheek.

Lena misses her Brooklyn neighborhood and her friends. Soon she will have a new neighborhood, new school and new friends.

Chapter 11

The newspapers continue to run stories about the upcoming Caruso appeal. They summarize the events of Joey's death and the murder of the doctor. The scheduled appeal is for late summer or early fall. Rumors spread that Defense attorney Voss will be replaced. He makes statements to the New York press, but they are more subdued than the remarks he did earlier when Clarence Darrow first offered his services. He is no longer, and maybe never was, in favor of his involvement in the case. He tells the press that the appellate court will not rule in favor of a counsel change at this late date. It would be an unjust ruling and would diminish his client's confidence in him.

* * *

Maria does not want to deal with her Brooklyn memories. She asks Marky to find an apartment in Manhattan where she can have some privacy. Finally, an apartment is located in Manhattan. This day, Mrs. Snyder is on her way again, possibly for the last time, to tell Maria and her family that if she likes the apartment, it is available. The superintendent will hold it for her viewing.

"Mrs. Snyder, please come in," Pepi tells her and motions her to sit at the dining room table with the family.

She says, "Maria, I have good news for you. We have an apartment for you to consider on 106th street in Manhattan. We can see it today."

Maria tears up. "Mama, Papa, How am I going to do it alone? I'll be all alone." Maria and her mother cry.

Pepi who understands the situation, turns to Maria and says, "Maria, now you know how Cheech feels. He's been alone since February."

"I know, Papa, I know Cheech is alone; I miss him. I've missed him since he left with the doctor's body lying on my kitchen floor. Maybe I'm just selfish, but I can't help thinking that you and Mama won't be with me anymore."

Pepi hugs her. "My little girl, you have a life. No matter what happens to Cheech, you have to go on. Mama and I are visitors in your life, only visitors. One day, we will leave, but you must be there for your husband

and children. Of all my children, you, Maria, are the strong one. Lena is just like you. You and she will be friends always, even after she marries. Cheech needs you both."

"Thank you, Papa. I love you. Is this the way you won Mama's heart?"

"No, Maria, she won mine. When I rode my horse up to her, it was over for me. I still haven't won her heart after all these years."

Annette scolds, "*Basta*, enough you know better *mi amora*. Don't talk like that!"

Maria gets ready to look at the apartment. Meanwhile, Mrs. Snyder talks to the Privitera's about the progress in the case, and the confidence Mr. Marky has in the upcoming appeal. It lifts their spirits, especially Pepi, who next to Maria misses Cheech the most. It is good news; it renews his hope that his daughter and son-in-law will survive this terrible time in their young lives.

Maria has just a few things from her old flat in Brooklyn. The only things she wants are important papers, photos and the planter in the master bedroom, a gift from her parents. The police confiscated some things for evidence. As her request, O'Hanlon sells and gives away the rest.

In the next few weeks, Mrs. Snyder and Maria shop for furniture for the little apartment. The move affects Lena more than it does Maria. Lena's hope to return to Brooklyn and her old school and classmates is shattered. She knows she will never see them again. She cries on Maria's chest in the new kitchen. "Mama, I'll never see my friends again, Florence and the others, never again."

Maria strokes her daughter's hair. "Lena, what would I do without you? Do you know how much Mama needs you? You are a joy to me. How brave you are. Your grandfather is right. You and your Mama are peas in a pod. No matter where you go in your life, you will have good friends because you are honest and strong. Someday, Mama will take you to visit your old friends in Brooklyn. Would you like that?"

"I don't think so, Mama, thank you . . . well, maybe Florence."

"Lena, I'm so proud of you. I worry about you growing up too fast; I don't want that to happen."

Lena looks at her mother with tears in her eyes, "Mama I won't grow up too fast, I promise you. I won't do that."

Maria gives her a strong hug. "I know you won't, Lena, thank you." She releases her and says, "Lena will you help me? We need to shop for food. Help me get your brother and sisters ready to go out."

"Okay, Mama, I will." Lena straightens herself up and heads for the bedroom where the children are playing. Maria watches her little daughter walk into the bedroom. She knows that Lena will not be the same when this is all over. She makes a pact with herself to make a special place for Lena in her family, a place of honor and respect. She knows it will not be easy; this will scar Lena for life.

* * *

It's June 17, 1927; the newspaper headlines read:

Mrs. Caruso Makes Radio Plea for Aid

Caruso's Daughter begs Court to spare her father from the electric chair

Killing Scene re-enacted

Lawyer, in dialect of doctor's killer, tells of boy's death and the attack.

* * *

Maria adds her voice to the campaign on behalf of Cheech for the first time. Marky arranges for one hour of Radio time at station WGL Manhattan, New York for her and others to ask the public for assistance. Marky begins the broadcast. "Lady's and Gentlemen, most of you know about the murder of Doctor Andrew S. Pendola last February 13, in Brooklyn. Tonight we present the wife of Francesco Caruso. She will tell you about what happened that day last February, a very sad and heart wrenching story. Caruso's eight-year-old daughter Lena will speak to you about what she and her brother and sisters feel about their father and everything that has happened. Charles a. Schneider, the former deputy Attorney General of New York, who volunteered his services, will read a letter written by the condemned man Caruso in his cell at Sing Sings death row. Caruso has been learning how to read and write while on death row. His sentences are short and very touching. Now ladies and gentlemen, I would like to introduce you to a very strong young woman, Mrs. Maria

Caruso the wife of Francesco Caruso." Maria is hesitant, but she walks over to the microphone. Marky say's, "Maria, We know you're not accustomed to speaking to a radio audience. It's okay to be nervous. It's okay if you need to stop. Just say what's in your heart."

Mrs. Snyder worked with Maria on the radio talks. Maria looks around, clears her throat and starts. "I am Maria Caruso the wife of Frank Caruso." In a husky, hesitating voice with a heavy accent she blurts out, "I'm alone all by myself. I lost my little six-year-old boy Joey, gone forever, no more! Last month my four-month-old Ida died." Maria breaks down.

Mrs. Snyder wants to go to her. Marky stops her and says in a low whisper, "No, that's exactly what we want. Watch, she is doing fine, just watch."

Maria gathers herself. "I sorry I cry. Forgive me. My Ida was sick . . . very sick. I was scared to take her to the hospital. I thought a doctor would kill her too. I keep her home to take care of her. I tell God I will never let another of my baby's die by a doctor as long as I live, never again. I keep her home and she die. God, forgive me. God, forgive me. God, help me." She fights the tears. Her shaking, little hands hold her handkerchief in front of the microphone. "I have four children left in my home. They need their father in their life. I need him. I love my husband very much. He is good. I feel terrible for Mrs. Pendola. Everything happened so fast that day. I don't know exactly what happened. That poor man, I am so sorry for his wife." Maria loses control of her emotions. She turns to leave the Microphone, but turns back. She speaks barely above a whisper. "Please help me. Please save my husband. Please help me save what is left of my family. I beg of you. I beg you . . . please."

These are the worst of the words that the beautiful and proud Maria says. It is her nature to be the help giver, the one people turn to for help. This is especially difficult for her, but she knows the consequence if she refuses.

Marky meets her at the microphone and tells her so the radio audience can hear, "Maria, thank you. Mrs. Snyder, please help Maria to her seat." He speaks into the microphone. "Now I want you to meet pretty, little Lena Caruso." Mrs. Snyder brings Lena to the microphone. "Lady's and Gentlemen of the WGL listening audience, it is my honor to introduce you to Caruso's oldest daughter, eight-year-old Lena." He smiles at Lena and says, "Don't be nervous; just speak into the microphone."

"I'm not nervous, Mr. Marky!"

Surprised by her straightforward and positive tone, he say's, "Oh, okay young lady, speak to the nice people listening. They want to hear your voice."

"Hello, I am Lena. I'm eight-years-old. I love my Papa so much. I really miss Papa, and I want him to come back home. My sisters Josie and Anna and my little brother Sal miss Papa too. Please help us. I will never see my brother Joey again in my whole life. My sister Ida is gone too!" Lena turns away and starts crying.

Maria rushes over and hugs her. "Lena, please don't cry; you make mama cry too! Are you finish?"

Lena gathers herself. "No, Mama, I'm not finished." She faces the microphone again and says, "My papa is good. He didn't mean to kill the doctor. He was sick. Papa was sick; he didn't know what he was doing. The doctor did wrong and my little brother died. Joey protected me when we walked to school. I don't have him anymore. I miss him . . . a lot! I need my Papa. Please help us. We need your help. Please help us save Papa. Thank you." She hurries over to Maria. Maria wraps her arms around Lena and they cry together.

Marky snaps back to reality and rushes over to the microphone. "Pardon me for a moment, Lady's and Gentlemen, while we tend to Maria and her little Lena. It will be but a moment." After a short pause, he says, "Lady's and gentlemen, at this time I'd like to present former New York Deputy Attorney General Charles A. Schneider. He will present to you the chain of events that lead to the murder of Doctor Casper S. Pendola. Mr. Schneider, the microphone is yours." Schneider takes the microphone.

"Thank you, Mr. Marky; I'd like to tell you the tragic events that brought about the murder of doctor Pendola. Joseph, the dead boy, was ill for a little over two weeks. A cold turned into a sore throat and Diphtheria. The child took a turn for the worse. Someone posted a quarantine sign on the Caruso's door. The sign came to Frank's attention, the father, when he opened it in the morning to go to work. As soon as he saw the sign, he stepped back into the flat and told his wife of the sign. They both knew that it meant someone would come to tend to the child and they knew they could not leave the flat. They abided by the law. No one came. A week went by; the boy was worse. Frank knew Joey was dying. He broke the quarantine to find a doctor. None was available because it was Saturday, so Doctor Pendola's pharmacist brother called him for Frank. The doctor arrived at the Caruso flat and gave Joey a shot. He sent Frank to his brother's pharmacy to have a prescription filled for the boy.

The pharmacist told Frank that his brother should not do things like that. He said the medicine was too strong for a child. Yet, he gave the medicine to Mr. Caruso anyway. Back at the flat, Frank questioned Doctor Pendola. He told him his brother said the medicine was too strong for Joey. Showing his arrogance, Doctor Pendola told Frank that his brother did not know what he was talking about and that he should mind his own business. Then he gave Joey the medicine. He promised to return the next morning at ten o'clock to check him, and he left. Joey worsened over night and Sunday morning he died in Frank's arms. Before he died he told his daddy, 'Papa, I'm dying please don't let me die. That shot the doctor gave me is killing me. Please help me, I don't want to die.' Frank promised his little boy that he would not let that happen, but it did. Joey breathed his last. Imagine how it would feel to have your child die in your arms. I pray it never happens to me or to any of you.

"Frank sat on the floor and rocked his dead son whom he wrapped in a warm blanket. The morticians found him rocking back and forth. They took Joey away. There was no premeditation on the part of Francesco Caruso. This poor man was out of his mind with grief. To this day, he cannot remember all that happened when he killed the doctor. The quarantine sign on the door disappeared after the murder. No one in authority will tell you it was there. The Caruso's, along with everyone else on the third floor, saw that sign. The neighbors cooked for them so they would not have to break the quarantine. How far will the medical community go to protect one of their own? Will they do it even if they feel there is a possibility this doctor may have made a serious mistake that may have cost Joey his life? What in Gods name ever happened to the Hippocratic Oath? Is that protecting someone's life, if so, whose?

"I volunteered to work gratis for Francesco Caruso, not for sentimental reasons or pity, but as a simple matter of abstract Jurisprudence . . . nothing more. I believe the courts overstepped their authority. It is obvious to me that the courts and the medical community conspired to make a long-lasting example of Caruso. Lady's and Gentlemen of the listening audience, this man does *not* deserve to die for this killing. Leopold and Loeb did not die for a deliberate cold-blooded murder. Their reason for killing that young man was to see what it felt like to kill a human being. They sit in prison waiting for the time when they can be free again. Francesco Caruso will die unless you help us. I have evidence not heard in the first trial. The appeal will be different. I will prove that it was *not* a premeditated murder. All we need is a chance! Thank you and Good night."

"Please people, I have an announcement to make before we close for this evening," Marky speaks into the microphone. "I have initiated paper work to have Mr. Schneider take over the Caruso case. Mr. Schneider will handle the appeal this fall, and he will handle the case after the appeal. The great criminal defense attorney from Chicago, Clarence Darrow, will assist him. He also volunteered his services gratis. We not only want Mr. Caruso removed from death row, we want him released from prison with all charges dropped. We want him free and restored to his family. There has been enough death in this story. It must finally end. The station manager signaled that my time is almost over. Before I go, I would like to remind all of you about other broadcasts regarding the Caruso case. Please listen to them and give us all the support you can. We will do it with your help. I am Alexander Marky. Thank you and good night."

Mr. Marky tells Maria and Lena how proud he is of them. Maria asks him how many times she has to do this. "As long as the money lasts we will continue. Pray that it doesn't run out. Cheech's life depends on it."

Mrs. Snyder drives them home. Now that Maria and the children live at 106th. Street, it is much easier for Mrs. Snyder to prep and transport the family back and forth.

* * *

Marky arranges a dinner at the Hotel Belmont to raise money for the appeal and retrial. In attendance are Maria and Lena. They shake hands with people and thank them for coming. They sit at the table with Marky, Schneider and a new attorney who volunteered to join the Schneider, Darrow team. His name is Howard Hilton Spellman, a former district Attorney.

As they eat, people drop by the table to meet Maria and Lena. The show of support by the guests is heartwarming to Maria. For the first time, Lena realizes she and her mother are among friends. A short, stocky man walks up to Maria. "Pardon me, Mrs. Caruso, I am Congressman Fiorello LaGuardia. It is an honor to meet you. I would like to help you in your fight to free your husband from prison if I may."

Not knowing what to say, Maria looks at Marky for direction. He rises and walks around to Maria's side of the table to meet the congressional representative. He extends his hand to the man.

"Congressman LaGuardia, it is a pleasure to meet you, Sir. My name is Alexander Marky. I'm the director of the Caruso Defense Fund. Mrs. Caruso and the rest of us are grateful for your support."

LaGuardia tells Marky that he will be in touch with him. He turns to Maria and points to a poster of Cheech on the wall. Mrs. Caruso, is that your husband?

"Yes, Mr. LaGuardia. That is my husband."

"Well I'll be. I believe your husband and I met about fifteen years ago or so. I used to volunteer to help the new immigrants as they came through Ellis Island station. It gave me a chance to meet them and help them because I speak Italian. One day a strong and handsome young man about eighteen or nineteen stood in line. He was going to make a left turn that would have put him in the line to go back to Italy. I stopped him and asked him to come to my desk. He told me his name, and I explained that he did not want to go that way because he passed the examination. He had to go the other way. I could tell by the tag on his lapel. He thanked me. I always wondered how he did. You can count on my help, *Seniora.*"

Marky gives the Congressman his business card. LaGuardia promises to get back to him. He leaves, but not before telling Maria not to be disheartened. "Things will be fine."

"Maria, do you know who that was? He will be the next Mayor of New York!" He shakes his head and says, "They're coming out of the woodwork. We just have to stand still and they come to us. We're on the right track, Maria." Schneider and Spellman nod their heads in agreement.

The next morning, LaGuardia's office calls to make an appointment. Marky agrees to meet LaGuardia at his office in the afternoon. LaGuardia steps out of his office to welcome Marky. "Good afternoon, Mr. Marky, please, come in and sit down!"

"Thank you for making an appearance at the dinner last night. Were you asked to attend, Sir?"

"Mr. Marky, I followed this story since it came to my attention by the very first news article. I pursue it on my own. I gladly attach my support to your effort to save this man's life. The court did not do him justice. Last night when I saw his photo and recognize him as the young man I assisted years ago at Ellis Island, I felt obligated to do anything to help him that I might be able to do. After listening to his little girl last night, I could not turn my back on him if I tried. To be honest, if I am wrong about this case, my association with it could ruin my political career. Sometimes there are things a person must do regardless of the consequences. Indecision can lead to regret years later. Now, how can I help Francesco Caruso and his family?"

"Well, Congressman, next week we are having another fundraising dinner. It would be a big help, if you were to attend and possibly make a short speech. Then if you would pose for a photo session with Caruso's daughter Lena, it would be very helpful to our cause. Public support from someone of your stature would certainly help us get the results we need to continue with the appeal and retrial."

LaGuardia agrees. He tells Marky it will be an honor. They spend some time speaking about how the events occurred. After a lengthy conversation, LaGuardia has to leave for another appointment. He tells Marky to call his secretary with all of the details and assures him that he will be there.

All of the famous people getting involved impress Marky. He meets Clarence Darrow, Warden Lawes, public officials Schneider and Spellman, practicing attorneys, an old childhood friend who has since become one of the most powerful Broadway moguls, and now Congressman Fiorello LaGuardia within a two-month span. LaGuardia is destined to become one of the most prolific mayors of New York City.

* * *

At his cell on death row, Cheech's state of mind reverts from one of despair and the will to die to one of hope. He appreciates the affection and genuine caring. It helps him to cope with a frightening and final place in the world, the death row cell of any prison, anywhere in the world. From the very start, Cheech realized that this popular warden of one of the most notorious prisons in this country has a conciliatory tone in all of his conversations with him, a convicted murderer. The guards are more than generous in dealing with him. They invest their own time to teach him how to read and write the English. Each of the guards is Irish. They bring his friend O'Mally to mind all the time. He constantly thinks of his friend O'Mally. The guards bring a newspaper and sit by his cell while he reads what he can of the story of the day. Many of the articles are about him. His story, the story of Joey and the struggle people are going through in his name. He feels the constant humiliation of Maria and little Lena going on display to save him. He knows what his introvert Maria is going through. He recognizes the special strength of his little girl. He pays them back the only way he can. He sings songs to them, happy songs, sad songs and

Italian love songs. He sings songs like *O' Sole Mio and Amapola.* When a guard asks, he sings Al Jolson's songs. A strange thing happens when he sings Jolson. In imitating the great singer, he loses his Italian accent. Never before have the halls of any death row echoed with the sounds of music. It is an unusual time and place for a convict to be on death row. The warden allows the prisoners to enjoy singing, applause, laughter and conversation. They call out messages from one end of death row to the other to get a response from Cheech. They all know as Warden Lawes does, that Cheech will not be in their presence long. Bittersweet feelings permeate their comments and hopes.

The warden often appears at the desk of the guard at the entrance to death row. He brings his work with him, and hums along while being entertained by this unusual prisoner. He studies the reaction Cheech's heartfelt songs have on the condemned men, especially since it comes from one of their own. The warden leans back in the chair, eyes closed, hands behind his head, feet on the desk and listens to Cheech sing. Warden Lawes is an unusual warden. No warden ever displayed the radical opinions of this one. In the beginning of his short command of Sing Sing Prison, the guards and prisoners are not that receptive. They do not believe he is what he represents himself to be. Now they do, because they are witnesses to his genuine spirit and concern for the average prisoner. Cheech, who has been on death row for such a short time, cannot appreciate him to the extent of the other death row inmates. Later, he comes to understand their appreciation of this very special man. For now, he has too many personal emotions to deal with. However, the time is coming, and he will learn.

* * *

Mary hands Marky a letter. "You may have an important letter here, Mr. Marky. It's from Sing Sing Prison stamped and all!"

He opens the letter and reads aloud. "Dear Mr. Alexander Marky." He looks at the awkward handwriting, and then skips to the signature. "Jesus, Mary, this is from Cheech! I thought he couldn't write English? What is going on here? Am I the last one to know everything?"

Mary says, "Do you want me to call WGL Radio?"

He grins. Mary, "You're reading my mind!"

She runs back to her desk to call. While waiting for someone to pick up, she calls, "When should I ask for?"

"Any week night at eight o'clock will do."

After a brief conversation, she calls out, "Friday the 24th okay, Mr. Marky?"

"Are you kidding? Take it." As he reads the one page letter from the man he never met, he feels like he knows him.

Friday night finds Marky sitting before the microphone at WGL again. The Borax commercial ends. The station director points to Marky. "Good evening Lady's and Gentlemen. This is Alexander Marky. Today I will talk about Francesco Caruso again. By now, I am sure you're familiar with our cause. I will tell you why we want to save this man. I sat in the courtroom all through the trial. It was the poorest excuse for a trial that I've ever witnessed. The court withheld evidence from the jury. The court-appointed defense attorney did not participate in jury selection. The doctor's widow took the stand even though she was forty miles away when the murder was committed. At one point, the police imprisoned and held as a witness Caruso's wife Maria. They thought about using her against her own husband. Even though Caruso had problems speaking English, the court denied him an interpreter. Well . . . I have some good news about this case that has held our attention for the last three months. The court of appeals granted us permission to dismiss Caruso's present team of attorneys and replace them with a new team specially gathered for the upcoming appeal. New York's court system will be under a magnifying glass for this session. The new team handling the Caruso appeal and retrial will be Clarence Darrow, Charles A. Schneider, Howard Hilton Spellman and Walter H. Pollak. While Francesco Caruso has been on Sing Sing's death row, he had the opportunity to learn to read and write English. He sent me a letter that he wrote himself from his cell on death row. For the very first time, he tries to tell us in his own words what happened on that sad and tragic day in February when two people lost their lives. It starts:

'Mr. Alexander Marky: It is hard for me to write into words what I have in my heart. I know because of what I did, many people have suffered. Joey is sick very bad and I go to Mr. Joseph Pendola the drug man. He is a good man, he help me. He send his brother the doctor to take care of Joey. He say the medicine his brother give to my little boy is too strong for a baby. I ask the doctor what his brother say and he say his brother should mind his business. He don't know what he talking about. He give the medicine to Joey and Joey dies. When I tell him Joey is dead, that he killed my boy, he laugh at me. I go crazy mad. He say he want to pay me to keep quiet, not tell anybody he was here. He say he will pay me to keep quiet. Everything go black. I can't stand it. I yell at him and he hit me in the face. I grab him by the throat. I hit him again-and-again, and I no let go. Before I know what I do, he no move no more and I drop him on the floor. Same place where Joey die. Same place. I no remember what he says and what I do for a long time. Some time I remember little bit and some time I forget. It goes away. It makes me sad that Mrs. Pendola lost her husband. The little *bambina* will never know her Papa. I lost my beautiful boy and now I lose my baby girl Ida. I want to thank all the American people who help me and my family. I say thank you to Mr. Clarence Darrow for his help. I am grateful to Mr. Alexander Marky for his work for my family and me.

Francesco Caruso.'

"Lady's and Gentlemen, I ask you. Does this sound like a man who planned to kill Doctor Pendola? Does this sound like premeditated murder as the jury ruled? At this very minute, Caruso is sitting on death row awaiting electrocution. He should *not* be there. We must all do whatever we can to stop this execution. Once again, I ask you; donate to the Caruso Defense Fund. Please help save this man. Thank you and good night."

* * *

A week later, the audience of The Sons of Italy Club of Brooklyn awaits the evening's guest speaker, Congressman Fiorello LaGuardia, to take the stage. As the crowd enters the converted dance hall, the noise is louder. The crowd quiets when the curtains on the little stage move. Behind the drawn curtain are Marky, Maria, Lena and LaGuardia. He is a fast-talking little man who speaks in short, animated voice phrases. He has Maria and little Lena laughing, a needed change of mood for them.

"Maria, I will speak to you last." His voice is serious and soft. We laugh now but out there," —he points towards the audience— "we will be sad. We have sad and hard work to do. I know the court system wronged your husband. He didn't mean to kill the doctor. I will ask you questions; you answer them as well as you can." Speaking to Maria in Italian, he says, "We speak in Italian tonight. These people want to hear you speak Italian because many people here speak and understand Italian better than English. We speak Italian tonight, Okay?"

"*Cie,* Mr. LaGuardia."

"*Bene,*" he replies. Jokingly he turns to Lena and speaks broken English to make her laugh. "And you young-a lady! We will-a speak English, *gabish?*"

Lena smiles, "I can't talk like that!"

"Miss Lena," he grins, it was a joke to make you smile. I don't want you to talk like that." He tells Marky. "It's show time."

Marky walks to the podium and signals the stage man to open the curtain. The curtain opens. The audience rises to their feet to applaud when they see LaGuardia, Maria and Lena. The audience sits when the applause dies down. Marky thanks them and says, "Lady's and gentlemen, I'm afraid I am the only person here who does not speak Italian. I understand how Cheech felt last February in that courtroom when they denied him an interpreter. Lena Caruso and I will speak to you in English tonight; however, Congressman Fiorello LaGuardia will honor you in your tongue. Listen to all the words of Congressman LaGuardia and Maria Caruso so you can spread the word to your neighbors, friends and relatives about the court's unjust actions to Francesco Cheech Caruso, a friend to many of you here tonight. It is an honor to present to you the next mayor of New York City, Congressman Fiorello LaGuardia."

LaGuardia raises his arms to quiet the crowd's applause. "*Gradsia! gradsia everyone!* Thank you; thank you. I am undecided about running for mayor, but how can I refuse you wonderful people. I think I'll do it!" In appreciation, the people break out in applause again. "Thank you, thank you. Please, please." LaGuardia winks at Marky as if to say, "I know this is not a political rally."

Chapter 12

LaGuardia continues in Italian. "Ladies and Gentlemen, I came here tonight because I want to help. To kill someone or die, no matter what the reason, it is bad. It is especially bad for us Italians when it is one of our own. It displeases me that this terrible thing happened in our community. There are always reasons why things like this happen. There was a reason in this case. Even more despicable than the crime of a tormented man, is the crime of AMA officials whose job is to guide the medical profession to be understanding and compassionate in a case like this. That crime occurred when a small group of people marshaled all of that organization's power to send a poor man like Francesco Caruso to the electric chair when they know he was out of his mind with grief when he killed one of their own. To cover up the truth, to know there was no premeditation on the part of this man and to proceed to deny him all of his rights to a fair trial purposely and deliberately, are what constitutes a calculated and deliberate premeditated crime, a crime against the very people its oath promises to protect.

"If Francesco Caruso is electrocuted, the AMA is guilty of a far more serious crime than that of Mr. Caruso. Can you imagine how your heart would feel if your beloved little son died in your arms saying, 'Papa, I'm dying. Don't let me die! Please, Papa!' How terrible that must have been."

His voice quick and animated breaks up in the emotion of the moment. The crowd is quiet and attentive. "God help him. That is why we are here tonight. We ask for God's intervention, and we ask for yours as well. We are here to help Francesco and save the AMA from making a terrible mistake. The Caruso family found an apartment in Manhattan so they can be nearby when the appeal and retrial comes up, and it most certainly will. Last week, according to Mr. Marky, some photographers and reporters were at the Caruso flat to write stories and take pictures for the newspapers. I have a recent picture of the Caruso children that I will pass around to you."

He motions for the stagehand and hands him several copies of the picture to pass through the crowd. "Look at two-year-old Anna. Look at the holes in the bottom of her shoes. It's terrible. This poor family has been through enough. We must all do what we can for them. We need you to call your friends, your relatives, your congressional representatives, the governor and anyone else who will listen. You need to do these things as much for yourself as for Francesco. Many of you have known him for years. I met him in 1911 at Ellis Island when I helped him as an immigrant from Sicily."

LaGuardia points to Maria sitting on the stage. "Look at his brave and beautiful wife. Look at his oldest daughter Lena. You will have a chance tonight to hear them talk about their husband and father. I want you to know, to see and feel what they have been through by their own voices. As long as you live, you will remember what you hear from them tonight, their story. Please help the Caruso's. I would like to introduce you to Caruso's oldest daughter Lena. She is an eight-year-old who will impress you with her maturity when she speaks. She will speak to you now. Come, Lena."

Dressed in a pink dress, Lena walks over to LaGuardia. After the audience stops clapping, he asks her, "If I get a chair, will you do me the honor of sitting on my lap, young lady?"

She turns to Maria; Maria shakes her head in approval. Lena says, "Okay, Mr. LaGuardia."

LaGuardia lifts the microphone from the podium while someone brings a chair onto the stage. He sits on the chair and lifts her onto his lap. "If I let you hold the microphone, will you let me use it too?"

The audience, touched by the interchange between the child and the very popular LaGuardia, smile as Lena tells him, "You're funny, Mr. LaGuardia. You can hold it if you want?" They laugh.

"Lena, it looks like you're the boss tonight. They like you better than they like me!" She smiles, something rare. In his almost comical rapid speech, he turns to the child. "How old are you, Honey?"

"I'm eight-years-old, Mr. LaGuardia."

"I'm gonna ask you a hard question, Lena, and if you don't know the answer, maybe your mama can help . . . okay?"

Her look is serious when he asks her how old her sisters and brothers are. "I'm the oldest. Josie is seven, Joey was six, Anna is three, Sally is two and Ida was four-months-old when she died." The audience claps.

When they quiet down, LaGuardia say, "Lena, maybe I should sit on your lap!" Again they laugh. "Lena, do you miss Joey?"

"Yes I do, Mr. LaGuardia. I do. I love my brother." Her eye's water, bottom lip quivers.

LaGuardia wipes away her tears. "Tell us about Joey."

"He was smaller than me, but he walked me to school and protected me. Now I walk by myself. I think about him all the time. I miss my Papa too."

"Tell us about you baby sister Ida."

Lena quietly cries. No one in the crowd makes a sound. "Ida was really sick. Mama did what she could for her." Crying she tells him, "Mama was afraid to take Ida to the hospital; she said the doctors would kill her because they hate my Papa. Ida died in her bed all by herself." Lena covers her face to hide her tears.

"You love Joey and Ida, don't you, Lena?"

"I do! I think about them and I cry. Mama cries all the time. She doesn't think I see her . . . but I do!" She glances at Maria. Both are crying. Lena jumps off LaGuardia's lap and runs to Maria. They hug and cry while white hankies flash from the audience.

LaGuardia shakes his head as he walks to the podium. He places the microphone in its holder. He quotes Lena. "'Mama was afraid to take Ida to the hospital; she said the doctors would kill her because they hate my Papa. Ida died in her bed all by herself.' Lena is eight-years-old Lady's and Gentlemen. No one can make a child of eight say things like that. Her mother did not know Lena saw her crying. Saints preserve us; she was afraid of doctors. Let's take a break. When we come back, we'll talk with Maria, a very special woman." LaGuardia leaves the stage shaking his head and blowing his nose as the curtains close.

After a brief break, Maria is the next to share the stage with LaGuardia. Once again, she relates to the audience the events of February last, her needs, wants and present situation. Prepared by Marky, her comments mirror her talk to the radio audience of last month. She will repeat it many times.

* * *

In her new home at 113 East 106th street, Lena adjusts to her new school. Most of her classmates are friendly and do not speak to her of her fathers situation. Not having the company of her brother Joey to walk her home, she walks alone.

"You're Lena aren't you?" a boy of about 11 asks her. She walks around him, but he moves in front of her. "Where do you think you're going? Yea, you're the jailbird's kid aren't you?" He knocks the books out of her hands. Lena cries.

A man from across the street comes to her aid. He tells the boy, "Beat it, Stupid, if I see you do this again, I won't talk to you. Do you understand?" He asks Lena if she is all right and walks her home. As they approach her building, she points to a stoop and tells him that she lives there and thanks him. "Do you want me to go with you and tell your mother what happened?"

"No, Sir, thank you for your help. I don't want Mama to worry. Thank you for walking me home."

The man smiles at Lena. "I live on the street where the boy stopped you. My apartment faces the sidewalk you use to go back and forth to school. I will watch you from my window for a while, in case something like this happens again. When I see you coming, I will open the window so you can see me. If I have to, I will call the police. Go on upstairs. What is your name?"

"My name is Lena."

"You aren't Lena Caruso are you?" When she does not answer, he says, "Lena, go ahead, upstairs!" She turns and runs up the stairs to the second floor flat. Not wanting to worry Maria, she does not mention anything about the incident. True to his word, the man opens his window and waves to her everyday as she goes to and from school. Lena, carrying her books in her crossed arms on her chest, waves her fingers to him. Her smile brings a smile from her self-appointed guardian in the window across the street.

On this afternoon, the man watches for Lena. He observes a small group of about six kids waiting across the street. He wants to position himself in a better place, so he leaves his flat, crosses the street and waits in front of a drugstore.

Lena approaches. Before the man can react, the small gang of kids encircles her and calls out names like murderer and jailbird. One of them knocks her and her books to the sidewalk. She cries and attempts to defend herself. Their are too many. The man runs to her aid, grabs two of the children by the back of their coats. "You little bastards, I ought to whip the hell out of you." The others scatter and run. He shoves the two boys he grabbed. "This is your last warning. There are no more! The next time I will call the police." He helps Lena to her feet and gathers her books for her. "I'm sorry, Lena, I couldn't get here any faster, I'm sorry. Are you okay?"

She wipes her eyes. "Yes, I'm okay. Thank you."

He kneels on one knee in front of her. "Lena, if this happens one more time, I will have to tell your mother. She would want to know." She nods to the man and he escorts her to her home again.

On another day, Lena waves to her friend in the window. A well-dressed man with a hat almost immediately confronts her.

"Lena, I have a message for your mother. If I tell you, can you remember it and tell her?" She glances at the window across the street, but he is not there. She looks back at the man. "Tell your mother that the appeal will not be granted. Your father will die for what he did. Tell Mama it's over."

Her friend quietly moves up behind the stranger. She looks, causing the stranger to turn. Her friend speaks with a no-nonsense tone, "I will tell you only once. You had better have a good reason for stopping this child in this manner."

"Who the hell are you?"

"I'm this child's guardian angel." The stranger reaches behind his back. Lena's friend grabs his throat and pushes him against a parked car. "Maybe I didn't make myself clear, Asshole; one more attempt to ignore my question and I will rearrange your face." He reaches to the small of the stranger's back. Nothing is there. He picks the stranger up and flings him over the hood of a car into the street.

Getting up, the stranger yells to the self-appointed guardian angel, "You have no idea who you're dealing with! You haven't heard the last of this." The stranger hurries away.

The protector turns to Lena. "Okay, Lena, it's time for me to visit with your mother. Agreed?" She shakes her head. He accompanies her home.

At the door to her apartment, Lena opens the door and invites him in. "Please, come in. I'll get mama."

Maria hears voices and enters the parlor. She sees Lena standing next to the stranger and looks to her for answers. "Mama, I don't know his name, but he wants to speak to you." Maria nervously watches the stranger.

He says, "I know you are Maria Caruso and your daughter is Lena. My name is Santo. I know about your family's misfortune. I live across the street from the sidewalk that the child takes back and forth to school every day. Two weeks ago, I saw a bigger boy stop Lena. He knocked her books out of her hands and pushed her. I chased him away. Last week, a group of older children attacked her almost in the same place; I chased them away, too." Maria is listening and watching Lena. "Today a man stopped your daughter. He frightened her. I took care of him and sent him on his way. I want to keep protecting Lena, unless you disapprove. Something must be done about this before she gets hurt."

Maria looks directly at Lena. "Is this true, Lena?"

"Yes, Mama, it is. I didn't tell you. I don't want you to worry."

"Of course I would worry! That *is* what Mama's do. You should have told me," she scolds. "Mr. Santo, I don't know how to thank you. You are a good man. I will talk to my lawyer, but there is no one else to help us. Are you married?"

"No, Mrs. Caruso, I'm not married."

"Would you come to our home for dinner Sunday?"

"Thank you, Mrs. Caruso. I would enjoy that. I will watch Lena until you can do something about this problem. Thank you." Before he leaves, Santo tells Lena that he will be in the window every morning and every afternoon.

Maria explains to Lena how proud she is of her and makes her promise that she will tell her whenever something bad happens. She sternly tells her, "No more secrets!"

Maria is unsure how to deal with the problem. She is unaware that O'Mally will stop by in two days to leave her some money for the month's expenses.

The next day, Maria leaves Josey, who does not attend school because she is retarded, Anna and little boy Sally with a neighbor so she can shop for food. She hurries because she does not like to stay away from her children too long. Returning home carrying her purse and two bags, she climbs the poorly lit steps to the second floor. A man comes down. In an instant, he throws her to the steps. His hand is on her neck so she cannot scream. As her groceries spill from the paper-bags and roll down the steps, he rasps, "your husband's appeal will not be successful. Even if it is, he will die anyway. So will you and the rest of your children." She is in shock. Grabbing her by the throat and shoulder, he lifts and slams her back onto the steps almost rendering her unconscious. "There will be no more warnings you goddamn Wop!" He runs down the steps and out of the building.

Neighbors hear the cans rolling down the steps. Some open their doors to see what the commotion is. A man runs up to stop Maria, who is semiconscious, from sliding down the steps. People rush to her aid gathering groceries and helping her up. A man carries her up the steps and into her apartment. He places her on the couch. "Mrs. Caruso, are you okay? Should we call a doctor?"

The mention of a doctor gets Maria's attention. "No, no I will be okay now, please, no doctor, please. Thank you all for your help."

A woman, friendly to Maria asks, "Maria, what happened to you?"

"I don't know what happened, Millie. It was all at once. I was carrying the groceries up the steps. A man grabbed me and threw me down on the steps. He threatened all of my family, including my husband. He called me an awful name and then he ran off. I don't know who he was." Crying, Maria assures everyone she is fine. She thanks each one for coming to her aid. As they leave, they tell her they are there for her. She just has to call if she needs anything.

All alone, she sits at the kitchen table crying. She does not know what to do. First Lena is threatened and now all of them are. She prays that Mr. Santo will be at the window for Lena, but she makes up her mind that she will also watch her daughter from the entrance of the building each morning. She can see all the way to the school gate.

* * *

O'Mally stops by Marky's office after his shift to pick up Maria's money for the month. As if angel-sent, he knocks at her door. Maria opens the door. She cries, "O'Mally, oh, oh, it's so good to see you. You are a Godsend!" She glances up. "Somebody up there is looking out for us." She pulls him into the flat and shuts the door. "O'Mally, I don't know what to do. First Lena is threatened . . . now me. We are so scared. We don't know what to do."

O'Mally frowns. "When did all this happen, Maria?"

"Yesterday to me; about two weeks ago for Lena, but I didn't know. She knew I would worry. A nice man down the street is helping Lena. He brought her home the other day and made her tell me what has been happening to her. I don't know what to do."

"Tell me exactly what happened to you and Lena."

"Mr. Santo said that bigger kids hit and pushed her down. They called her names like jailbird and murderer. Then a man stopped her and told her that her father was going to die. Mr. Santo chased him away and brought her home. Yesterday a man knocked me down on the steps. He threatened the whole family, including Cheech. He called me names and shouted at me. I'm so scared I don't know what to do."

O'Mally assures her he will take care of it this day. He wants to meet with Mr. Santo. He asks Maria where he lives and assures her everything will be okay, not to worry anymore. He hands her the envelope. She thanks him and asks, "How long will this keep up, O'Mally, the money?"

"As far as I know, it is for as long as Cheech is behind bars." As he leaves her building, Maria waves to him from the porch at the entrance. O'Mally walks to Santo's building. He introduces himself and asks him about the attacks on Lena. Santos tells O'Mally everything. He assures him that he will continue to watch out for Lena. O'Mally thanks him. He heads for Brooklyn and Giovanni's. He enters the restaurant and heads to the back to speak to Antonio.

"O'Mally! *bona seeda*, good evening, so soon?" He invites O'Mally to sit at the table and partake of wine and food. They discuss the trials of Maria and Lena. Antonio assures O'Mally he will take care of it. O'Mally bids his host goodnight and returns to his home.

Antonio reports to D'Aquila. He arranges to find the man who approached Lena and the one who attacked Maria. They enlist neighborhood toughs to find the boys who roughed up Lena. Someone visits the principle of the school Lena attends.

* * *

The newspapers report that Supreme Court Justice Levy ruled it permissible for the team of Schneider, Darrow, Spellman and Pollak to replace the legal team of Voss and Price in the Francesco Caruso case. Mr. Schneider is the attorney who sent the letter of request to the appeals court.

Voss, Cheech's attorney from the very start, is very angry at the ruling. The newspapers quote him as saying he is opposed to the ruling on the grounds it is contemptuous, unethical and unprofessional. He shouted to reporters at the press conference, "This action was instigated by Alexander Marky, a publicity agent. In an underhanded and calculated manner, Marky brought Clarence Darrow into the case."

Because he is not related, Alexander Marky is unable to visit with the man whose life he works to save. With the change of attorneys approved by the appeal court, brought about by his efforts solely, he feels he can finally request an appointment to meet Cheech for the first time. Mary connects Marky with the warden's office at Sing Sing Prison. "This is Alexander Marky's office calling. He would like to speak to Warden Lawes please."

"One moment please, I will connect you."

Mary cups the receiver and calls out, "Mr. Marky, quick, she's connecting me, hurry!"

He picks up the phone. "Hello, Mr. Marky, how are you? I thought you'd never call!"

"I'm fine. What did you say?"

"I said I thought you'd never call, Sir! I've been expecting your call."

"Why would you expect my call? I think everyone, but me, knows what's going on around here."

Warden Lawes chuckles. "Let's just say you're a busy man. I've read all about your exploits."

Once again sensing the run around, Marky changes subjects and gets right to the point. "I would like permission to visit Caruso. I need to gather information for his attorneys as they prepare for the appeal of his case this fall." He hopes this explanation works.

"Mr. Marky, you will be allowed to visit with the prisoner for the stated purpose. Cheech is eager to meet you. He is thankful for all you have done.

Again, people surrounding this case surprise Marky. "Thank you, sir. When can I meet with him?"

"Tomorrow's fine if you can make it. The sooner the better as far as Cheech is concerned; how about after nine in the morning?"

"Warden Lawes, I don't think tomorrow will be possible. I need some time to get a stenographer, interpreter, an attorney and a witness together. With your permission, I would like to use this occasion to get Mr. Caruso's statement about the events that lead up to the murder."

"I understand. Let me know when you're ready."

"Thanks, Warden, I'll do that."

"Thank you, and good day to you."

"Mary, get me that steno and the interpreter on the phone and then get me Schneider. Guess who the witness is going to be?"

Mary calls out, "Will do, Sir, and thank you. I would love to meet and hear this man's story!" She dials the phone. "Hello, may I speak to Mr. Clarence Darrow please?"

"Hello, this is Clarence Darrow."

"This is Mr. Marky's secretary calling on his behalf. He would like to know of any information you discovered for the appeal hearing for Mr. Francesco Caruso."

"I'll send the folder today. Tell Mr. Marky that with what I have accumulated in this folder, we could revive a dead man! I'll see Mr. Marky before the hearing." Mary thanks him and leaves a note for Marky.

A clerk for the Appellate Court calls Marky's office and tells him the appeal hearing will take place in two weeks. They receive the folder from Darrow, and Marky calls Schneider, Spellman and Pollak to bring about a meeting of the minds. The request for a new trial will depend on Clarence Darrow's findings, and on how the information is used.

* * *

The October 26, 1927 New York Times headline reads:

Caruso Appeal Set for Tomorrow

Arguments begin tomorrow in the appeal of Francesco Caruso. According to a clerk, a brief filed in the appeal cites 14 legal errors. The main legal argument in the brief states there is no proof of premeditation in the first trial, and that the court ignored important evidence. Council will also show that Judge McLaughlin erred when he allowed the victim's wife to testify and when he denied Caruso an interpreter.

Schneider will site twenty-five instances when the defendant, because of his lack of ability to understand the English language, clearly did not understand the questions.

They will argue that, at the beginning of the trial, the Kings County Medical Society sent a petition signed by thousands of people in the medical field to District Attorney Dodd asking for a vigorous prosecution of the trial on behalf of the Medical community of New York. They will argue that the court obtained Maria Caruso's statements to the police and read them illegally at the trial . . . indirectly causing Maria Caruso to be a witness against her own husband. They will present these and other arguments at this very important hearing.

* * *

The appeal hearing begins. Judge Benjamin Nathan Cardozo is appalled at the number of discrepancies in the court's conduct and conviction of Caruso as he listens to the proceeding. During the appeal, the name of Clarence Darrow comes up in reference to the files presented. The judge is interested as the attorneys bring the facts to the surface.

The attorneys are confident as they prepare to leave the hearing. The court clerk asks them to follow him to the Judge's chamber. The conversation with the judge is favorable. They know they must progress with their work for a retrial. They thank the judge and head for Marky's office where they call Clarence Darrow. They brief him about the appeal, and tell him he needs to come to New York to prepare for the new trial.

* * *

The November 24, 1927 headlines read:

Caruso Wins Appeal
New Trial Ordered
Appellate Court reverses first Degree Conviction
No Grounds for Premeditation in Caruso Case

Marky and the defense attorneys make statements to the newspapers. They predict the eventual release of Francesco Caruso. The Medical community is angry and shocked by the ruling.

O'Mally reads the news accounts and contacts Marky. They agree to meet at Maria's apartment to tell her the good news. They arrive to discover that Santo beat them to it. Lena is sitting on Santo's lap. He tells her, "Your Papa will be home soon."

For the first time since Cheech's arrest, Maria is happy, hopeful and smiling. The mood is festive as neighbors drop by with food to help feed the many guests. With the door open, in comes the funny little man with the clipped speech and animated voice saying, "Where's the food? I'm so happy, I can eat a horse!"

"Mr. LaGuardia, thank you. I'm so happy you came. The food is in the kitchen, wine is on the table. Please, please help yourself. This is wonderful. Thank you, God!" The children are playing and running around the flat. Maria is so happy. She seeks a moment away from people to think and to be thankful for her blessings. She excuses herself and walks into the kitchen. She is lost in thought as she straightens up and washes dishes.

"Mrs. Caruso."

She jerks and turns. "Mr. Santo, you startled me."

"I'm sorry, Mrs. Caruso, may I talk to you?"

"Of course, talk."

"In the last three weeks I have been approached by friends of yours. The first was your friend O'Mally the police officer. I spoke to him about the attacks on Lena. He told me all I had to do is ask if I need anything. Three other men questioned me about the attacks on Lena and you. I told them everything I knew. They said if I ever need anything, I should go to Giovanni's restaurant in Brooklyn and tell the bartender I am a friend of Cheech Caruso. I wanted to talk to you about this because I don't know what to make of these people."

"Mr. Santo, come with me." She leads him to the back bedroom. She closes the door and stands with her back against it. "Mr. Santo, O'Mally is a dear friend of my family. If he said he would help you, you can count on him to do that. He is a good man. The other men . . . well, be careful. They have the power to grant you anything you want; however, I must warn you that there will be a bill to pay. They are Cheech's friends, too."

As they leave, Santo thanks her and tells her he will be careful. "I made it this far without anyone's help. I will go forward on my own."

As they walk down the hall to the kitchen, Maria says, "My husband will want to meet you."

Santo nods his head, "Of course."

* * *

At Sing Sing's death row, the guards bring the good news to Cheech. Even off duty, guards arrive at the prison to bring Cheech messages of good will and little gifts from them and their families. Cheech hears "I told you so!" many times. He finally feels, for the first time since Joey's death, that maybe life *is* worth living.

Warden Lawes walks up to the cell's open entrance. It has remained open since the news arrived. The warden stands with his hands on his hips, "Well, Caruso, need I say more?" He steps in to shake Cheech's hand. "It won't be long now, Cheech. I can't speak for anyone else, but I know I will miss you very much. Death row will never be the same again. You must have this same mesmerizing effect on everyone you meet."

Cheech's smile lights up his handsome face. "Thank you, Warden, thank you for everything. I can read and write English now because of you. What a shame I had to come to death row to learn, but I did learn and only because of you. Thank you!"

* * *

Marky sets up the meeting with Cheech to give his statement in the presence of a steno/interpreter, Marky, Schneider and Mary as a witness. The guards and the warden will view it as well. His biggest supporter is the Warden.

At this first meeting of Cheech and Mr. Marky, Cheech brings Marky to tears by his warm embrace and sincere expression of appreciation. The session takes about an hour. These loyal friends and acquaintances hear for the first time what really happened. Cheech remembers everything that happened that day, something he could not recall in the past due to a serious concussion he suffered on that fateful day.

As the session ends, Warden Lawes announces that the paperwork is arriving by mail that will affect the transfer of Cheech from Sing Sing to the Raymond Street Station. "Things will never be the same around here again." He asks Cheech, "I think this calls for a song. Mr. Marky has not heard you sing, Cheech. Do you think you could do that for us? Maybe *O Sole Mio?*"

"*Signor*, Sure!" he answers.

They sit on the floor or anywhere they can find a seat. The other death row inmates hang on the bars of their cells to get a better look. Cheech takes Mary's hands and seats her on his cot. He kneels on one knee in front of her. "*Signora, quest e per tuo,* Madam, this is for you." He breathes deeply and sings to Mary, eyes nearly closed. She blushes since no one ever sang to her before. The blush is still there as the song ends.

Applause and cheers follow. Marky says, "Cheech, that was beautiful. Thank you very much."

"Thank you, Mr. Marky, thank you!" Cheech replies.

Chapter 13

Many Italian clubs and organizations, from the very beginning, show their keen interest in the Court's actions against Cheech. They launched, almost as extensive an effort as Alexander Marky to get an appeal. The ruling by the appellate court is as much to appease these various groups as it is to right a wrong. They bring an enormous amount of pressure on everyone who had a role in the first trial.

Prosecutor Gallagher, District attorney Dodd, the judge in the first trial, as well as Judge McLaughlin, refuse to give statements to the press. They all say they must wait until they have an opportunity to read the complete order. Everyone associated with the first trial, who worked with the prosecution, feels the heat and the negative attention.

A newspaper article states that Caruso acted hastily in a time of bereavement when his mind was not in a normal state; therefore, it is not comparable to a cold-blooded murder. Groups send many petitions to Governor Smith's office emphasizing the Caruso family's financial state. The public and governor are fully aware of petitions sent to the prosecutors by the Medical Community. The prosecutor's office and the office of the Governor receive hundreds of letters from private physicians claiming they will refuse to attend unknown patients at their own residence unless they are sure of their own personal safety.

An innocent bystander caught up in the tragedy of the whole incident is the saddened widow of Doctor Pendola. The successful appeal affects her, too. Married only eighteen months when her husband was murdered, she has not known the support that Maria has known. A mother and an infant live with her at her heavily mortgaged home, now a maternity hospice to help pay expenses.

Reporters interview the young widow at her home. They quote her as saying, "The decision by the appeals court is preposterous. The court gave him every protection and opportunity. He had two of the best lawyers in the city. It was a fair trial. A lawyer I know who was at that trial said Caruso received a very fair trial. I cannot see on what grounds the court could grant a new trial. Now we must go through it all over again! I am just now settling after the shock of my husband's death and the agony of the trial. About a month ago, I started this maternity hospice. The shock of this decision has me so nervous I can hardly carry on my work here with only one patient." Mrs. Pendola denies she is well off. "People talk of the difference between Mrs. Caruso and Me. They speak of me as fixed with a home and money. They are wrong. The furnishings I received on a credit with the proposition that I make good. I owe for everything I have. Yes, I hate to see so much sympathy for the Caruso family with every effort put out to save the man who killed my husband in the prime of his life. Did you know that Mrs. Caruso had a party in her new home? It was festive with family, friends, photographers and political friends in attendance. Congressman LaGuardia was there. Rose D'Andrea of the Bronx district attorney's office brought the Caruso family a turkey and sent a second one to the prison for Mrs. Caruso's husband. The Grand Adirondack Temple of the Knights of Pythias also sent Mrs. Caruso a turkey."

We know that both women suffer from the events of that fateful day in February. The AMA's actions against Francesco Caruso are not activated out of concern for the doctor's grieving widow, but for selfish and self-serving reasons on behalf of the doctors and medical community as a whole. No one offers to assist Mrs. Pendola. She fends for herself as she cares for an aging mother and infant daughter. The people she trusts abandoned her. The powerful AMA and all its groups are in a frenzy as they try a last ditch effort to salvage what ever they can of the original sentence, but Mrs. Pendola is abandoned.

On the other hand, Maria Caruso sees her fortunes brighten. The public has no idea how much support and assistance numerous groups helped in the dire need of the Caruso family. People like Alexander Marky, Clarence Darrow, and Fiorello LaGuardia, good friend Sgt. O'Mally, neighbors, friends and many groups helped. The Mafia, under the direction of Cheech's friend Salvatore D'Aquila, puts a plan in place to take care of Maria and the children regardless of what happens to his friend.

Two organizations, each selfish to their own cause, one sworn to save life, the other sworn to take life, do not reflect the result most expect. The AMA falls short of compassion for self-serving reasons. The Mafia shows compassion and commitment for justice.

Which crime is more serious, more flagrant? Is it the vicious murder of a grief-crazed mind, or is it the calculated legal murder by an organization, whose oath is to protect human life? The AMA representatives misguided the trust of a grieving young widow. They took advantage of her broken heart and spirit by convincing her that what is good for their organization is good for her.

* * *

Friday November 25th 1927 the newspapers report:

Caruso's Have Real Thanksgiving Feast

Family Rejoices at Reversal of Verdict

Visitors added to the cheer as Caruso's children enjoyed Grandmother's turkey and chatted with eager anticipation for the return of their father.

* * *

It truly is a day of joy for the Caruso family. They have not experienced a happier day since several weeks prior to Joey's death. The Privitera's come in from Fort Lee the day before the holiday. Maria and Annette prepare the meal. They anticipate extra guests. All day long people come. They include a few new friends in their new home, such as Millie downstairs and Santo from up the street. Many of the old neighbors from 36th street in Brooklyn used the holiday to travel and visit with Maria and her family. O'Mally brings his wife for the first time along with the O'Hanlon's. Lena visits with her friend Florence. Merchants from the Brooklyn neighborhood visit. Reporters pop in and out all day.

The custom in New York in 1927 is for children to dress up for Thanksgiving in costumes of tramps, beggars and hobo's. Children, dressed up for this day, fill the streets. The exceptions are the Caruso children who want to be with their mother and grandparents on this joyous day.

* * *

At Sing Sing, Warden Lawes approaches the cell on death row, which has housed Cheech since the beginning of the year. He dreads the change in atmosphere after Cheech leaves. He enters the unlocked door to the cell. Cheech stands. "Cheech, I just sent a telegram to your wife. You'll be leaving us Tuesday the 29th to be taken back to Raymond Street. They'll hold you there until your trial."

Cheech smiles, and thinks that maybe life is worth living. Perhaps there is hope after Joey. "Thank you, Warden. I hope I provided some joy with my singing while I have been here. It's the only way I can thank you for all you've done for me. Not just the way you've treated me, but for giving me hope. Thank you, Sir."

"Thank you, Cheech, for the difference you've made here, not only with your songs, but by the way you carried yourself. The death row inmates will surely miss you. I told you when you first came that you didn't belong here; the courts confirmed my opinion. I will miss your company, Mr. Caruso." They shake hands and hug. "Be ready to leave early Tuesday morning. The guards will be here to pick you up. Cheech, do you realize that once a man is on death row he usually leaves one way?"

Cheech looks at his friend for what may be the last time. "I know, my friend, that's what the guards say to me since the appeal. They bring best wishes from the wives and families. Look at the bags of letters and postcards I get all the time. For once in my life, I am lucky. I will not disappoint you, Warden Lawes."

"I know you won't, Cheech. I'll say goodbye to you before you leave." He heads for his office.

Marky visits Maria to tell her she will receive a telegram from Warden Lawes stating what time Cheech will leave the gate of the prison. It is a gesture by the warden to allow her to sit behind Cheech on his train trip back to the Raymond Street Station. She can greet him at the gate and speak to him for the first time since he left the murder scene. She will have time to visit him at the Raymond Street Station house.

Before Marky leaves, he asks Maria to call Mrs. Snyder when she knows the time of Cheech's departure from the prison. He says that Mrs. Snyder will take the children to Fort Lee to spend the day with their grandparents and then return to drive her Sing Sing Prison where Maria will follow the transportation van to the Ossining train station, which will take Cheech to Raymond Street. She will sit in the seat behind the prisoner on the train. Marky tells her, "I will pick you up at the Raymond Street train station and drive you to the Raymond Street Station House. When your visit with Cheech is over, Mrs. Snyder will be parked outside the station house to take you home." This will be the last time Maria sees Mrs. Snyder.

* * *

The telegram arrives on November 26, 1927, the day after the joyous Thanksgiving feast. Standing in the doorway, the little Western Union boy asks, "Are you Maria Caruso?"

"*Cie*, I mean yes." She signs for the telegram and tips the boy. He thanks her and leaves. She tears the envelope open hurriedly. Unable to understand it all, she runs out into the hall and calls down to her friend Millie. "Millie, Millie, please come up hurry," she shouts.

In an instant, Millie responds, "I'm coming, Maria, I'm coming!"

Inside the apartment, Maria hands the telegram to Millie. "According to this telegram, your husband will come through the Sing Sing Prison Gate at 9:00 am on November 29th. You will be able to speak to him and sit behind him for the whole train ride back to Brooklyn. When he's placed in a cell at Raymond Street, you may visit with him."

"Oh, Millie, I'm so happy. Thank you for reading the good news for me. Millie can I use your telephone please?"

"Sure you can. Come on!" Maria tells Millie that she has to tell Lena to take care of the children and she tells her that she will be right back. They rush down to the second floor and Millie's apartment.

Maria calls Mrs. Snyder to tell her the good news. Mrs. Snyder says she will be there on the afternoon of the 28th to take the children to Fort Lee, and that she will return the morning of the 29th at 07:00 to pick Maria up for the ride to Ossining New York and the prison. Maria hugs her friend and runs upstairs to tell the children the good news. She calls the children into the living room to tell them that Papa is leaving Sing Sing for his return to Raymond Street and the trial that will be soon.

The morning when Maria finally gets to see and talk to Cheech arrives. She does not sleep well the night before in anticipation. When Mrs. Snyder comes, they are both so excited that they hug and share tears of joy together. Before they leave, Maria says, "Mrs. Snyder, I don't know how to thank you for all you have done for me and my family this past year. What would I have done without you? You helped me be strong to speak at all those awful places. It was so humiliating to Lena and me. When Cheech is home I will forget the humiliation, but I will not forget you. Not ever."

Later, they reach the main gate of the prison. They sit in the car, engine running on this brisk morning. At 08:30, the morning sun shines with new hope for the Caruso family. With so much love in her heart, Maria cannot conceive of another terrible thing happening. Hope fills her heart. Her love for Cheech wipes out the possibility of anything going wrong. She just wants to be with him.

At precisely 9:00 am, three guards and Cheech step through the gates. Cheech points to the car. "That's my Maria!"

Maria gets out of the passenger side of the car. She thanks Mrs. Snyder. She walks over to where Cheech is standing handcuffed to one of the three guards. Mrs. Snyder calls to Maria, as she walks away, "Maria, don't forget, when you are through speaking to your husband, return to the car and we will follow the van to the train station." Maria shakes her head and waves.

One of the guards tells Cheech, "Give her a hug if you want."

"*Gradsia*."

Maria approaches. Cheech reaches out with his free arm to draw her to him for the first time in a while. As the tears roll down his cheeks, Maria speaks softly in his ear, "*Che', Di' voulio bene, Che'*, I love you." In their most intimate and private moments as man and wife, she calls him Che'. It is a private name for only her to use. In public or around family she calls him Cheech.

"Maria, you will sit in the seat behind me on the train, no?"

"*Cie, Che'* I will be there." After their first embrace since the tragedy, Cheech releases her and she runs back to the waiting car. The guards escort Cheech from the van into the station. Maria is right behind. They go through the turnstiles and board the train. As the train starts to roll, Cheech turns to Maria, "How are the children and everyone else, Maria?" Over the 30-minute ride, she tells him everything she can think of. She really needs this time to clear her thoughts. She tells him about everyone who helped over the months. The long list that includes so many prominent people raises the interest of the guards as well.

The ride ends. The guards take Cheech is to a waiting van. Maria runs to Marky who is waiting for her as Mrs. Snyder told her he would be. The vehicles head for the Raymond Street Station. Marky gives Maria an admiring look. "Maria, your beauty is radiant today. I don't believe I've ever seen you smile like that before."

"Oh, Mr. Marky, I'm so happy. Thank you. Thank you for everything. I depend on you as no one ever before. God works in strange ways. Thank *you*, God, and you, too, Mr. Marky."

As the prison van and Marky's vehicle approach the Raymond Street Station House, people line the sidewalks on both sides of the street at times overflowing into it. Police try to keep the orderly Caruso supporters in check as they direct traffic in front of the station house. Cheers ring out and the crowd of a thousand or more chant and cheer, "*Viva, Caruso, Bene*'" Others shout, "Good luck, Francesco, we hope you get out!"

The crowd's enthusiasm moves Cheech. He offers a subdued smile in appreciation. This is his largest audience, and yet his own emotion will only allow him to show his appreciation with a small-suppressed smile. The crowd tones down its rousing support to prevent an unintended altercation between them and the cops trying to manage them. As Cheech and the guards enter the building, the group turns its attention to Maria. She speaks to them in Italian trying to show her appreciation for their show of support for her husband and his family. Still, this tiny woman also thinks of Mrs. Pendola and offers a silent prayer for her.

Strangers and friends alike shake hands with Maria and offer her congratulations and words of hope. They applaud her as she leaves. Marky calls out that he is leaving and that Mrs. Snyder will be waiting for her. She enters the station house, and the crowd disburses in a peaceful manner.

A police officer shows her to the commander's office. "Mrs. Caruso, I am Commander Johnston. I hoped your husband would win his appeal. As long as he is with us, you may visit him as often as you wish. I know Warden Lawes quite well. He told me your husband is a good man deserving respect. I wish you, your husband and your family all the luck in the world and look forward to the day when I can release him to you."

"Thank you, Mr. Johnston, Sir. Thank you very much."

The commander tells her that it will be a few minutes before she can see her husband. She thanks him and sits in the hall to wait. In the bag she carries, there are a few sandwiches, with ham and provolone cheese. She thinks how far things have evolved and wonders how long it will be until he is home again. She wonders how she can ever thank all the nice people who helped bring things to this point. Once again, she thinks of her young counterpart, Mrs. Pendola, and makes a vow to pray for her every time she prays the rosary. A gentle tap on the shoulder brings her back to the present. "Mrs. Caruso, you may see your husband now. Please follow me."

"Oh, oh yes, thank you, thank you." She recognizes the long passageway where, what seems so long ago, police led her handcuffed as a suspect because of her own admission to the police that she murdered the doctor.

Approaching the cell, the guard points to it and tells Maria that he will be back in a little while. She walks in to Cheech, the first time they have been alone in the past year.

"Cheech, quick before the guard comes by, take these sandwiches and hide them, quick!"

Smiling he tells her, "It's okay, Maria, they won't care. They have been good to me since I've been locked up. Warden Lawes allowed me to learn how to read and write English while I was on death row. They will not stop you from bringing food to me. Bring some for them too."

They hold hands and speak about many subjects, but Maria does not mention the attacks on Lena and her. Rather than worry him, she carries the burden by herself.

The guard returns to tell her visiting time is over. Maria thanks him. She kisses her husband for the first time in a year and promises to return daily to see him. Everyday at 11:00 am, she will leave the kids with her friend Millie and take the subway to Raymond Street. She turns and waves goodbye to Cheech.

He says, "*Domani*, tomorrow!" She nods yes and winks.

Later, the guard comes by to tell Cheech that the Commander said Maria can stay as long as she wishes from now on. Cheech thanks him.

Maria looks around and spots Mrs. Snyder's car across the street. She enters the car. An excited Mrs. Snyder asks, "Did you see him Maria? How is he?"

"Oh, he's wonderful. I touched him, and kissed him and smelled him. She burst into tears.

"Maria, what happened? What's the matter?"

"Mrs. Pendola, she will never see her Cheech again. Her little baby, she will never know her Papa. She will never know him."

"Oh, Maria, I know. Neither will you and your family see little Joey. Now you are making me cry."

Mrs. Snyder starts the engine and pulls away from the curb.

When they reach the apartment, Maria thanks her again. She tells Millie and the children how well she found him and how nice the police were to her. All this kindness is something that overwhelms her.

Darrow returns to Manhattan at the request of Schneider and Spellman. He first stops by Governor Smith's office. After an hour long meeting, the two men part and Darrow is on his way to the 1.440

Broadway offices of Schneider and Spellman. Since he cannot practice law in the state of New York, he early on requests the assistance of Schneider, Spellman and Pollak. From the start Darrow works in the background, his name is the cutting edge of this effort. The very mention of the great attorney's name opens doors that would have remained closed if he were not known to be involved. Though the three men are capable learned attorneys on their own, they are in awe of Darrow. They adhere to his every request to the last detail. Their lifetime thrill is not only to meet the man, but also to be forever associated with him.

The newspapers report:

New Trial Date Set for Doctor's Killer

Trial is set for January 30, 1928 as Appellate Court overturns Caruso's conviction

It goes on to give a brief description of the events that lead up to the killing and the results of the original trial.

Clarence Darrow, who works quietly behind the scenes from his Chicago home, since his enlistment to take on the Caruso case, manages to use his famous name as a tool to stir up interest at the appropriate time. Spending much time with Schneider, Spellman and Pollak, he grills them on how the trial will proceed.

People involved in the original trial and representatives of the New York AMA give statements to the press to the affect that nothing will change in the new trial. The new team led by Clarence Darrow will not go for a reduction in sentence; they will demand freedom for Cheech. All of the arguments and motions raised at the appeal are the framework of the famous attorney. The defense team lead by Schneider will use the temporary insanity plea in the upcoming trial. Everything is ready.

A publicly known fact about Clarence Darrow is that throughout his famous career he is a staunch supporter of the abolishment of the death penalty. He argued for twelve hours in the Leopold and Loeb case that their heinous and deliberate crime should not incur the death penalty. In his opinion about Cheech, he feels that a temporarily insane man most assuredly does not deserve the death penalty, nor does he deserve punishment at all.

He knows better than anyone does the circumstances and events of the first trial. He studied it from all points of view, the AMA's defense of doctor's rights, the role Cheech played in it, the pharmacist's statement, and the understandable anger of the young widow. He studied the kangaroo court atmosphere of the first trial, the denial by Judge McLaughlin for an interpreter, the use of the doctors wife as a witness (even though she had never been in the Caruso home), the reading of the defendant's own wife's statement into evidence as well as the shutting down all of the defense's objections. He contemplated how much the statement of the doctor's brother contributed to Cheech's decision to kill the doctor. "My brother shouldn't do things like this. This medicine is too strong for a child!" What affect did those words have on a man already mourning the loss of his baby boy? He studies it all as he sifts through every possibility and viewpoint, the widow's testimony and its affect on the jury, Maria's read statement over the objections of Caruso's lawyer . . . all of it.

Darrow sits back, hands behind his head at the office of Schneider. He says, "We need to go by Maria's place. She's the only one alive, outside of her husband, who was actually there at the time of the death. She saw it. She opened the door and watched the altercation. Then we need to speak to the O'Hanlon's. Frank trusted them. He turned to them, and he trusted them to cover his tracks. He went there directly after the killing. We also need to speak to the mutual friend of both Frank and the O'Hanlon's, Sergeant O'Mally. Lastly, we need to get a statement from Frank now that he's back at Raymond Street Station House. It is my understanding that he learned how to read and write English at Sing Sing. His statements for the first trial were incomplete because he was suffering from a concussion. The question is, why wasn't he offered treatment before the trial, and was it by design. If possible, we must make all of these appointments for this coming week. Then we will have enough time to incorporate the information for the trial."

Schneider tells Spellman, "Get Pollak. Set up all of the appointments for this coming week."

"I'll start right now." Spellman hurries off to the other office and his telephone.

"One more thing, Schneider, I want Alexander Marky at all of these meetings. Please see to that."

* * *

Maria keeps her word to Cheech. With the help of Millie and other good friends, she spends all of her lunchtimes at Raymond Street with her Che. In this worst time of times in their relationship, she loves this man, this man whom she did not wish to marry when she first met him. Not because she didn't find him attractive, but in a silent pledge to herself never to marry after losing the love of her life in Sicily. In spite of it, she knows in her heart that he will never truly love her. This is the essence of Cheech. He has a strong effect on everyone he meets, yet many of these meetings end in disaster.

Raymond Street for Cheech is a replay of Sing Sing. The cards and letters come into the station house in bags wishing luck and best wishes often with money. The guards help Cheech with the mail. They welcome Maria's visits in anticipation of the treats she brings for them. Commander Johnston enjoys her home cooking for his lunch at least once a week. He complements Maria on her cooking. Cheech told Maria not to bring the children to visit him while he is behind bars. The Commander, upon hearing this arranges for Cheech to visit the children unsupervised in his office.

Cheech grabs all of the children in one hug and lifts them off the floor. They all hug and kiss him with big happy smiles. He puts them down and reaches for Maria. The children watch them embrace in a promise of things to come. It is the first time they have all been together since Joey died. They watch Cheech tell Maria some very important and deserved words, "Maria, you are a good woman. I hope the day will come when you forgive me for what I have done to you and our family. *E yeda batsa*. I was crazy. I don't know if I will ever get over Joey and Ida."

"I know, Che', I know. We have each other and the kids. They need us."

Cheech sits on the commander's desk chair and invites Lena to sit on his lap. "What would I do without you Lena my little boss? Can I ever make it up to you? Can you find it in your heart not to grow up to fast . . . for me?"

"Papa, I love you, know what? I sat on Mr. LaGuardia's lap, and we talked to a lot of people with a microphone. Mama helped me."

"You did?" Teasing her he says, "Who is Mr. LaGuardia?"

Lena knows he is kidding. "Papa, you know; he's a congressman!" He hugs her and smells her new clean scent. Lifting her off his lap, he opens his arms to Josey.

She walks to him saying "Hello, Papa." He lifts her and says, "Josephina, my special little girl." Josey was born mentally retarded. "What have I done to you? What in Gods name can I do for you? Did you miss Papa?"

"No, Papa, you're always with me. I see you all the time. I see Joey too. He visits me every day."

Tears trickle down Cheech's face. "Josephina, I wish I was you! I miss Joey all the time. I'm going *batsa*!"

"I will take you to him tomorrow. He is always with me. Honest, Papa, he is."

Several tears trickle down his face when he says, "I believe you my special, little Angel. Papa will let you do that. I promise, when I come home."

Sitting on his lap Anna almost four and Sally almost three look at each other and at the man that they cannot remember. Maria tells Lena and Josey to help by standing close to them. She knows that the littlest one will be more comfortable with them there.

Cheech says, "Maria, how am I going to do it. How can I ever make it up to these children? In Gods name, how will I?"

"We will do it together, Che', you and I." We will do it together." The visit ends. Cheech kisses and hugs all of the children and Maria. He hugs Maria the way a man hugs the special woman in his life.

Chapter 14

People who participated in the different meetings are ready. The final details in this yearlong effort are completed. There will be no more hidden facts. Unknown to Cheech, in this month of October 1927, he will have two meetings of his own that will drastically change things for him. One meeting is from his best friend O'Mally and the other is from a man who calls himself Mario Caruso.

* * *

"You have a visitor, Frank." Cheech looks up from his cot to see O'Mally stop in front of his cell. His cell door is shut, not locked.

Cheech opens the door as the guard turns to leave. O'Mally looks at the open door and then back to his friend, "Does that mean that you can go home any time you want?"

Cheech laughs. "You know better, *Piason*." They hug and slap each other on the back, something O'Mally never did before he met Cheech. "What's the matter, *Piason*? Can I take some of that weight off of your shoulders?"

"Jesus, Cheech, I should be saying that to you!"

"You have been my *Piason* for a long time; many times we have helped each other. Now what's the matter?"

The two men sit beside each other on the cot. "First things first as you say. You are going to have a visit from your brother Mario. Antonio called me. That is the name he will use, your visitor. The visit is tomorrow. I told the commander your brother is coming in from Sicily. So do not act surprised when you see him, *Gabish*, Cheech?"

"*Cie' E' gabish*; thank you my Irish *Piason*, thank you."

"Now, Maria asked me not to worry you with this, but you have to know because she doesn't understand. Some people attacked Maria and Lena in the last few months."

"What the hell do you mean attacked, by whom?"

"Calm down. Let me explain, Cheech. The attacks started on Lena first, but she had help from a man who lives on her way home from school. I spoke to him. They were bigger boys picking on Lena. Santo is a good man. He sits at his front window watching the people going by. He lives alone. He said that at first, it was just kids and then it was a man. At first, Lena kept it from Maria; she didn't want to worry her. After the man incident, Santo accompanied her and insisted she tell her mama. He chased the kids away and beat the hell out of the man.

"It turns out that the kids were children of doctors and nurses from the area. Santo said the man looked familiar, thought he was either a doctor or lawyer. He knew him from somewhere, possibly the newspapers. He still watches Lena from his window. Then there was the attack on Maria. She was carrying some groceries up the steps when a man knocked her down. He pushed her around, roughed her up and left in a hurry. He was gone when the neighbors looked. He called her names and told her that you were going to die no matter what Darrow did. He told her she and the children were not safe either, that she should stop fighting the original sentence. Then he was gone. The neighbors came out and took care of Maria."

"You went to see my friend?"

"Yes, I did; everything stopped. It has been quiet since I went to Brooklyn. That's not all."

Cheech's expression is hard. "What else?"

"Last month Mary left me. She took the kids. I don't know where she is. Then last week I got a call from a friend telling me he heard there is a contract on me . . . not by your friend. Either from Vannie's (Irish Mob) bunch or the AMA grunts. Can't think who else it could be. I have assurance that it is not your bunch. Antonio told me, hands off!"

"O'Mally, I give you some advice like at brother. Don't run and don't turn your back. Neither one of those two groups have the will or the organization that Salvatore has. I tell you this. As long as he is the *capo*, no one will do anything. Because they know we are brothers, you still have time. For now, you are safe. If someone targets Salvatore as I told you he would eventually, then you disappear. Your pension is no good if you are dead."

"Yeah, I Understand, Cheech. I think I spent too much time with you."

"No, *Piason*, you learned well. You will be okay. Now I tell you something; be smart; stay away from me."

O'Mally understands his friend's advice. O'Mally grabs his friend, which is in all likelihood to be their last moments together, "Jesus,

Cheech, I love you. You should have been my brother instead of the asshole I have for one."

Wiping their eyes, Cheech tells him, "I know. I love you too. You be good. You still can live a good life. Love to live. Now get the hell out of here, *Piason!*" There will be one more meeting for the two friends, but neither knows it at this time.

Cheech is restless that night thinking about Salvatore D'Aquila's pending visit. He knows that D'Aquila is behind everything that happened since his conviction. He remembers the note O'Mally delivered to the mobster. He did not want to involve the Mafia in his problem, even if it led to his death. At the time, dying would have been easier. Now he ponders what he will say to Salvatore if he asks him to join with him, something he respectfully and courteously managed to put off so many times in the past. Being a made man in Sicily before he left for America, he has kept it a secret from everyone. But now, with all that D'Aquila has done for Cheech, he feels a pressure, an obligation that was not there before. With all that has happened in the last few days, Cheech has many reasons to be grateful.

Early the next morning, a guard tells Cheech that his brother is waiting to visit with him, and he will be in shortly. Still uncertain, Cheech decides to be honest with D'Aquila. He is Hopeful Salvatore will understand.

The guard accompanies D'Aquila to the cell. D'Aquila says, "*Walune!* Kid! *Coma sta?* How are you *Frada?* Brother?" The guard lets Salvatore into the cell. Cheech embraces him in a *piason* bear hug. Dressed in a gray suit with light gray spats over black pointy shoes, Salvatore looks quite dapper.

Seeing the brothers' joyous reunion, the guard leaves them to some privacy. Out of site from the guard, Cheech breaks the hug and kisses the back of Salvatore's hand. He speaks quietly. "*Gradsia, Salvatore, Gradsia bi tuta mia avata.* For all you have done for me." They sit on the bunk and talk softly. Cheech does not wish to display his displeasure at his powerful friend's decision to save him from execution, so he acts gracious.

Salvatore scrutinizes him. "Are you okay, Cheech?"

Cie, Pardroni, Boss! "Saunyo bona, I am good!"

In Sicilian they continue. "You had me worried, Cheech. Did you expect me not to help you?"

"Well, *Pardroni*, this is not family business. I didn't want you to become involved. You have enough on your mind with the business."

"The business, ah the business will kill me one day. For once, I do something special. I help a friend and I fuck the AMA. It makes me happy, not as much for you as for me. I call the biggest producer on Broadway and ask for the best publicist and organizer, and you know I got Alexander Marky. I call Chicago and Alfonzo sends Clarence Darrow. I make more calls and the District Attorneys and their deputies, Lawyers and all kind of good people come out of the woodwork. There is money enough to support you and your family for the rest of your life." He smiles. "The telephone is a wonderful thing, Cheech, just wonderful!"

Although Cheech is aware of the reach of the Mafia in Sicily, it is nothing compared to what is happening in America. He is surprised at how many people in different positions and business's Salvatore has in his pocket.

D'Aquila continues. "We have all but taken over the business from Vannie Higgins (The Irish Mob). Your friend O'Mally is in trouble. He is a mark for any loyal Irish thug. It is difficult for us to monitor. I will take care of the contracted hit man for your friend. They cannot stop me. Consider it done. He has no fear from the hit, but I cannot control any other action. The best thing for him is to lie low and then disappear. Maybe go to Chicago. You tell him what I say."

"Thank you, *Padroni*, I will."

"Cheech, I will not ask you to join me again. Not that I would not like it, but because there have been threats to kill me and they continue. My luck cannot last forever; eventually they will catch up to me and bang bang, that's it, *Gabish*?" Cheech nods. "You have a decision to make that is very important." Cheech listens intently, curious. "I will be killed someday. When I'm dead, you will be on your own and at the mercy of any hit. With the money and the memory that the AMA has, it could be a long time threat. If Darrow proceeds with a temporary insanity plea, you will die. Like me, who knows when, but you will die. Maybe your family will be at risk. Let me offer the court a deal on your behalf for a lesser charge. I will see that Lawes takes care of you, that your family has money to live on while you are at Sing Sing. When they release you, you will no longer have any threat over you. You will be able to live as you wish. You can tell me now or later, but not too late."

Cheech gives Salvatore an intent look. "Make the deal for me, *Pardoni*. For me I don't care. My family has suffered enough. No more!"

D'Aquila beams showing his pleasure. "Good! *A fata bene*'! You did well! I knew you would. I took care of it already, *Piason*. At the trial you will be dressed in a new suit with patent leather spats on dancing shoes; you will stand up and shock everyone in the room with your decision."

Cheech smiles, "Thank you, *Padroni, Gradsia, and bene.*"

"I feel it in my heart that I will never see you again, Cheech. Sometimes I hear the clock ticking in my head. Then bang! It is over. I will always remember you, *Piason*. The loss of Joey must have made you *batsa*, crazy! *Mea desbiaga*, it displeases me."

Cheech kisses the back of his friend's hand, this *Capo*. He knows he is on his own again, alone to cope with the sadness in his heart.

Salvatore is the first to rise. Cheech stands. The men embrace in a show of mutual respect. The mobster reaches to Cheech's cheek and with his fingers wipes away the tears trickling down his cheek, "I will take your tears of love with me forever. I will miss you, Frank. Never will I forget you." D'Aquila opens the door to the cell and walks away not looking back.

Cheech sits on his cot with his head in his hands crying.

"You must love your brother, Cheech," the guard says. "He is a handsome man. Can I get you some water?"

Cheech wipes his eyes. "Yes, I do love him. Thank you, no water, I am fine." He ponders how to explain it to his petite and beautiful Maria, a stronger person than she was a year ago and quite capable of handling anything. He will tell her tomorrow when she comes for lunch.

* * *

The first of the three meetings set up by Clarence Darrow is with Maria. He and his two cohorts head for her apartment. She is preparing a homecoming party for Cheech, even though she is tired of heart and sad of spirit. When she left Sicily twelve years earlier, she never imagined what lay ahead of her in this land of plenty, this new country with so much promise. The dreams are mostly gone, but still there is hope. She wonders if all her tomorrows will be as tainted by all the yesterdays since Joey and Ida died. She answers Marky's knock. She opens the door to see three men standing in her doorway, "Mr. Marky, please come in, *wana, wana*. Come in, come in!" She seats them at the kitchen table. As Cheech would have done, she brings four glasses to the table and fills them with wine from the icebox. She sits at the table next to Marky and lifts her glass in a toast. "Please, let me say this to you, Mr. Marky. When I met you last spring, I didn't hear your words or see your face. When you spoke to me, I didn't hear you. I was like a lost soul unable to think or feel. I accepted your help because Mama and Papa were nodding to me. The look on their faces hurt my heart. It was hard to breathe. To you and their confidence in you, I drink to you my dear, Mr. Marky. There are many kinds of love. You are one of them. I love you.

They lift their glasses in the toast. "Thank you, Mrs. Maria Caruso. I can tell that you are your husband's wife. He taught you well. He is a special man, a beautiful man, and you, My Dear, are beautiful, too. People like you give the heart cause to live. The two of you are Broadway's loss. I've never heard words used as you two use them. I'll never forget either one of you."

Schneider tells Marky, "Wow! Alex, you're not so bad yourself. I believe you just met this guy one time . . . right? I can't wait until I get a chance!"

Nodding his head, Darrow says, "Me, too, Fella's. But if you don't mind, I'll stand behind you Schneider until after we're introduced!"

They all laugh and lift their glasses one more time. With another clink of the glasses Maria says, "Moments like these, moments of the heart are what the bouquet of life is made of, feelings of love."

"Maria," Marky says, "I'd like to introduce you to the attorney from Chicago who continues to direct your husband's trial. This is Mr. Clarence Darrow." As Darrow reaches across the table to shake Maria's hand, Marky introduces Schneider. "This is Mr. Schneider. He will do the work in the courtroom." She thanks the two men for working with Mr. Marky.

Maria stands and says she will clear the table for the food. She asks them to retire to the living room for a while. A short time later, they are back around the table. Usually grace is said in the Caruso household, but out of respect for guests, they forego it. She invites the men to commence eating.

Darrow says, "Mrs. Caruso, I thought Italians say grace."

"We do, Mr. Darrow, but my husband feels that in offering our hospitality to guests, we should not impose our beliefs on others who might not appreciate them as we do."

This family's sensitivity impresses Darrow, a confirmed agnostic. The men compliment Maria's cooking. After lunch, the men sit back while Maria clears the table for the discussion that is coming.

Maria takes her apron off and sits next to Marky. Darrow starts the conversation. "Maria, we need to know everything that happened last February 13th and all of the events that lead up to the death of Doctor

Pendola. First, I would like to ask you a question that I need to know. Did you actually see the doctor die? Did you see the instant he stopped breathing?"

She closes her eyes for a silent moment then speaks. "Yes, I saw it all. As soon as Cheech started shouting at the doctor, I opened the door and saw the whole thing. I saw the poor man die."

"We'll talk about that later, but for now start with when your Joey first got sick and don't leave anything out."

She places her elbows on the table and closes her eyes and starts, "Joey was a smart little boy. Two years younger than my Lena, he used to wait for her in the morning and in the afternoon to walk with her to and from school. He would say it was his job to protect her. He did it for Cheech. Joey was so smart, that he often helped Lena with her homework.

"About three weeks before he died, he was waiting outside the door to the school for Lena to come out so they could walk home together. It was raining; he didn't put on his hat. His head got wet. He caught a cold and it just didn't get better. His cold turned into a sore throat; he couldn't stop coughing. Cheech went to the Pendola drugstore and got some throat swabs for his throat. Joey got real bad. Nothing seemed to help my baby. Then we could see that he had diphtheria. We knew what it was. We saw it on the forth floor and our floor and the second floor. A week before he died, we told some of our neighbors in the hall that we thought Joey had diphtheria and that they should call the doctor and they said they would.

Cheech kept going to work for a while because we needed the money. One morning on the way out, he saw a quarantine sign on our door and some of the neighbors on the floor opened their doors to tell Cheech that they would take care of the food for us, not to worry. He thanked them and closed the door. He told me about the sign and I saw it."

Darrow interrupts, "Did anyone else see the sign besides you and your husband?"

"Yes, Mr. Darrow, everyone on our floor. Everyone knows what it means."

"Go on, Maria, please."

"We waited all week for a doctor or nurse to come by, but nobody came, not ever. The neighbors kept putting the food outside our door for us. Still, nobody came, no one. Cheech kept telling Joey help was coming, but nobody came." She cries, then wipes her face. "Joey's throat was worse. His little voice got so raspy that he didn't sound like a little boy anymore. Then he could barely talk. When he tried to speak, foam and bubbles came from his mouth, little bubbles . . . poor Baby. Cheech and I took turns sleeping a few hours at a time. We swabbed his throat all night and day. We kept the other children in the back bedroom away from Joey so they wouldn't catch it too. My poor little Lena took care of them all by herself. Since I was helping Cheech with Joey, I couldn't go back to the bedroom to see the children. I worry about Lena. How will all this affect her later in life? We didn't know what we were doing anymore. Cheech and I were sleepwalking, and still nobody came. Saturday morning Joey got even worse. Cheech refused to wait any longer. He left to get a doctor for his son. He knew it was against the law, but he was so afraid of losing his little boy. When he came back, he said we had to clean Joey up a little for a doctor who was on the way. We washed Joey up a little and got the room ready for the doctor. Cheech said that he couldn't find a doctor so Mr. Pendola called his brother for us. The doctor came and looked at Joey. When he saw how bad Joey was, he yelled at us for letting him go too long; he said we should have called for help sooner. Cheech grabbed him by the wrist and told him to lower his voice. He said he would not tell him again, and the doctor was nicer. Cheech told him we didn't look for a doctor sooner because the hospital put a quarantine sign on our door. They knew Joey was sick. We don't know who called them.

"The doctor said Joey must go to the nearest hospital. Cheech told him that he did *not* want his boy in the hospital. Then doctor said he would try to help Joey at home; he gave Cheech a paper for medicine. He told him to take it to his brother and bring the medicine back, that he would wait. Cheech left. The doctor helped me with Joey. A little later, Cheech was back with the medicine. I know he ran back. He was out of breath, breathing hard. He gave the medicine to the doctor. He told him that his brother was upset with him and said the medicine was too strong for a child. He said his brother said he wished his brother wouldn't do things like this.

"The doctor seemed upset. He told Cheech that his brother didn't know what he was talking about and that he should mind his own business. He was a little nasty with Cheech. Then he rolled Joey over and gave him the needle in the back. Joey burst out crying, and we comforted him. The doctor said he would be back next day (Sunday) at ten o'clock in the morning, and then he left. At first, Joey seemed a little bit quieter. Then about midnight, he started getting very sick again. We were up all night with Joey. Poor Lena took care of the younger children all the time we couldn't leave the house from the quarantine.

"By seven-thirty the next morning, Joey was terrible. It broke my heart to see him like that. Shaking and coughing, he moved his head from side-to-side; he would not stop. At eight o'clock, Cheech couldn't stand it anymore. Once again he went to find a doctor. He did not like or trust Doctor Pendola. He returned about 10 o'clock, but this time because it was Sunday, he couldn't find another doctor. Joey was deathly sick now. When he tried to talk, we couldn't understand him too good. He grabbed his Papa by his arm with his little hands. I could understand him, but Cheech had a hard time understanding his little boy. Joey told him he was dying, that the shot the doctor gave him was killing him. He asked Cheech to help him; he didn't want to die. He said, 'Please Papa, please don't let me die. Help me, Papa." He said, "I am leaving now.' Bubbles came out of his mouth. He let go of his Papa's arms and stopped breathing. His eyes stayed open; his head went back. He was gone! Joey was dead."

She cries for a little while and resumes. "I stood up and cried, but I don't think I had a voice. It was like in my stomach. Cheech broke down and held his little boy. I couldn't understand him; he was hollering and yelling. Then he stopped. He played with Joey's fingers and kissed them and he said, 'Please, Joey, don't do this to me. Not again, this can't be happening again.' I knew he meant about his father. Back in Sicily he did something, and his father wished him dead. When his father mistakenly heard that Cheech was killed in an ambush, he dropped dead of a heart attack. Joey looked like his grandpa, so Cheech named him after his father. Now he lost his son, too. It was too much for me. I ran around straightening the house. The children started crying and came out of the bedroom. I told them to stay in the room. My little Lena helped me get them back in. I went back into the kitchen. Cheech was wrapping Joey in his death sheet. He picked up Joey, hugging him tight. He walked backward to the wall and slid down with his back until he was sitting down on the floor. He cried. His face was all red and puffy like he was going to blow up. Then he rocked back and forth, easy rocking as if he was putting Joey to sleep. Then he banged his head on the wall when he rocked back. He kept banging it harder and harder until it splattered blood. I tried to stop him, but he was too strong for me. I yelled for help. I ran to the door. I yelled out into the hall that Joey was dead. I yelled that Cheech was killing himself. I yelled for someone to call the wagon—no one came to help me. When I got back to Cheech, he had stopped rocking and banging his head. I thought he was dead too. Joey was on his legs and Cheech's arms were hanging by his side. He didn't move. Then he moaned. Blood was everywhere, all up the wall onto the ceiling. Most was where he banged his head; it looked like a big red star. I got a wet rag from the sink and put it on his face. Then I fainted and fell on Joey. I woke up on the couch in the parlor where Cheech had carried me. Joey was on the floor next to me wrapped in the blanket. Cheech was lying next to him crying. I took the rag off my head and wet the back of Cheech's head with it. He didn't care. I don't think he knew what was going on. Then, I was going to open the kitchen door; he told me not to do it, so I returned to him and Joey.

"Somebody knocked at the door and Cheech got up to answer it. He let some men in from the wagon and they looked at Joey and asked us questions. Cheech couldn't answer too much, so I did. They put Joey in a bag and strapped him onto a carrier and they left telling us that there would be some people coming to check the rest of the children. After they left, Cheech and I went into the kitchen and sat at the table. We were in shock. We couldn't believe what had just happened. Joey was gone forever. We sat at the table and had a drink of wine. I looked at the blood going up the wall and Cheech said not to look at it. He said he didn't know if he had the strength to pick me up again. I tried not to look, but it was hard. Some of our neighbors came by and knocked at the door. I know the O'Hanlon's came by. We told them we were okay. We wanted to be alone, so we didn't open the door. Cheech asked me if he kissed Joey before they took him away. I told him he did. He cried again. He said he killed his Papa, and then named his first-born son after him, and now he killed him too. I tried to console him. It was like make believe. Nothing was real, but it was. Joey was really dead and gone.

"There was another knock at the door. It was about one-thirty in the afternoon. Cheech got up and told me to go into the back bedroom with the children. Then he closed the door to the kitchen.

I went back to the kids, but I didn't go close to them, I didn't want to make them sick. I told them to be real quiet. bedroom door was cracked so I could hear Cheech open the door. I heard Doctor Pendola ask Cheech what was the matter. Cheech sounded real angry when he told the doctor that it was over, that Joey was dead. The doctor said that he tried everything he could and asked why we waited so long to get help? Cheech got real mad. He told him that we waited for help for a whole week and it never came. Then he told the doctor that his medicine killed Joey, not the sickness. He said that his brother was right about the medicine being too strong for a child. I heard the doctor ask Cheech if they could talk in private. They went into our bedroom and closed the door. I ran to the door to listen. I heard the doctor say that if Cheech would not tell anyone that he was ever there, he would take care of our loss with money. Cheech blew up. I never knew that he could be that way. He was crazy. He cursed at the doctor. I can't tell you what he said!"

Marky says, "Maria, you must tell Mr. Darrow everything."

Maria takes a deep breath and quotes Cheech. "He said, 'You no good son-of–a-bitch, you no good Bastard, you good for nothing piece of shit! First, you yell at me for not taking care of my baby, then you say your brother don't know what the hell he's talking about, then you kill my Joey! Now you fucking Bastard, you want to pay me for my loss! Are you a real doctor? Do they teach you that at school for medicine how to kill people? How many people have you killed?' I cracked the door open and I saw the doctor drop his black bag to the floor. He hits Cheech on the face. Cheech grabbed the doctor by his lapels and threw him across the room. The doctor broke a chair in the corner when he landed. He stood and Cheech grabbed him again. He punched the doctor on the face over-and-over-and-over-and-over. He threw the doctor over the bed and on the floor. He ran over to him and kicked the bed out of the way. The planter fell over.

He told him, 'now I'm gonna kill you like you killed my son, you no good, Bastard.' The doctor tried to protect himself, but he couldn't. Cheech sat on him and punched him a few more times; then he grabbed him by the throat and squeezed. I could see the doctor's legs sticking out from behind the bed. They were kicking. I could hear his arms moving, and then there was no more. All the noise stopped; it was quiet. All I could hear was Cheech breathing. He moaned again, like when he was banging his head on the wall. He was coughing and crying. He got up very slow and came to the door. He led me away from the room saying not to go into the room. He could not lift his head up. He said it hurt so much. He went into the kitchen and got a knife out of the drawer. I told him 'No, Cheech, please no, no more please.' I couldn't stop him. I ran after him and stopped at the door to the bedroom. He knelt by the doctor's head. He said, 'Now I do a good job you filthy Bastard.' He stabbed him in the throat and then lifted his head up by the hair and he cut his throat. I ran away and stopped in the parlor. I was sick! He dragged the doctor's body into the kitchen and dropped him on the floor right where Joey died. Then Cheech came up to me and said he had to go, that he was leaving. I asked him where he was going. He didn't know. He was just going. He didn't know what he was doing. He put on his hat and a coat and he said he would see me in court and he was gone.

"Somebody must have heard the noise. As soon as Cheech left the house, the police were at the front door. They banged on the door and broke it in. They ran around the house with their guns yelling and ordering us around. I was so upset I think I was crazy. I never saw anybody die before." She closes her eyes and whispers, "All that blood. All of a sudden, I saw two people die. When they asked me where my husband was, I yelled that he didn't do this; I did it. I don't know why. I just said so. I told them that my husband was a good man that loves his family. I was going crazy. They arrested me, took the children away from me and locked them in a broom closet because of what their father did. I was in the jail when my poor babies were in a broom closet all night long—no light—no food—no water, all night. The next day, my brother Louis came to jail to get me. We rescued the children, and then went to my parent's place at New Jersey.

"I was crazy after my sweet little Joey died. I saw Cheech crying for his child, and I just went crazy. I didn't know what I was doing; I didn't care. Neither one of us knew what was happening. It was horrible. When he left me, he didn't know where he was going. He wasn't escaping; he didn't know what was going on."

Maria runs over to the sink to throw up. Marky is by her side saying, "It's over, Maria, you don't have to talk about it anymore. You did very well."

She excuses herself so she can go to the bathroom to freshen herself up a little. While she is in the bathroom, the three men exchange looks. Marky says, "It been terrible for me learning a bit at a time over the last year. I can't imagine how this woman survived witnessing all of that. She swallowed her pride to stand in front of people and beg for her husband's life, like a beggar on stage. She and her daughter faced ridicule. They were both threatened and attacked. God knows when this will end for these poor people. Probably never I guess."

Darrow says, "No question that we are speaking of temporary insanity. I would imagine something more than that. With the description of him slamming his head against the wall, there probably was some damage to his thought process. Hell, it's hard to think when you have a headache. It is worse if you have some kind of damage. What an amazing story. It moved me. I just don't know what to say to her when she comes out of the bathroom."

Marky says, "If I know Maria, when she comes out of the bathroom you won't have to say anything."

Maria returns to the table with a bottle of wine. She fills the glasses again. She sits and lifts her glass in salute, "To love and life." They all raise their glasses and sip of wine. "Gentlemen, that was terrible. I mean this is the first time since Joey died in his father's arms that I have allowed myself to think of everything that happened to us that day so long ago. It was like living through it again. If my husband comes home tomorrow, I don't know if we can make it. I know he is suffering more than I am. He came to this country with a bag full of troubles; it did not help him."

"Maria," Darrow says, "I have handled many kinds of cases, but nothing like this one with mistake after mistake made repeatedly. There have been many wrongs done here. No matter what the outcome is, no one wins. You lost two of your children, one by overdose and the other because you were afraid to take her to the hospital for treatment. I cannot say how you, your husband and your family will survive. There is someone else affected by it, too. That is Mrs. Pendola. She, too, has a child. That child will never know her father. I just cannot express to you how sad this whole affair makes me."

Maria gets up and leaves. She returns quickly holding something. "Mr. Darrow, this is Joey's rosary from his confirmation. Every night, I pray the rosary for Joey, Ida, Doctor Pendola and his family. It is a nightly ritual. I don't know if you believe in God . . . but I do! God *will* help us, the ones of faith."

"Mrs. Caruso, I respect your beliefs, but I find it difficult to believe in a God who would allow things like this to happen."

"My dear Mr. Clarence Darrow, God didn't do this. We did. We were perfect at one time, the human race. We fixed that too. We do these things to ourselves. The Catholic Church teaches that it is better to give than to receive, and that means thanks too. I will give Him my thanks whatever my lot is at the end. Can you understand that?"

"I understand that you are a firm believer in God. I can see it. You'll forgive me for mine."

Maria looks at him and quietly says, "I will forever find a word in prayers for you Mr. Clarence Darrow. I know of your work in this life, and I will do it. I will pray for you of my own accord. You do not need forgiving. God works in different ways."

"Maria, as I told you earlier, many wrongs have been made here. The things we are concerned about now are the illegal wrongs committed

by the courts to your husband. Our investigation brought these illegal
actions to light. The Appellate Court agreed. On November 22, Justice
Cardozo issued the Appellate Court ruling that granted a new trial. We are
no longer trying for a lesser judgment. We are going to get a complete
release from all charges. His defense team of Mr. Schneider, Mr. Spellman
and Mr. Pollak will use a temporary insanity plea in the new trial. We will
need to know all there is to know about the state of your husbands mind
after Joey's death and before the death of the doctor."

"Oh no, Mr. Darrow, that cannot be. He will not let you do that."

"Mrs. Caruso, we have no choice. If we do not issue a plea of
temporary insanity, your husband could face execution. He can
conceivably receive the same ruling he got in the first trial and be back on
death row again. Do you understand that?"

"*Cie*, I understand, but you do not understand. He will not let you do
that. My husband is very sensitive about the use of the word crazy. He *will*
not do it." Shaken, Maria gets up and walks to the sink.

Darrow walks up to her. "Mrs. Caruso, being in the temporary state of
insanity is not the same as being crazy. There is a big difference. It is not
the same. If we do not use the plea, we cannot win. We do not have a
choice."

Not knowing what to say to him, she turns and tells them all "promise
me that you will tell him of your intentions before the trial. Please promise
me you will speak to him first." They each assure her that before the week
is out, they will discuss it with Cheech.

Once again, they all sit at the kitchen table to discuss the state of
Cheech's mind on that fateful day. Maria tells them how much time
Cheech spent with Joey after the quarantine sign went up. "For the next
week, we take turns treating Joey and sleep in shifts. By the end of the
week, the lack of sleep wears us out. We are in a state of the unreal. One
hour feels like the other. Even in his sleep, my baby Joey calls for his
Papa. Cheech wakes up to come to his side. The two are inseparable. I
send Cheech is so worn out, I send him back to bed as soon as Joey falls
asleep. There are times when Cheech doesn't know what he is doing. Me
too, I got that way, too. When Joey dies in his arms, he is crazy, banging
his head and saying things that don't make sense, things going back to
Sicily and his papa, his brothers and Valenta his childhood sweetheart. He
is like a crazy man!" Realizing what she just said she places her fingers
over her mouth and closes her eyes.

Marky says, "See, Maria, he was that way, he was out of his mind when Joey died and understandably so. Do you see that for a while he was out of his mind?"

"Oh my God protect us, please, oh my God, my poor *Che*'! *Yeda patsa!* Was crazy!"

Chapter 15

Darrow says, "Maria would you please continue, please."

"The wagon took Joey away. I went into the kitchen to sit and be quiet. I saw all of that blood on the wall where he banged his head. It was terrible. He told me not to look at the wall. I tried to clean the back of his head with a rag and water. It was so hard. He cried out and moaned when I touched it a little bit. I was careful not to hurt him. He was changed. The O'Hanlon's and others knocked on the door. We just sat and looked at each other. Tears came out of his eyes, but he didn't cry. Then there was that awful knock at the door. I will never forget it. I knew it was the doctor. The look on Cheech's face changed no longer calm. He told me to go into the room with the children, but I did not. I closed the door to the children's room and listened from the end of the hall. I could tell that Cheech's head hurt by the way he got up and how he walked, crooked like. He was *not* well. Cheech told him that it was too late. Joey was gone. He was dead. The doctor got fresh, loud and told Che that he should have called him sooner. He said that it was his fault. He yelled at Cheech. My husband told him to stop shouting, to holler no more, not one more time. He told the doctor that he killed Joey with the medicine and that his brother was right, it was too strong. He was crying and holding his head.

"The doctor asked can they talk in private, so they went into the front bedroom and closed the door, but I could hear them. He told Cheech that if he didn't tell anybody that he had been here, he would pay money for our loss. Madonna Mia, Cheech went crazy. He yelled that first the doctor holler at him, then he kill his Joey and now he gonna pay money to lie. I cracked the door open and looked in and saw the doctor's face in the dresser mirror. He was smiling. He dropped the black bag and punched Cheech in the face, but Cheech didn't move. His eyes were red, face tight. He grabbed the doctor by the neck and punched him again-and-again. He threw him across the room and attacked him more. He yelled at the doctor that he was a no good son-of-a-bitch en *bastia,* and that he was going to kill him. The doctor yelled that it was his brother's fault, not his or Cheech's fault. Madonna, he was crazy. *Yeda patsa!* The poor man was screaming for his life and Cheech kept on hitting him like a *patsa,* crazy man. When he took his hands off the doctor's throat he did not move. The doctor was dead. Cheech got up, limped like a cripple into the kitchen for a knife and cut his throat. Then he dragged the doctor to the kitchen like a rag doll, head hanging down. I was so nauseous. He threw him down on the same spot where Joey died and kicked him. He said that was where his son died and so did the doctor. Blood trailed from the bedroom to the kitchen where the doctor lay. The smell of blood was everywhere.

"Cheech calmed and slowed down. He could hardly move. He told me to get his hat and coat. I put them on him; he could hardly talk. He said he was leaving, that he would see me in court. I said 'Where you going Che'?' He said he had something to do and he left." She covers her face and cries, "Che', Che' my poor Che' how we gonna live past this? You killed that poor doctor, *Poo'ida Bastia*, poor bastard."

The room is silent. Marky squeezes Maria's shoulder. "Maria, my life will not be the same either. I will never forget you, Cheech and your story. My life changed by it. I think and feel different now than I did last spring."

"Mr. Marky, I am sorry for you. I hope you can get past it when this is all over."

Darrow says, "Maria, thank you; that's enough. I can't listen to anymore. I am too emotionally involved, not good for me. We will leave you alone if you are all right. I mean so we can leave. Are you okay?"

"Yes, Mr. Darrow, I am okay, I will be fine. But promise me you will speak to Cheech, please."

"I promise you I will."

The men head back to Marky's office on Broadway and plan their visit to the O'Hanlon's. Before taking them out to dinner, Marky calls O'Mally and asks that he be present at the O'Hanlon's apartment the next morning. At this time, the money in the Caruso Defense Fund is estimated at over a million dollars and growing. No one but D'Aquila and Alexander Marky know its exact value or location.

The next morning the four men enter O'Hanlon's flat. O'Hanlon and O'Mally greet each other. O'Mally does the introductions, "Frank, this is Alexander Marky, this is Attorney Schneider and this is Clarence Darrow.

They settle at the dining room table and O'Hanlon calls in his daughter Florence. Marky starts, "Mr. O'Hanlon and Florence, it is important that we know everything Cheech said to you and how he acted when he stopped in on you last February 13. By telling everything just as it was, you help Cheech and us. Why don't you start, Mr. O'Hanlon?"

Frank says, "Cheech is a good man. I would do anything for him. When my wife, God rest her soul, died three years ago, Cheech arranged her funeral and handled the expense. I don't know where he got the money, but he did. I wasn't working because I had a heart attack the year before. I had no money. He stopped the property manager from throwing my daughter and me out on the street. I'm not the only person he helped. It didn't make any difference that I am Irish. He is the peacemaker around here. People go to him before they go to the police. That day you asked about, I was sleeping when he knocked on my door. Florence opened the door. She saw him all doubled over so she helped him in and yelled out for me. Cheech was in trouble. When I came into the foyer, he had blood all over him. Florence ran off to throw up. I helped him into the kitchen because he could hardly stand. I told Florence to get a shirt and pair of my pants for Cheech. When she felt better, she brought them out to us. Cheech looked pale like he was going to throw up so we brought him over to the sink. He was sick. He kept saying his head hurt bad. The back of it was bad. I asked him what happened and he told me not to ask. The less I knew the better off I was. He did say that Joey was dead. Florence started crying. I asked him what happened to Joey and he said 'Diphtheria.' That's all he would say. I told Florence to leave the room for a while and I helped him out of his bloody clothes. He said he had to get going fast, that the police were after him. I washed his face and hands. Florence washed his shoes off. He felt a little better. He put his coat on and said that I didn't know anything. In a while, the police were going to talk to all of the tenants, that I should say that I was sleeping. He said that Florence should go out to the hall and tell the police that he was here, that I was asleep and that she gave him some money and that he left. He was concerned about my weak heart. He did not want me involved with the police. There was something wrong with Cheech when he first came in. He was walking funny and throwing up spit. He's not like that. The man is an ox. Nothing bothers him to make him throw up. He was in that flat for two weeks with Joey. Joey was his life. Around his boy, he was real sweet, kind and gentle. Otherwise, nobody messed with him. I mean nobody."

O'Mally chimes in, "That's my Cheech. Never knew anyone like him."

Continuing O'Hanlon tells them, "Cheech thanked us. He said to make sure O'Mally knows what happened to Joey. Then he took off to his brother's place on Staten Island. I felt so sad for him when he left here. I went up to his flat earlier when I heard the ambulance people up there, but

Cheech and Maria wouldn't open the door. I could hear crying in there, but I guess they wanted to be alone. Later that day, O'Mally came by and told us everything. I was glad that they didn't kill Cheech. Most Irish cops don't like Italians. I was sick after O'Mally told us what had happened. How sad. That wasn't Cheech; he must have had something wrong with him. I'm so glad they took him off death row; he didn't belong there. The man has a golden heart, not saying he's an angel, but he's a damn good man."

They ask for confirmation from Florence. They tell the O'Hanlon's that they won't be called to testify. The information they gave is enough. O'Mally verifies everything they said, and adds his own confidence and loyalty to the man. The session ends.

* * *

December 1927 finds the little Caruso flat decorated and full of hope that the man of the house will be back home soon. New neighbors of the 106th street block come by to drop off Christmas treats and gifts for the children. Friends from Brooklyn remember the Carusos as well. They bring by some of the family's favorite Italian cookery and treats.

* * *

Before returning to Chicago for the Christmas holiday, Darrow has one more appointment to keep, the one with Cheech. The day arrives and O'Mally, the attorneys and Alexander Marky drive from Manhattan to Brooklyn where almost a year ago this whole story started. They park in front of the Raymond Street Station House and walk into the building. The head for the commander's office, Alexander Marky greets him extending his hand, "Commander Johnston, I am Alexander Marky. These are Mr. Caruso's attorneys and you know Sergeant O'Mally. My secretary made arrangements for us to meet with Francesco Caruso."

"Of course, Mr. Marky."

Marky introduces the visitors. "These are attorneys Schneider, Pollak and Clarence Darrow."

"I know Sergeant O'Mally. Gentleman, welcome to Raymond Street. Follow me." The commander leads them to Cheech's cell.   He says, "Cheech, you have company."

A solemn Cheech welcomes Marky and the others. Opening the door to his cell, he invites the group in, "Come in. Please come in." He smiles at O'Mally. "*Piason*, I'm so glad to see you again!"

O'Mally smiles, "All they had to do was ask."

"I know, *Piason*, I know!" A guard brings some chairs. He leaves after Marky thanks him.

Marky says, "Mary, my secretary, told me to tell you that she will never forget your song. She runs around the office all day singing O Sole Mio."

"That's sweet, Mr. Marky. Please tell her I will not forget her, too. You are a lucky man. My friend, sit here next to me."

O'Mally sits next to Cheech on the bunk. Cheech gives his cheek a gentle, brotherly slap. "Let me introduce you to these gentlemen, Cheech. These two gentlemen are Mr. Schneider and Mr. Pollak, they are the attorneys who will handle your second trial." Cheech stands to shake their hands. He thanks them for the work they have done for him and his family.

Marky turns to Darrow. "Cheech, this is Clarence Darrow. It is my honor to introduce him. He is the man who gave you another chance at life. His hard work brought about the Appellate Court decision to give you a new trial."

Cheech gives Darrow his straightforward look for a moment. Then he walks up to him, right hand extended and grasps his hand in a grateful grip.

Darrow says. "Glad to meet You Mr. Ca . . . ."

He is cut short by one of Cheech's patented left-handed bear hugs. Darrow is taken aback by this show of affection and gratitude by this short 5' 6" bull of a man. Darrow looks over Cheech's shoulder to see O'Mally smiling.

Darrow tries to straighten; he tells Cheech, "They warned me about you, Mr. Caruso. I see what they mean." Everyone is laughing as Cheech finally lets go of the almost six foot man allowing him to stand straight. "Can we sit down now, Mr. Caruso?"

Cheech points to the chair, "Sit, Mr. Darrow, sit." Darrow is a little embarrassed. He smiles. "Mr. Clarence Darrow. My wife she tells me that you are a wise man. That you do much good for poor people and others who are less fortunate than you."

Darrow interrupts him this time. "And I have heard of you. You are a very strong and most persuasive gentleman." O'Mally and Marky smile knowing Cheech has made another of his unforgettable introductions.

Cheech says, "Mr. Darrow, I understand that you do not believe in God?" The smile disappears from everyone's face. Not knowing what to expect, Darrow straightens up in his chair. "My wife told me of your meeting with her. I asked her if she imposed her saying of grace before meals. She told me she did not. I did good Mr. Darrow? I taught my wife long ago not to impose her beliefs on people when we offer them the pleasure of our hospitality."

Darrow tells Cheech, "No, Mr. Caruso, she did not do that, and I appreciate it very much. That was kind of her."

Cheech, taking command of the conversation, as he always does has O'Mally quietly expecting some very honest opinions to come out. He wonders if Cheech truly understands who he is speaking to.

Cheech continues, "Well, Mr. Darrow, my wife she tells me you do not believe in God, and I tell her many times that I do not believe in God, too. I tell her many times that I do not believe in the afterlife also, many times. You are a smart man Mr. Darrow, smarter than me."

Darrow interrupts, "I think my friend Warden Lawes did a good job on you while you were on death row, but you had to help. You speak beautifully, Mr. Caruso."

"Thank you, but it is not important to me how well I speak English. Even when I would speak funny, I still make people feel good, because I speak honest. For what you do for me, I do something for you. It is something more important than what you give me. He asks O'Mally to slide over so he can sit directly across from the great lawyer. "I believe like you all my life. All life is, is what it is now, what we are now, when we die we don't go any place but in a hole in the ground. I believe that all my life. I believe that life is only what I can see or hold in my hand. I believe that always as a young man. Then one day I lose my Joey, my chance to live and love again. I lose him forever. I cannot take that. I lose my head. I killed that poor doctor when I could have picked him up with one hand and hanged him on a coat hook, to stay and make him listen to me until I let him down when I am done. A *bambina* lost her papa, and a pretty young lady lost the love of her heart. I cannot change nothing. Nothing! It is beyond my way. I can do nothing to make it better. Life is funny. We think we are in control of it, but life it just happens to us. One day we realize that we do not control our fortunes. We just think we do, but we cannot do anything.

"My Joey, I will not see again in this life. Now, I have to believe that there is a life after. I need too believe. Perhaps you have no need, but I do. I see that now. I can wait however long it is until I die. I *will* see my Joey again. I know he waits for his Papa. Not here, but he waits. I need to believe in a life after death. I need to know that we will be together again. I need to believe in God. I need that, or I would kill myself for nothing now. I will bide my time in this world. My day will come. My heart hurts for you Clarence Darrow, because I know what you do for people, and you do not know what I know. You do not know that there is a God. There is a need for such a thing in people's lives. Maybe you will never know or have a need, but you are Godsent, I know. In his way, maybe God is just. Maybe what makes you so special is that you can never think of God. It could be if you did, you would find it difficult to do the things you do. More than the things you do for Francesco Cheech Caruso, the things you do for mankind. Who said ignorance is bliss? Maybe it, too, is just. You are a very special man. It is my honor to meet a man like you. I am sorry if I embarrass you in front of your friends, but I want you to know my heart before you say anything. If before you die, you start to understand what I say to you today, then I did a good job. If you do not, then Maria won't be the only one praying for you. Now you may speak Mr. Darrow."

The cell is quiet. Feeling lectured by a very caring and compassionate man, Darrow turns to Marky. Not quite knowing how to respond, he raises his eyebrows, "Well, I know where to come if I need a special presentation. I can see how you win so many people over to your side, Mr. Cheech Caruso; you are special, too. Now we need to get to the matter at hand. That is your upcoming trial. Since the appeal, we spoke to people we will use in our effort to have you set free. We are no longer trying for a reduction in sentence. We have spoken to Maria, to the O'Hanlon's, to O'Mally here, and now we need to speak to you. Mr. Schneider and Mr. Pollak will handle the trial in the courtroom. I will be there as an adviser."

Marky speaks up, "Cheech it has been a long saga since last February. I am so pleased for you, Maria and the rest of your family. Do you know how few men walk away from death row? Especially at Sing Sing? You are the first, the very first to cheat the chair. We will present a temporary insanity plea. Anything else and it will make it possible for Judge McLaughlin to re-institute the original sentence."

Cheech glances at his long time friend O'Mally, looks down at the floor and gets up. He walks over to the wall between the cots and places his hands on his hips. Not knowing what this all means the three attorneys look at each other in bewilderment. Cheech turns to face the group. "You will not speak to me; you will listen. *Basta, basta*, enough, that's all, no more, please!" Now they are confused. Even O'Mally cannot figure out where his friend is going with it. "Mr. Marky, Mr. Darrow, Mr. Schneider, Mr. Pollak and you, my *Piason*, it's over, *finito*, done. There is no need for a trial. There will not be a death sentence, it's been decided, and it's over."

Darrow declares sternly, "Mr. Caruso, the people involved in the first trial made so many mistakes that you can be a free man within days of the start of your new trial, which I may say you deserve, if you will allow the trial to proceed. There is no doubt that the AMA railroaded you and that you were not of a sane mind when you committed the murder. We can prove there was no premeditation on your part to commit murder that day."

Cheech, just as stern says, "Look, my friends, it is over. There are forces here that are stronger than right or wrong. There is a time when a man has to make a decision; no one can do it for him. This is easier for me than it is for you, I know that, but it must be this way. I have made up my mind. I make decisions like this all the time. I just make them, and I go on. I made my mind up once before, and allowed good, well meaning people to change my mind for me. Now I know better. That will not happen again. I already talked to Maria. I told her not to expect me home after the trial."

Marky gets up from his chair, "Please. Cheech, don't do this. You're a free man; we will win."

"Please, Mr. Marky, sit. You don't understand. I can only be a free man if I *don't* care about my family. Someone attacked and knocked down my wife. One of my children was harassed. This happened to me while I was protected. Sometimes unexpected things happen, unavoidable things. They just happen. Then you can only react. Well, I will not allow something terrible to happen to my family. Enough things have happened already. I will prevent that and protect them the best way I can. I will do this. You didn't create this situation . . . I did. To make some kind of peace, I must do this. I have no choice. It will give me time to think about what I've done, the way I have lived. The doctor's widow can have some peace. She is hurt enough. She needs to go on with her life. The baby, God forgive me and help her. She will need it. Yes, it is finished, Gentlemen, *finito.*

"When I was at Sing Sing, Warden Lawes, another special man like you Mr. Darrow, he tells me that I have no business being there on death row. He knows I was sick when I killed the doctor. He tells me that when I am released a free man, I should find a way to salvage the rest of my life and make a good life for my family and me. I told him that I knew I would not die for what I did, but I would never be free either. He tells me that I have many smart and strong people protecting me, but he don't understand what he says. When I come here, everybody wants me to win my freedom back. Sometimes, Mr. Marky, when we try to make things better, we only make them worse. I think things cannot get better than this. I lost two children, my Joey and my Ida. Maria and I will not have them ever again in our lifetime. Poor Maria saw everything. Will she learn to hate me? The widow lost her husband. She will not have peace in her life again. Maybe if I go to prison, she can heal and live a little. The *bambina,* when I think of her, she hurts my heart. How can I live with that? It is too much for me, *basta!*

"Now please listen to me, and then you go. I made a deal, agreed to by everyone. At the trial, I will plead guilty and be returned to Sing Sing. It will not be bad for me. Warden Lewis Lawes will take good care of me. I can be with my wife and children on the weekends; I will be a trustee. Warden Lawes and his wife are my friends. He tells me I will be out in seven years. He is a good man. He is both sad to see me again and happy. He understands. While there, I will go back to death row to sing to my friends again. This time I will pray for them, too. When I am released from Sing Sing, no one will know and I can sneak away and disappear quietly. No one will miss me. I will lead a good life. I accepted this agreement. The story is over. Please . . . try to understand."

Schneider looks at Cheech nodding his head in disbelief, and in a serious and saddened voice says, "In God's name who in the hell was this so called deal made with, and who was the driving force?"

Cheech pauses for a moment. With a half-hearted smile, he tells Schneider, "If I could tell you, don't you think I would have told you by now?"

"If what you say is fact, there is no need for any of us to work on this case is there? You and your family will be okay?" Cheech nods his head yes. "Then I will give all of my files to Mr. Spellman and let him represent your case, though I will be in the court with him."

Clarence Darrow looks at Cheech, who is apparently in charge of his faith, and tells him, "I'd be incorrect if I told you that I understand, but if this is your final word on this matter, I will honor your decision. Just tell me, I need to hear you say it."

To which Cheech replies, "Mr. Darrow it is my wish that this affair end as it is about to. You did your job well. I will not die in the Sing Sing electric chair. I thank you for that very much. God bless you, Sir." The cell is hot and silent. Cheech breaks the silence, "I would like for Mr. Schneider and Mr. Spellman to stay here, and I would like for the rest of you to wait until I call you separately, please gentlemen. I would like to speak to each of you alone." Schneider and Spellman remain seated and the others file out to the outer office. Alone with the two attorneys Cheech says, "I thank you for coming forward when it was not the thing to do. Acting on what you believe is right is so important. I cannot pay you, but I hope that you will accept my affection for you and the wish I hold in my heart for you and your families." He gives each one a strong hug. The two men accept the affection, though they might not often react this way. He asks them to send in Darrow and O'Mally.

The two men sit down. "O'Mally, my friend, my *piason*, I did not expect to see you again. Thank you for the gift, Lord. I want you to hear what I will tell Mr. Clarence Darrow today and remember it for always. Don't say anything. I know in time you will understand. I want you to disappear after this visit. You must do what I will do when I am released from jail." He turns to the great Clarence Darrow, "Mr. Clarence Darrow, I told you that you are able to do the things you do because you do not believe in God. I will show you what I mean. You would defend me if I were guilty of murder because you do not believe in the death penalty. A God fearing man could not do that. Well my dear Mr. Darrow, I do believe in the death penalty. I think it is necessary. I don't know if it will put your mind at ease, but I was absolutely out of my mind when I murdered the doctor. I have come to know that. If I believed in God at the time, maybe, just maybe I would not have done it. Do I confuse you?"

"No, Mr. Caruso, I understand you. I regret to say that I find it a little frightening."

Good then, *gradsia*. Your great name cheated the electric chair one more time. You should be happy with your work. You are a great man, and you are not finished with your work. I have a favor, one more thing to ask of you if you will allow me to ask, Sir."

"I will certainly try."

"Good, thank you. When you return to Chicago, I wish that you go to Colosimo's Café and speak to Alphonso for me, *gabish*? Ask him, for me, to look out for my friend Sergeant O'Mally and keep an eye on him. Tell him that because my friend O'Mally helped me, he is in trouble and has to stay quiet, out of the way. Tell him that after I am released from prison, I will meet with him. Tell him Salvatore D'Aquila speaks for my loyalty. Do you understand me, Sir?"

"Yes I do, Mr. Caruso, consider it done."

"You will not be offended if I hug you again?" Cheech asks the great attorney.

"No, Cheech, I would not disrespect you that way, but I will be careful when I'm around Italians from now on." Laughing, the two men hug for the last time. They share a moment of silence together, each knowing they won't see one another again. Cheech thanks him again as Darrow leaves.

"O'Mally, we will say our goodbyes one more time." They face each other. They both have tears in their eyes.

"Thank you, Cheech, thank you for everything. I don't know how life will be without you there."

"*Piason*, you and me, we are different than all these people around us, no? You listen to your friend. The money will continue to come to Maria for all the time I am in prison; it will not stop. Marky will have you drop it off to her. When he cannot reach you any longer, I will know that you disappeared, *Gabish, Piason*?"

"*Cie*, I understand Cheech." Cheech reaches out and grasps O'Mally for what will be their last embrace. Eyes squeezed shut the tears continue.

"*Mio frada,* O'Mally, *di voulio bene'.*"

"Me too, Cheech, I understood that."

Cheech tells his friend, "Be good, *mi dispaga dou mouguiada di lachada*, it displeases me that your wife left you. *Chio, amigo!*"

"*Chio*, Cheech, *chio!*" Cheech tells O'Mally to have Marky come in.

"Mr. Marky, Mr. Alexander Marky, poor man, you did the most; yet you knew the least. You saw what they did to me in the courtroom. There were others there who saw it too. Did you ever wonder why you were asked to sit in on my case? Well, a childhood friend of yours is an important friend of an important friend of mine. They put their heads together and it came up Alexander Marky. Maria tells me you are a good man, a respectful man. You understand how hard it was for her to do the things she had to do to save my life. She said you are smart, very smart.

Those are the reasons they picked you. From now on, you can do anything you feel you would like to do. You will be only as successful as you choose. Maybe you will marry Mary. She looks at you too much." He grins at Marky's expression. "The time will come when you cannot reach O'Mally. When that happens, I wish for you to call Warden Lawes and tell him that you cannot reach O'Mally. He will tell me. This is important to me, Mr. Marky."

"I will do that for you, Cheech, I promise. The money will continue to go to Maria while you are in prison. Don't worry, there is plenty of money. More than I ever imagined. It will last longer than the time you will be incarcerated."

"Good then. God bless you, Mr. Marky. Thank you. You go now; I have kept you too long." Starting with a handshake, the two men embrace. Cheech tells him to go and then sits on his cot. He sheds tears, sad. There is no other alternative for him, no other way to find peace and safety.

As the trial date of January 30, 1928 closes in, rumors are rampant that a plea for a lesser charge will be granted. The AMA and all who were behind the kangaroo atmosphere of the first trial are upset and making daily statements to anyone who will listen that there will be no deal. The loudest of the voices is that of Judge Alonzo G. McLaughlin. Trying to force their will this time by trying to influence the public's opinion is futile. He refuses to accept anything except first-degree murder, but nothing can change the deal of the cards—not this time.

The trial date of January 30, 1928 arrives and the jury is selected. Intelligent people comprise it. They include Bankers, realtors, a furrier, a builder and a manufacturer. Rumors abound that someone placed a call to one of Cheech's attorneys the day before the start of the trial, but no statement is forth coming. Attorney Spellman finally speaks to the business of the call, but refuses to give the source of the call. The next day, the trial is underway. People anticipate a number of motions by the defense, but as soon as the trial gets underway, Spellman drops a bomb on the courtroom. He stands and asks for the jury to be excused from the courtroom. He tells Judge McLaughlin that his client wishes to avert a second trial by accepting a plea of first-degree manslaughter. The judge is frustrated and angry. After heated discussion, the plea is accepted. February 1, 1928 the New York Times headlines are:

Court Lets Caruso Plea Manslaughter

Court Accepts Defense Request.

The Second Trial in Killing of Doctor Ends Abruptly

Sentencing is set for February 14, 1928

Maximum Sentence Fifteen Years

Judge McLaughlin Requests aid for Mrs. Pendola.

Exactly one year and a day since the death of Doctor Pendola, the saga is over for Francesco Caruso. Money raised by the Caruso Defense fund and the Mafia help the family survive while the breadwinner is in prison.

The pleas of Judge McLaughlin and others on behalf of Mrs. Pendola have no effect. The Mafia organization pledged to take life . . . saved one. The AMA organization pledged to save life . . . tried to take one.

Due to appeals in the coming weeks, the sentencing date is changed. On February 28, Judge Alonzo G. Mclaughlin carries out the sentencing. Cheech stands as the judge reads it to him. The newspapers report that he is as motionless as he was in his first trial. He is wearing the suit and patent leather shoes that Salvatore D'Aquila ordered. The judge asks if he has anything to say. He looks away in defiance. As he is led away in shackles to be transported to Sing Sing, he winks at Maria and smiles at Lena and Florence O'Hanlon seated next to her.

The newspapers report that he is as motionless as he was at his first trial of April 4, 1927.

Mrs. Pendola attends the trial every day. She opts to sit out in the hall. A guard tells her the results. She leaves the court building without comment.

Papa's decision to accept the advice of his friend Salvatore was a good one. The two would not see each other again. Joe Masseria ordered the murder of Salvatore D'Aquila on a Brooklyn street corner on October 1928, only eight months after he met my father. Papa wore the same suit and pumps that Salvatore gave him when he left Warden Lawes and Sing Sing in 1934 after serving seven years.

As promised, the money kept coming to Mama for the full seven years and then some. One day it just stopped. Papa had a hard time finding jobs after his release from Sing Sing. Because he was a felon, he looked for jobs that required no identification. For the same reason, he never applied for a driver's license or chanced buying a home. He and Mama were afraid that an ex-con would be deported.

As Papa advised, O'Mally disappeared, he did just that but not like papa had wanted for his close friend. On one of Mama's visits to Sing Sing, she told Papa that she had not seen O'Mally for a few months, and that Marky stopped by to see what she knew about his disappearance. Papa never heard from O'Mally again. He often wondered what happened to his *frada*, brother.

Until papa died in 1968 at the age of seventy-four, he would burn a church candle on his dresser every February 13 for Joey, Ida and the doctors little girl, Catherine. It would stay lit until it burned out by itself.

Uncle Louie liked to play the tough guy . . . and he did, many times. It was risky. If he got hurt of disfigured, it would most likely mean the end of his dancing career. I owe Lou (Louis Privitera) a debt of gratitude. Without him, I would have never been able to tie Papa, D'Aquila and Darrow to Colosimo's Café' and Al Capone in Chicago. He told me that Darrow, Caruso, Durante, Tucker, Valentino and Al Smith (Governor of New York) and others frequented the famous nightspot. He told me all of this in 1976. He died in 1978. His wife and dance partner Anna died years earlier.

Rosario, Papa's brother and our family got together one more time in 1949 with disastrous results. Rosario swore that he would never again come to our house. He was true to his word. He died in 1977.

Warden Lewis Edward Lawes wrote a book in 1934, which was a smashing success. The warden and Papa were inseparable for the seven years. Often he spent weekends at the warden's home with his family. Papa loved the warden's children. In 1937, Catherine Lawes, the warden's wife, died in a car accident. Papa went to the funeral and bought a flower wreath from our family. He was such a respected warden that the gate was opened, and any prisoner who wanted to pay final respects to Catherine was allowed to. They all returned to the prison yard. There were no escape attempts. He passed away in 1947. Papa was not aware of his passing.

Fiorello LaGuardia became Mayor of New York City in 1934, the same year as Papa's release from prison. One of New York's favorite Mayors, he became even more popular during a newspaper strike when he read the comic strips to a radio audience. He also died in 1947.

Judge Benjamin Nathan Cardozo, the Appellate Court judge who reversed the ruling in papa's first trial, went on to become a respected

Supreme Court judge in 1932 replacing the seat on the bench that Oliver Wendell Holms vacated by his death. He served until 1938 when he died. Herbert Hoover appointed him.

Clarence Darrow, the famous attorney, continued writing books and gave speeches until his death in 1938. Apparently, none of Mama and Papa's wishes and prayers worked. He would remain an agnostic to the very end. He had his ashes strewn over the pedestrian bridge and spread in a lagoon at Chicago.

In the end and seventy-five years later, it is my hope that the Pendola family fared better than the Carusos. This surely has been a cross to bear.

Endnotes

For those of you who have wondered why, early in my story, Mama confessed to cutting the doctors throat I submit the truth to you.

In 1972, I went to my sister Lena's place at Fishkill, New York to help her redo her condominium. Everything from electric to plumbing to painting, decorating and general fix up. I was there for two weeks. We were about halfway finished with the work when we sat on the floor to look at old family pictures. As we sat there, she started crying after showing me a picture of her daughter Camille, Sissy. I was taken aback because we had just had a laugh about one of the pictures we just looked at, and Lena just didn't cry. She was the strong one, Papa's right hand man. I took her hand and asked her why she was crying. She decided at this time, after many years of knowing of my intentions to write Papa's story, to tell me this story. So help me God.

She wiped her eyes and proceeded to line up the pictures of her husband Jim, son Jimmy and daughter Sissy in a row on the floor. Pointing at the pictures she said, "Jim died at 51, Jimmy died at 47 and Sissy died at 47. Do you know why?

I replied, "Yes, I do. Jim died from a heart attack, Jimmy and Sissy died of cancer."

She looked at me for a while, "Yes, but do you know why they died?" I did not know what she was getting at. "I don't know if I should be telling you this, but I need to tell someone! The only people in the last forty-five years who knew what really happened were Mama, Papa and I. When the doctor and Papa went into the front bedroom, Mama put us kids in the back bedroom and went to the front bedroom to listen to them. I heard Mama walking away. I opened the door to see where she was going. I saw her open the bedroom door just a little bit and look in. I tiptoed up behind Mama. She didn't know I was there at first. I heard everything Papa and the doctor said. There was a terrible fight and a lot of noise. Then, all of a sudden, it was quiet. I grabbed Mama and hung on to her legs. She knew I had heard every word. I looked around her into the room. I saw Papa sitting on the doctor's stomach punching and punching him. I snapped and ran into the kitchen. I got the biggest knife I could find in the drawer and ran back to the bedroom. I slipped past Mama who was still at the door with her hands on her mouth. I ran up to Papa and handed him the knife. Mama made a loud gasp! Papa looked up from the doctor. Then he looked at the knife I held out to him. Then our eyes met. He took the knife and ordered me to leave the room., which I did immediately.   I ran out and sat in the hallway, closed my eyes and covered my ears. I heard a loud thump and opened my eyes. Mama fainted at the doorway to the master bedroom. Papa came to the door and picked Mama up. He put her into a sitting position up against the wall in the hallway. He had blood all over him. He went back into the bedroom and dragged the doctor out by the front of his shirt. The doctor's head was dangling and swinging from side-to-side as Papa dragged his body out to the kitchen. He dropped him on the spot where Joey's cot was, the exact spot where Joey died. I will never forget the look in Papa's eyes when I handed him the knife, as if he expected it of me, his girl. We bonded that day; that is why I was his second in command." She looked at me, "Don't you see, Dom, I believe that because I gave the knife to Papa, God punished me. That is why I lost my husband and both of my children much too soon."

I was stunned. I didn't know what to say to my sister. It was quiet for a while. I asked her, "Did you ever tell anyone else?"

"I told Jim one night when we were in bed. I was so ashamed."

I told Lena that I did not believe God did things like that to children. I know she really believed it, and who was I to convince her of anything else?

She looked at me. "He didn't do it to a child. He waited for me to grow up."

I could not think of anything to say to my tormented sister. What could I have said?

Now I know this is why Mama, in her confusion at the time of the doctor's death, volunteered to take the blame for his murder. It was not to protect Papa as everyone surmised. It was to protect her Lena, who was more like Grandma than she was Papa. It must have been very difficult for her to live with this knowledge all her life. I have only known it since 1972; it took me this long to put it into words. I am still not sure I should be telling anyone about it. I will never know if is the right thing to divulge, but at my age, I have a feeling I will find out soon enough.

I remember when Papa passed away. I received a call from my sister Lena telling me the bad news. She said he asked for me. After I hung up the phone, I told my wife Catherine about it. I went to our bedroom and closed the door. I lay down and cried for two hours and thought of many things. The first thought that came to me within the very first minute was a realization that I had never told my father how much I loved him. I did not realize until then that I had not told him. From that moment to this very day, I carry the terrible burden of that cross on my heart. There is no relief for me—not now—not ever.

Papa and I never got along. There was no father and son relationship between us. I did not know or understand why. I grew up by myself and quite by chance. As a child and a young man, I had a violent nature. I know there was more than one effort by at least thirty-nine guardian angels to direct me. Just because I knew guardian angels watched over me does not mean I always listened to them. I did not want too.

I remember papa crying one time when he did not realize I could hear him. He told Mama they were going to do to his son as they had done to him. He was speaking of me. Years later, I came to realize that his "They", was the penal system, the medical community or both.

When I was sixteen-years-old, I quit school. Papa took me to the Hicksville, Long Island Courthouse to apply for my working papers and social security number. It was that day that I noticed for the first time that I had no first name on my birth certificate. It read Male Caruso. I did not question it then and not for many years afterwards. One day, years after Papa's death, I asked Mama. At first, she did not respond, except to shake her head. Finally, I did get her to tell me. She said that I was born because papa wanted to try to make another Joey. He wanted one more chance. When I turned out to be a male, Papa told the mid-wife to put the name of Joseph on my birth certificate. Mama became so upset with him that the mid-wife did not know what to do, so she filled in my name as Male Caruso. She said they could change it later.

Mama said that she would not allow papa to place a terrible burden like that on a child. It has remained the same to this day. I went through working papers, Social Security Number, driver's license, draft card and the United States Navy. No one ever questioned it, not once. The old adage: What is in a name is meaningless to me. Am I angry with papa? No not now, nor have I ever been, nor will I ever be. It is true what they say about planting potatoes and getting potatoes. My father and I were alike. I know it is not right to favor any of the children in one's family, but I cannot help but favor one child. I know in my heart now how he must have felt about Joey. I'm sorry I couldn't be Joey for him, but I don't begrudge him his special love for my brother. I now understand it better than ever. It is and was a special love.

Grandma was something. She told me something one day when I was six-years-old that took me a lifetime to figure out. She sat me on her lap and said that I was a special little boy and that I was never to forget it. She asked me if I understood her and I told her I did. I didn't really. I looked at Mama standing close by. She smiled. Twenty years later, she explained to me why my birth certificate read Male Caruso. I finally understood what Grandma meant, what she was saying. She was right, my Grandma, I *am* special.

People have sometimes described my writing of this book as airing my family's dirty laundry. Well for the first time in seventy-four years, my family's laundry is clean and aired out. This is something I think I have always known I had to do. I regret the fact that Papa asked me to help him do it years ago, and I refused him. I did not have the courage to do the only thing he ever asked me to do for him—I could not do it for the man—I denied my father.

Now in my seventies, I have few regrets, except for that. When my time comes, I will leave this earth a far better person than when I entered it. I have lived through a life of hell and torment. I would not give up my parents, my siblings or anything else that makes me a Caruso for anything in this world. I have come to accept everything that I am; I love and respect my parents and everything they gave me. I am blessed. I am special just like my Grandma said. I love my life, but I will not mind leaving when my time comes, because I know Grandma will be there, and I will finally get to meet her handsome Italian police officer who rode a horse. I will meet my Grandpa who died before I was born.

Mama and Papa will be there, too. I made sure I told Mama I loved her before she left us. I will not waste any more time telling Papa that I love him. I know he is waiting to hear it, and I know he knows that I love him. Josey, my mentally retarded sis, will not have to ask for me anymore or say I was just there with her. I will be there with her again as I used too be.

Uncle Lou and his beautiful ballroom dance partner and wife Anna will be there too. They retired from dancing professionally before I was born, so I never saw them do the tango. Who can forget Uncle Frankie? He wanted to turn me into the next dance sensation, but leukemia beat him to it. In the 1950's, when I was cool, and rocking and rolling, that was not me. It was the best imitation I could do of Frankie.

Finally, there is Joey my brother and my sister Ida. The brother and sister I never knew. I know Joey is with Mama, Papa, and Ida. They are all together again after all these years. I cannot wait to meet Joey. I have but one question. Will Joey be six-years-old? Will he be fifteen years my senior? Well, either way I do not mind. He is either a kid brother or a big brother. Either way I win. Ida died so young, only four months old. What a shame that I know nothing about her, but I will sit her down and find out everything about her when I get the chance to meet her.

There is one other thing. I cannot wait to see Papa's face light up the way Mama used to say that it did when he saw Joey. Joey was like an extension of Papa's own self. I guess, as only one sperm can penetrate; only one heart can mend another. I want that for Papa's heart. I want Joey to mend it, papa's sad heart. I think I know how he felt now. If any one knows how Papa felt outside of Mama, I do. With all my love to you Papa, I cannot wait to be with you again, your son, Dominic Caruso.

Last of all, although I have included in previous pages how Joey died and how it affected Papa, what you will read in the following pages is a copy of Papa's testimony as he took the stand on his own behalf in the first trial of April 4, 1927.

The testimony of a man not accustomed to speaking to people of his heartfelt emotions in public. They are the compelling, heart wrenching and mournful words that the court ignored that day. Upon reading these words, my heart was free for the first time in my life. At age sixty-five, I started anew with an understanding and appreciation for life not known to me before. I am sure that this is what Mama and Papa wanted for me. I can hear Papa saying, "Write the words I say Dominic. No change them! *Justa? Justa*! Right? Right!"

I present to you, a copy of my father Francesco Cheech Caruso's testimony, word-for-word as he spoke it eighty-years-ago in the presence of a deaf jury, a kangaroo court. This 1927 Appellate court copy has not been edited or altered in any way .

Judge Cardoza wrote the opinion. He would later take the vacated seat of Justice Oliver Wendell Holmes on the supreme court of the United States of America.

390

(246 N. Y. 437)

159 NORTH EASTERN PEPORTER

PEOPLE v. CARUSO.

Court of Appeals of New York. Nov. 22, 1927.

I. Homicide tS=~332(3), 342—Court of **Appeals,**   reviewing conviction for murder in first degree, may weigh evidence, and, if necessary, grant new trial.

In reviewing convictions *for* murder in the first degree, the Court of Appeals has broad powers in seeing that justice is done both to accused and to the state, and it is the duty of the court, not only to weigh evidence, but to grant new trial, if it believes justice requires such a course.

2. Criminal law c3=338 **(7)—Testimony that** deceased sang his baby to sleep and questions as to defendant's citizenship held improper appeals to sympathy and prejudice.

In prosecution for murder of doctor, alleged by defendant to have been committed under be ife that (doctor had killed defendants child by an overdose of antitoxin, permitting widow of deceased to state that, on return from call, deceased sat on his baby's crib, and sang her to sleep, and questions as to whether defendant was a citizen, or had applied for naturalization, were incompetent and improper appeals to sympathy and prejudice.

3. Homicide ~I 69(2)—On defense that homicide was committed under belief that deceased killed defendant's child by overdose of anti-toxin, testimony that dose was not excessive was Inadmissible.

In prosecution for murder of doctor, alleged by defendant to have been committed under be ife that his child was killed by an overdose of antitoxin, administered by doctor, evidence that (lose was not excessive was inadmissible, since belief of defendant as to such fact, and not whether his belief was mistaken, was the question.

4. Homicide C=253(3)—Conviction **of** first **degree** murder held not justified, **In view of lack** of evidence of premeditation and deliberation.

In prosecution for murder of doctor, alleged by defendant to have been committed under be ife that deceased had killed defendant's child by overdose of antitoxin, evidence *held* not to justify conviction of murder in the first degree, in view of lack of showing of deliberation and premeditation.

Appeal from Kings County Court.

Francesco Caruso was convicted on the verdict of a jury of murder in the first degree, end he appeals. Reversed, and new trial ordered.

Walter II. Pollak, Charles A. Schneider. Howard Hilton Spellman, Ruth I. Wilson and Lewis A. Pinkussohn, all of New York City, for appellant.

Charles 3. Dodd, Dist. Atty., of Brooklyn (Henry 3. Walsh, of Brooklyn, of counsel), for the People.

(N.   Y.

ANDREWS, J. This judgment must he reversed.

[1] In reviewing convictions for murder in the first degree, the Court of Appeals has broad powers. It is to see that justice is done both to the accused and to the state. If guilt is clear, errors or instances of unfair conduct by the prosecutor may sometimes he ignored. The greater the doubt of guilt, however, the more likely are errors to affect the substantial rights of the accused. The more likely are appeals to sympathy or passion or prejudice to influence the jury. It is our duty, not only to weigh the evidence, but to grant a new trial, if we believe justice requires such a course.

Francesco Caruso, an Illiterate Italian, *35* years old, came to this country about 1911. He worked as a laborer, and in the early part of 1927 was living with his wife and six small children in an apartment in Brooklyn. On Friday, February 11th, one of these children, a boy of six, was ill with a sore throat. That day and the next he treated the boy with remedies bought at a drug store. The child grew worse, and at 10 o'clock of the night of the 12th he sent for a Dr. Pendola, who had been recommended to him, but with whom he was not acquainted.

What followed depends upon a statement made by Caruso and upon his testimony on the stand. Any proper Inferences may he drawn there from. The belief that what lie said was false, however, or any reasoning based upon his failure to call friendly witnesses, will not supply the want of affirmative testimony of the facts necessary to constitute the crime. Those facts, if they exist, must be inferred from his own admissions.

Some time between 10:30 and 11 in the evening Dr. Pendola arrived. The child had diphtheria. Caruso was sent out to buy some antitoxin, and, when he returned, the doctor administered it. He then gave Caruso another prescription with instructions as to its use, and left promising to return in the morning.

Caruso watched the child all night, giving remedies every half hour. "About 4 o'clock in the morning," he testified, "my child was standing up to the bed, and asked me to, he says, 'Papa' he said, 'I am dying.' I say that time, I said, 'You don't die.' I said, I will help you every time.' The same time that child he will be crazy—look like crazy, that time—don't want to stay any more Inside. All I can do, I keep my child in my arms, and I held him in my arms from *4* o'clock until 8 o'clock in the morning. Alter 8 o'clock in the morning the poor child getting worse—the poor child in the morning he was"

—(Slight Interruption In the testimony while

$. PEOPLE v. CARUSO **(1~ N.E.)**

• *-N.Y.)*

the defendant apparently stops to overcome his emotion). "The poor child that time, and he was asking me, 'Papa,' he said, 'I want to go and sleep.' So I said, 'All right, Giovie, I will put you in the sleep.' I take my Giovie, and I put him in the bed, and he started to sleep, to wait until the doctor came, and the doctor he never came. I waited from 10 o'clock, the doctor he never came."

Then, after trying in vain to get in touch with the doctor, he sent for an ambulance from a drug store.

"When I go home I seen my child is got up to the bed that time, and be says to me, 'Papa, I want to come with you.' I take my child again up in my arms, and I make him look to the backyard to the window, He looked around the yard about a couple of minutes, and after, when he looked around, he says to me, 'Papa, I want to go to sleep again.' I said, 'All right, Giovie, I will put you in the sleep.' I put my child on the bed. About a few seconds my child is on the bed, my child says to me, he says, 'Papa, I want to go to the toilet.' I said, 'All right, Giovie, I will take you to the toilet.' So I was trying to pick up the child, and make him go to the toilet, when I held that child I felt that leg

— that child started to shake up in my arms. My wife know about better than me—I can not see good myself in the face, so she tell what kind of shakes he do, and she has told me, she says, 'Listen, Frank, why, the child has died already.' I said, 'All right, you don't cry. No harm, because you make the child scared.' That time I go right away and put the child on the bed. When I put the child, before I put my hand to the pillow, my child said to me, 'Good-bye, Papa, I am going already.' So that time I put my hands to my head—I said, 'that child is dead. I don't know what I am going to do myself now.' That time I never said nothing, because I said, 'Jesus, my child is dead now. Nobody will get their hands on my child.'

About 12 o'clock Dr. Pendola arrived. The child has been dead for some time. He was told, and then Caruso says the doctor laughed, and he "lost his head." This seems incredible. Yet Caruso apparently believed it, for his testimony on the stand is a repetition of the same charge made in his statement that same night, before it is likely that a man of Caruso's mentality would he preparing a false defense. The probability is there was, from one cause or another, some twitching of the facial muscles that might be mistaken for a smile.

Besides the delay of the doctor and the smile was another circumstance, which, if true, would exasperate Caruso. He says, and again this appears in the statement as well as in his testimony on the trial, that, when he was buying the antitoxin, the druggist told him that the dose was too large for a child of the age of his son. This he told the doctor. The latter was indignant, and paid no heed to the warning. The druggist denied any such conversation, and apparently the dose was proper. But it seems probable that something occurred that left on Caruso's mind the impression that the death of his child was caused by malpractice. At least, immediately after the death, he told an am ife ce surgeon that Dr. Pendola had killed his child by an injection, and also complained of his delay in not coming that morning. And within a short time he made the same charge to others.

Then followed some talk. Caruso accused the doctor of killing his child. The doctor denied it. Caruso attacked him in anger, choked him until he fell to the floor, then went to a closet ten or twelve feet away, took a knife, and stabbed him twice in the throat, so killing him. Caruso then took his family to the janitor's apartment downstairs, and himself went to his brother's house on Staten Island, where he was arrested that night. He made no attempt whatever to conceal the facts of the homicide, and his departure cannot fairly be viewed as a flight, indicating consciousness of guilt.

[2] The case for the people was simple. Formal identification of the dead body was required. That Caruso committed a homicide, neither excusable nor justifiable, was abundantly shown by his own statement, and, indeed, was not denied. The real issue was as to state of mind of the defendant, whether he formed the intent to kill Dr. Pendola, and, if so, whether the killing was the result of premeditation and deliberation. What Caruso in fact believed and thought, what he had in mind at the time of the homicide, is the issue—not whether his beliefs were justified. And the jury, horrified at the conceded brutality of his acts, are still to decide this issue in a judicial temper. Appeals to sympathy or prejudice can but be harmful.

Mrs. Pendola, the widow of the deceased, was a young woman, placed upon the stand by the state. The right to use her as a witness for a proper purpose is not questioned, notwithstanding the natural sympathy her presence would arouse. But she knew nothing of the circumstances of the crime. She might have been asked as to the identity of the deceased, although he could be identified by others. She might give any other material evidence, notwithstanding any influence her presence might have upon the jury. Mrs. Pendola was not called for any such purpose. She was allowed to say she had been married

159 NORTH EASTERN REPORTER

for 18 months; that she had one child, 6 months old; that her husband was a medical graduate; she explained why his call on Caruso was delayed on Sunday, the 13th; she gave conversations with the doctor when he received the telephone call from Caruso Saturday night, and again after his return; she told how he sat on his baby's crib and sang her to sleep. All this had no materiality upon the issues before the jury. The object of the state is clear. Although, doubtless, the result of "well intentioned though misguided zeal," it was an "unseemly and unsafe" appeal to prejudice. Nor here can we overlook it as probably unheeded. And the object at the prosecution is emphasized by questions, ruled out it is true, as to whether the defendant was a citizen, or had applied for naturalization. They were so plainly incompetent; it cannot be believed they were asked in good faith.

[3] Testimony was given by an expert that the treatment of the child was correct, and the doses of antitoxin not excessive. The be ife of Caruso as to these facts was the question, not whether his belief was mistaken. Nor did this testimony tend to corroborate the denial of the druggist that he had ever told Caruso that the dose was too large. People V. Harris, 209 N. Y. 70, 102 N. E. *516.*

[4] But, passing the two questions already discussed, which would under the circumstances of this case require a reversal, there is also a fundamental reason requiring a new trial. Conviction here of murder in the first degree is not justified by the weight of the evidence. The jury might find that the intent to kill existed. While in his testimony on the stand Caruso denies such an intent, and says that in his rage he did not know what he was doing, yet in his statement he expressly admits his intent to kill, and the Inference that the intent existed might also be drawn from the two wounds in the neck inflicted with a large knife.

But was there premeditation and deliberation? This seems to have been the question which troubled the jury. They considered their verdict for six hours—twice returning for definitions of homicide and of deliberation and premeditation. Time to deliberate and premeditate there clearly was. Caruso might have done so. In fact, however, did he?

Until the Saturday evening Caruso had never met Dr. Pendola. Nothing occurred at that interview that furnished any motive for murder. Then came nervous strain and anxiety culminating in grief, deep and genuine, for the death of his child. Brooding over his loss, blaming the doctor for his delay in making the promised visit, believing he had killed the baby by his treatment, the doctor finally enters. And, when told of the child's death he appears to laugh. This, added to his supposed injuries, would fully account for the gust of anger that Caruso says he felt. Then came the struggle and the homicide.

As has been said, Caruso had the time to deliberate, to make a choice whether to kill or not to kill—to overcome hesitation and doubt—to form a definite purpose. And, where sufficient time exists, very often the circumstances surrounding the homicide justify—indeed require—the necessary inference. Not here, however. No plan to kill is shown, no intention of violence when the doctor arrived—only grief and resentment. Not until the supposed laugh did the assault begin. "If the defendant inflicted the wound in a sudden transport of passion, excited by what the deceased then said and by the preceding events which, for the time, disturbed her reasoning faculties and deprived her of the capacity to reflect, or while under the influence of some sudden and uncontrollable emotion excited by the final culmination of her misfortunes, as indicated by the train of events which have been related, the act did not constitute murder in the first degree. Deliberation and premeditation imply the - capacity at the time to think and reflect, sufficient volition to make a choice, and by the use of these powers to refrain from doing a wrongful act." People v. Barberi, 1.19 N. Y. *256,* 43 N. E. 635, 52 Am. St. Rep. 717. When the supposed laugh came, there was apparent cause for excitement and anger. There was enough to indicate hot blood and unreflecting action. There was immediate provocation. People v. Ferraro, 161 N. Y. 305, 375, 55 N. E.

981.   The attack seems to have been the instant effect of impulse. Nor does the fact that the stabbing followed the beginning of the attack by some time affect this conclusion. It was all one transaction under the peculiar facts of this case. If the assault was not deliberated or premeditated, then neither was the infliction of the fatal wound.

With due consideration of all the facts presented there is insufficient evidence to justify a conviction of murder in the first degree. Doubtless, on this record the defendant might be convicted of some crime, either murder in the second degree, or, if his testimony on the stand is accepted, manslaughter in the first degree. Either verdict might be sustained on the facts. Not the one actually rendered. The judgment of conviction should be reversed, and a new trial ordered.

Cardoza, C.J., and Pound, Drane, Lehman, Kellogg, and O'Brien, JJ., concur. .4 -392

Conclusion

I would like to acknowledge the assistance and support of the following people, without whose help so many times and so many long hours, I could not have written this story. They are Francesco Caruso, Maria Caruso, Theresa Lombardi, Lena Justo, Louis Privitera, Nick Savateri and Carol Kluz

About the Author

Dominic Caruso, the sole surviving son of Francesco "Cheech" Caruso is seventy-two-years old. At the age of sixteen he was approached by his father to write his biography. Unable to deal with it, Dominic put it off until he returned from Sicily in 1958. At that time he told his father that he didn't know when, but he would do it and he did write the story.

Born and raised in New York City, he served in the U.S. Navy for four years. After military service, he studied at the Professional Institute of Commercial Art at Reistertown, Maryland, specializing in commercial and graphic art, fashion illustration, advertising and animation. He later served as an graphics/animation instructor at the institute and authored an Animation 101 manual for use by future students. Mr. Caruso designed, developed and patented more than a dozen technological innovations.

The father of two daughters, Mr. Caruso lives in Maryland.

With the help of the governor of New York, he recently found and visited his brother Joey's grave as well as the grave of the doctor who met his fate at the hands of Dominic's father on the same day that Joey died. Interested readers can view the informative New York Times article by clicking on the dancing mouse at Mr. Caruso's website. www.wordsbydominc.com

Printed in the United States
137151LV00004B/13/P

9 780978 984038